THE *Hillier* GARDENER'S GUIDES
HERBACEOUS PERENNIALS

Andrew McIndoe and Kevin Hobbs

D&C
David and Charles

A DAVID & CHARLES BOOK

David & Charles is a subsidiary of F+W (UK) Ltd.,
an F+W Publications Inc. company

First published in the UK in 2005
Text Copyright © Andrew McIndoe and Kevin Hobbs 2005
Copyright © David & Charles 2005

Andrew McIndoe and Kevin Hobbs have asserted their right to be
identified as authors of this work in accordance with the Copyright,
Designs and Patents Act, 1988.

A catalogue record for this book is available from the British Library.

ISBN: 0 7153 2024 6

Printed in Singapore by KHL
for David & Charles
Brunel House   Newton Abbot   Devon

Commissioning Editor Mic Cady
Art Editor Sue Cleave
Production Beverley Richardson

Series Editor Sue Gordon, OutHouse Publishing
  Winchester, Hampshire SO22 5DS
Designer Robin Whitecross
Editors Lesley Riley, Jo Weeks
Proofreader Audrey Horne
Indexer June Wilkins

Visit our website at www.davidandcharles.co.uk

David & Charles books are available from all good bookshops;
alternatively you can contact our Orderline on (0)870 990 8222 or
write to us at FREEPOST EX2 110, D&C Direct, Newton Abbot, TQ12
4ZZ (no stamp required UK mainland).

ORNAMENTAL PLANT OR PERNICIOUS WEED?

In certain circumstances ornamental garden plants can be
undesirable when introduced into natural habitats, either
because they compete with native flora, or because they act
as hosts to fungal and insect pests. Plants that are popular in
one part of the world may be considered undesirable in
another. Horticulturists have learned to be wary of the effect
that cultivated plants may have on native habitats and, as a
rule, any plant likely to be a problem in a particular area if it
escapes from cultivation is restricted and therefore is not
offered for sale.

Contents

Introduction

Both of us are passionate about herbaceous perennials: Kevin about growing, introducing and discovering new varieties for our gardens; me about selling them, planting them and using them in my own garden and in gardens I have designed or have visited to give advice. With such a large and diverse group of plants to deal with, our problem has been selecting those to feature in this book.

We could not include everything. The number of varieties of our favourite perennials increases every year as breeders, hybridists, nurserymen and gardeners work their magic. The gardener looking for a specific plant should always be open-minded and prepared to accept a substitute. Perhaps the variety on offer is a more recent one, and an improvement on our recommendation. The selections Kevin and I have made for this book will undoubtedly change and be added to as time moves on.

We aim to whet the reader's appetite, to inspire the use of perennials in as many ways as possible. Perennials should be considered not only an essential element in the border but also serious contenders for use in any other situation in the garden. For example, they can bring colour to a woodland, add texture and interest in a low-maintenance gravel planting, and provide a luxurious display at the waterside. They are about flowers, certainly, but they are also about foliage, structure and texture. Most are easy to grow and maintain; some require special conditions and attention – qualities that appeal to the experienced gardener who likes a challenge. Grown with their own kind or mixed with other plant types, perennials have played a leading role in the garden for many years and will do so for many more to come.

Although the typical English herbaceous border is at its peak at the height of summer, you can have interest from herbaceous perennials for a much longer period, and this book will help you to achieve it. Because most perennials are available as container-grown plants, we are able to select varieties when we see them at their best. A plant in flower is easy to position in the garden, enabling creative combinations to be achieved.

Because of the variety offered by herbaceous perennials there will always be one that can be fitted in to even the most crowded garden. That quality is irresistible to any gardener. All of us who care deeply about plants want more of them, and when we find what we want we can always make room for it. We hope you find something new in this book, along with many old favourites that have proved their worth.

Andrew McIndoe

SELECTING HERBACEOUS PERENNIALS

The time it takes for a herbaceous plant to grow from hybridization to maturity is normally much shorter than for a woody plant. Therefore there are many more new cultivars of herbaceous perennials on offer than there are of most woody plants. Breeding of new cultivars has been spurred on in recent years by the interest in herbaceous perennials, the ease with which they can be accommodated in smaller gardens, and the desire of many modern gardeners to see virtually instant results.

Because of the fashionable popularity of certain plants, near alternative varieties are sometimes offered under the same name. If you are looking for a specific plant and no other variety will do, then be sure to buy from a reliable source. Choosing the plant as a large container-grown specimen later in the season, when the plant is in flower, may be the most satisfactory way of avoiding mistakes. The *RHS Plant Finder*, an annual publication well known to many gardeners, is an invaluable source of information on obtaining plants.

The Award of Garden Merit ♥

The Royal Horticultural Society's Award of Garden Merit (AGM) is a good indication of whether a plant is one to choose for your garden. Many of the plants in this book have been awarded the AGM (indicated by the symbol ♥).

So what does it mean? To qualify for the award, a plant has to have more than one point of interest and it has to have a unique property. It has to be easy to grow, be of sound constitution and, most importantly, be a good all-round garden plant. This is not to say that a plant without the AGM is not worth growing. It means that, to date, the Royal Horticultural Society has not trialled it or does not consider that the plant meets all these criteria.

LEFT: *Delphinium* 'Magic Fountains Lilac Rose' and *Centranthus ruber*

INTRODUCING HERBACEOUS PERENNIALS

Sometimes unfairly considered hard work, herbaceous perennials prove their worth with their reliable performance and, in most cases, ease of cultivation. Unlike woody plants, they do not need pruning, just a little tidying up.

Many perennials fill their space in the border in a season or two; some need dividing only rarely. Taller varieties must have support to give their best display. If you follow just a few rules of cultivation, perennials will reward you with a variety of form, leaf shape and flower colour unsurpassed by other plant groups.

RIGHT: *Iris sibirica* 'Flight of Butterflies'

What are herbaceous plants?

Understanding a little of the nature of herbaceous plants – what they are, why they grow the way they do, and where they come from originally – will help you to give them the care and conditions they need in your garden. In return, they will give you their very best performance.

The term herbaceous is applied to those plants that do not produce wood. Trees and shrubs, or 'woody plants', undergo a process called secondary thickening, whereby their stems are strengthened with woody tissue. This enables them to gain height year on year and to support leaves and flowers. As secondary thickening does not happen in herbaceous plants, their size may be more limited, although this is not always the case: the banana, for example, is a herbaceous plant. The 'trunk' of the banana 'tree' consists of layers of leaf bases, reinforced by fibres. Once the banana has fruited, the trunk dies, and is replaced by offsets that grow from the root.

DECIDUOUS OR EVERGREEN?

Most herbaceous plants from temperate regions are deciduous, that is, they lose their leaves and die down to ground level in winter. However, some are evergreen, their leaves having developed protective layers that prevent water loss and help them withstand extremes of temperature. Most herbaceous plants from tropical zones are evergreen: conditions in their native habitat allow the plants to continue to grow all year round so they have no reason to die down and go dormant.

PERENNIAL?

The term herbaceous can be applied to annuals and biennials, but it is usually used with reference to perennials. Deciduous herbaceous perennials survive from year to year by shedding their leaves and stems at the end of the

Some annuals and biennials such as the common foxglove, *Digitalis purpurea*, are grown as perennials because they survive in the garden from year to year by seeding themselves freely.

growing season, and overwintering by means of adapted stems or roots that store food and water in readiness for growth to start the following spring. This life cycle is either an adaptation to climates where there is insufficient light, water or warmth for part of the year to allow growth to be continuous, or it may be a result of habitat.

In gardens, the term herbaceous plants often includes annuals and biennials that seed themselves freely so are perennial in the garden, even if they are not perennial as individual plants. *Digitalis* (foxglove) and *Lunaria* (honesty) are two examples and these may be found in garden centres alongside true herbaceous perennials.

HABITATS

The herbaceous perennials that we grow in our gardens originate from a variety of habitats throughout the world: woodland, prairie, mountain, riverside, downland, bog. Their members include water plants such as *Nymphaea* (waterlily), which grow virtually submerged with only their flowers and leaf surfaces in contact with the air. At the other end of the spectrum are tropical plants that live entirely in trees; all parts of these plants are in contact with the air and they absorb atmospheric moisture by means of aerial roots.

As with all plants, knowledge of the natural habitat provides clues about the conditions a plant will enjoy in the garden and the contribution it will make to a planting scheme. For example, many herbaceous perennials, particularly those from woodlands, are adapted to grow, bloom, set seed and die down before competition from other plants robs them of water and light. *Corydalis flexuosa* ♀ is one such. Its light fern-like foliage appears from fleshy underground tubers early in the growing season. The foliage will work to replenish the food supply in the tubers, and as soon as it is in place, flowers are produced. In summer the flowers fade and set seed and the foliage dies down; the plant then becomes dormant below ground until the following spring. This is perfect timing as the foliage of the trees has by now stolen the light, and tree roots have drained the ground of moisture.

In some cases, the opposite conditions have led to similar growth habits. *Papaver orientale* (oriental poppy) is from Turkey and the Caucasus. It has long tuberous roots that enable it to grow, bloom, set seed and die back quickly in the early part of the year, before the fierce summer sun parches and bakes the earth in its native environment. The gardener needs to know this when positioning the plant in the garden, not only from the point of view of the poppy's preferred growing conditions, but also because of the gap it will leave in the border from early summer onwards.

(For more information about siting herbaceous perennials see pages 36–83.)

The waterlily *Nymphaea* 'Marliacea Chromatella' grows almost submerged, using the water as support for the stems and floating leaves and flowers.

HARDINESS

Because in winter most garden herbaceous perennials have no leaves to be desiccated by freezing winds or stems to be ruptured by frost, their roots and underground stems are generally able to survive the coldest days of the year. Exotic appearance is not necessarily an indication of a tender constitution. Herbaceous peonies, for example, are extremely tough; despite luxuriant flowers and lush foliage, they can survive temperatures of −20°C (−4°F) or lower. Some evergreen herbaceous perennials, such as agapanthus, are also fairly hardy, simply becoming deciduous when grown in cold areas.

However, winter wet can cause problems. It is an enemy of many plants from alpine regions: they are used to cold, dry winters and the protection of an insulating layer of snow, and when exposed to cold and wet are prone to rot and decay. In fact, most perennials, except those that require boggy conditions, are hardier in well-drained soils than they are on heavy clay.

The majority of our favourite garden perennials, and their modern descendants, are easy, accommodating plants that will thrive and reward regardless of how carefully, or not, they are tended. Gardeners seeking a challenge can experiment with modifying conditions in their gardens to create the right environment to grow the more demanding varieties.

Perennials in the English garden: a history

People have been gardening since Roman times but it is only in the last century and a half that herbaceous perennials have become a major feature of our gardens. Inspired by the work of key Victorian gardeners, modern plantsmen have taken up these versatile plants and shared their passion for them, so that today herbaceous perennials are more popular then ever before.

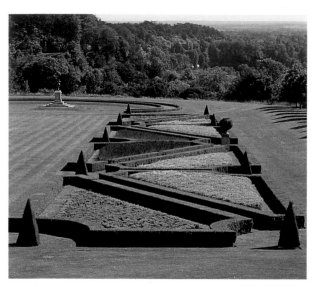

Topiary punctuates the parterre at Cliveden, Buckinghamshire. Trees and shrubs featured strongly in early gardens. Neat clipped hedges contained areas close to the house and joined the garden with the landscape.

The first plants cultivated in gardens were mostly those with a culinary or medicinal use. Even when gardens became more ornamental, gardening and collecting plants remained a pastime for the prosperous. And, because of the sheer size of the gardens of their wealthy clients, early designers often favoured trees and shrubs above herbaceous perennials, displaying them in open parkland settings; even smaller gardens or areas closer to the house consisted largely of shrubs, including neat clipped hedges in the knot-garden style. Nowadays, however, many of us have the opportunity to cultivate plants purely for their ornamental qualities, and here, to a great extent, lies the appeal of herbaceous perennials.

HOW PLANTS CAME TO GARDENS

Our passion for gardening has its roots in the early days of worldwide trading and the prosperity it generated. By the 16th century, the European seafaring nations were beginning to expand their empires, funded by wealth earned from trading foodstuffs, spices and materials from exotic crops. The 17th century saw many nations continue to flourish, and industrialization led to further trading. Many traders would have brought home plants found during their travels, perhaps via Cape Horn or South Africa; wealthy merchants travelling the world established gardens wherever they settled and brought specimens with them on their return to Europe.

In addition, there were those men who travelled specifically to study the flora of other lands and who brought back some of what they found. These 'plant hunters' were often the first Europeans to visit remote regions and they faced hardship and danger there. To add to their trials, much of the seed and plant material they collected perished on the journey home. Despite this, they made many successful introductions that have added to the glorious wealth of plants we now enjoy.

Tradescant senior and his son John are recognized as the most important of the 17th-century plant hunters. *Tradescantia virginiana* is a reminder of Tradescant senior's successful introductions of North American species while associated with the Virginia Company. In 1768, the *Endeavour* set sail from Plymouth, England, on its famous voyage of discovery of 'Terra Australis'

The Royal Botanic Gardens at Kew (left) were founded by Sir Joseph Banks on his return from Australia. David Douglas collected in America and introduced the Californian poppy, *Eschscholzia californica* (right).

The lovely *Primula bulleyana* (left) was introduced by George Forrest. William Robinson devised a new style of planting, using bold perennials and wildflowers in naturalistic settings (right).

under the command of Captain Cook. On board was Joseph Banks, a brilliant young scientist with a passion for botany. On his return to Britain, Banks founded the Royal Botanic Gardens at Kew with the help of King George III and so began the golden age of plant hunting, which lasted two centuries. The Royal Horticultural Society was founded in 1804 and, along with Kew, helped to fund a number of plant hunting expeditions. Commercial nurseries such as the famous Veitch Nursery of Chelsea were hungry for new plants to enrich their catalogues and sponsored expeditions.

The plant hunters brought back both woody and herbaceous plants. David Douglas is best known for woody plants and conifers collected in America, but he also brought species of lupin, penstemon, mimulus and the Californian poppy (*Eschscholzia californica* ♀). Robert Fortune travelled in the Far East and gave us such treasures as *Dicentra spectabilis* ♀ and *Primula japonica*. Ernest 'Chinese' Wilson introduced the beautiful *Lilium regale* ♀; George Forrest found *Primula bulleyana* ♀, and Frank Kingdon Ward *Meconopsis betonicifolia* ♀: the catalogue of introductions is seemingly endless.

ESTABLISHING THE ROLE OF HERBACEOUS PERENNIALS

It was not until the 1870s that herbaceous perennials evolved into their present role as a major ornamental part of our gardens. Using both wildflowers and bold

and beautiful herbaceous plants in a naturalistic setting, William Robinson (1838–1935) started a new era in planting, superseding the typical Victorian combination of dark evergreen shrubberies alongside formal colourful bedding schemes. Gertrude Jekyll (1843–1932) built on Robinson's ideas. Although known for colour-themed plantings, her borders also had structure, partly instilled through the repetition of bold plants such as acanthus, bergenias and stachys. She used subtle shades to enhance an effect, introducing yellow or white to blue plantings, for example, and often also introduced an element of surprise, such as orange lilies alongside blue delphiniums, to accent the planting. Plants that were more difficult to combine with others, such as ferns and hostas, were grown in pots, an idea that gardeners are just adopting today.

In her planting schemes for gardens such as those at Hestercombe, Somerset, Gertrude Jekyll used both soft and subtle colour progressions, adding bold surprises – perhaps orange lilies with blue delphiniums.

SPREADING THE WORD

Many herbaceous perennials and bulbs were introduced and promoted by E.A. Bowles (1865–1954). Known as a plantsman more than a gardener, he loved the rare and the unusual. He was also perhaps the most important garden writer of the early 20th century, and his thoughts and ideas are quoted by all influential plantsmen who have followed him.

The writings of Vita Sackville-West (1892–1962) about the garden at Sissinghurst in Kent further aroused interest in herbaceous perennials. Sissinghurst, now in the care of the National Trust, is still considered to be one of the best gardens in the world for herbaceous perennials: gardeners everywhere have imitated the plantings found there, particularly the associations created with fine old roses. Sissinghurst combines the formal design and structure devised by Harold Nicolson, Sackville-West's husband, with her informal and luxuriant style of planting. Their unusual lifestyle undoubtedly added an element of intrigue: successful gardens are often a reflection of the personality of the gardener, and perhaps the passion of a tortured artist comes through not only in the wealth of plant material at Sissinghurst, but also in how it is put together.

Hidcote Manor in Gloucestershire, now also owned by the National Trust, was the work of an American, Major Lawrence Johnston. Developed from 1903 onwards, the garden is renowned for its structure – a series of garden rooms divided by immaculate hedges – and for a number of plants that have been named after it. Johnston exchanged ideas with Sackville-West and other influential gardeners of the day. Within the strong structure of Hidcote, herbaceous perennials are used in sumptuous mixed plantings in both formal and informal settings. The red borders – a cocktail of red foliage and flowers – are perhaps the best known of the colour-themed plantings: a rich mixture against the dark yew hedges, which form the traditional backdrop of a herbaceous border. The woodland garden provides informal contrast with its hydrangeas and shade- and moisture-loving perennials.

CARRYING ON THE TRADITION

Gardens adviser to the National Trust for many years, the late Graham Stuart Thomas (1909–2003) carried on the herbaceous perennial tradition begun by these early pioneers. His books, published from 1940 onwards, have become the definitive works on old roses and herbaceous perennials. He was responsible for the establishment of the National Collection of old roses at Mottisfont Abbey, Hampshire. Here the visitor can meet not only his much-loved classic roses but also his herbaceous perennial 'old friends', as he knew them.

East Lambrook Manor in Somerset is another place that has been immortalized in the names of several excellent herbaceous perennials that originated there: *Euphorbia characias* subsp. *wulfenii* 'Lambrook Gold'♥, for example. The garden was the inspiration of journalist-turned-gardener Margery Fish (1889–1969), who had an enthusiastic interest in plant combining.

At Bressingham in Norfolk, Alan Bloom (1906–2005) pioneered the idea of island beds of perennials surrounded by lawn, a more informal and less labour-intensive approach. By selecting sturdy

Carol Klein's subtle and exuberant plantings have taught gardeners to look differently at perennials: the way they move in the breeze, the effect of light on both colour and outline, and how they work together.

varieties and using them carefully, he ensured that plantings were largely self-supporting and gave a long season of interest. As befits a nurseryman and plant breeder, he introduced many new varieties, work that is continued by his son Adrian and grandson Jason.

Two other important names in modern herbaceous perennial gardening are Beth Chatto and Carol Klein. Beth Chatto is well known for her writings on the selection and cultivation of herbaceous perennials for specific growing conditions, and for her clever use of foliage and plant forms. She has introduced us to many unusual plants. Carol Klein, through her enthusiasm and sincere interest in her subject, has taught gardeners to look more closely at the detail of plants: how they move in the breeze, the effect of light and the sheer wonder of their luxuriance.

As creative use of plants in gardens has developed, gardeners have gained the confidence to develop their own styles. Through his experiences in the garden at Great Dixter, in Sussex, Christopher Lloyd has become an advocate of bold experimentation with colour and form, asserting that subtle (or 'dull', as he describes it) is not the only option. Robinson would have approved of Lloyd's use of exotic plants such as cannas to enrich more traditional plant combinations.

NEW STYLES AND NEW VARIETIES

Meadow gardens and prairies are relatively new styles of planting that combine herbaceous perennials and bulbs with grasses. Emulating natural habitats, they bring a different kind of informality to the garden setting. In Europe, their early use in public parks and other open spaces was in stark contrast to the stiff, ordered coniferous plantings that preceded them. Through use of native species, these schemes also fulfil a conservation function and, with current levels of environmental awareness, the prairie and the wildflower meadow have become highly popular in the last few years.

Although herbaceous perennials are such a feature in English gardens, interest in them is by no means confined to Britain. From the late 20th century onwards,

Herbaceous perennials fit into any garden, even those with modern, minimalistic planting. This has led to increased interest in bold foliage subjects such as hostas (left) and rodgersias (right).

American nurserymen have been active particularly in the breeding of new hostas, daylilies and irises. Many parts of North America and continental Europe have very cold winters and warm summers; since deciduous herbaceous perennials die down in winter, they are often highly suitable for gardens in these areas, whereas woodier plants tend to find the contrasting temperatures and icy winds more of a challenge.

Even gardens with a minimalist, low-maintenance approach have space for herbaceous perennials. The foliage of architectural subjects such as angelicas, rheums and rodgersias is ideally suited to such a setting, the big leaves perfectly balancing strong architectural lines and bold masonry. In addition, these plants require no complicated pruning and training: just let them grow and give an impressive display, then clear up when they get knocked back in the winter.

THE FUTURE

In recent years herbaceous and evergreen perennials have gained ever increasing popularity. These affordable plants offer good value, reliably performing year on year. Many of them are extremely easy to grow and maintain, and they are available in such variety that there is more than enough choice for every size and type of garden. As gardens get smaller and fuller, perennials will become even more popular with enthusiastic gardeners. There may not be space for another shrub or tree, but there is always room for just one more herbaceous perennial

Speaking botanically

Latin names are essential for accurate communication. A plant's common name may vary from one area to another; and when it comes to using common names in a different country, the confusion can be greater still. The origins of botanical Latin date back to the 1700s, to the work of the Swedish botanist Carl Linnaeus. The dual name system he devised is still in use today.

PLANT CLASSIFICATION

FAMILY In plant classification flowering plants are divided into families. Each of these contains a number of genera that have similar characteristics. Members of the family Leguminosae, for example, all have pea-like flowers and carry seed in a pod (the Latin word *legumen* means pulse). Genera within this family include *Baptisia*, *Lathyrus* and *Lupinus*. A plant's botanical name consists of the genus and the species.

GENUS The generic name is something like our surname. The generic name always starts with a capital letter and is always a noun. It is often derived from names found in an ancient language such as Latin, Greek or Arabic. *Artemisia*, for example, is named after Artemis, one of the goddesses of ancient Greece. Other generic names commemorate people, in some cases the person that discovered the plant. For example, *Lobelia* is named after Matthias de l'Obel, a botanical author, plant collector and physician to James I, *Dahlia* after Anders Dahl, a Swedish botanist and pupil of Linnaeus.

SPECIES A plant's specific name, or epithet, is more like our first name, although it is written after the genus and always starts with a lower case letter. It cannot stand alone as a name. As a Latin adjective, it takes the gender of the generic name, so its ending agrees with the noun (although there are exceptions to this, as there are in any language). The specific name is descriptive, telling us something about the plant.

MEANINGS OF SPECIFIC NAMES

Specific names fall into a several categories, such as:

Describing origin: by continent, country, region; e.g., *europaeus, -a, -um*, from Europe (as in *Asarum europaeum*).

Describing habitat: from marshes, woods, fields, by water; e.g., *palustris, -e*, of swamps or marshes (as in *Caltha palustris*).

Describing the plant or a feature of the plant: its size, habit, leaf shape, flower colour; e.g., *ruber, rubra, rubrum*, red (as in *Filipendula rubra*).

Describing the use of a plant: many herbaceous plants have the specific epithet *officinalis*, meaning 'of the shop', referring to the apothecary's shop and the plant's use for medicinal purposes (as in *Pulmonaria officinalis*).

Commemorating a botanist, plant collector, famous horticulturist, patron: e.g., *fortunei*, after the 19th-century plant hunter Robert Fortune (as in *Hosta fortunei*).

SUBSPECIES, VARIETAS AND FORMA These are the botanically recognized subdivisions of a species where distinct forms occur in the wild. These are variously known as subspecies (subsp.), varietas or variety (var.) and forma or form (f.). For example, *Euphorbia characias* subsp. *wulfenii*.

Subspecies and forms are less common as cultivated forms of herbaceous perennials than they are in the world of trees and shrubs.

CULTIVAR A cultivar is a distinct form of a species that has been selected from wild or cultivated stock and has then been maintained in cultivation by vegetative propagation. In other words, all offspring come from one original plant. The cultivar name is written with an initial capital letter within single quotation marks, and follows the specific name. For example, *Campanula lactiflora* 'Loddon Anna'. Sometimes the cultivar name immediately follows the generic name. This often occurs with genera that have many garden hybrids, sometimes of uncertain parentage. For example, *Iris* 'Langport Wren' and *Hemerocallis* 'Gentle Shepherd'.

In gardening nomenclature, the terms 'cultivar' and 'variety' are used interchangeably. Often, too, the term 'form' is used in a general way to refer to a variety, subspecies or cultivar.

GROUP A cultivar shows little or no variation, because it has originated from a single individual. Members of a group can show considerable variation, but not enough to separate them botanically. For example, *Aquilegia* McKana Group include a range of hybrids of variable flower colour but with similar flower form.

HYBRID Species are collected from the wild; hybrids are usually born in gardens. Over the years, gardeners have interfered with nature by hybridizing species and, in some case, genera. Where a hybrid has originated from a cross made between two species, the new 'hybrid epithet' is always preceded by a multiplication sign. For example, *Nepeta × faassenii* is a hybrid between *Nepeta racemosa* from the Caucasus and *Nepeta nepetella* from Europe and North Africa.

In some cases, where two genera are closely related, it is possible to create a hybrid between them. In this case, the multiplication sign always appears before the generic name. For example, *× Heucherella alba* 'Bridget Bloom' is a hybrid between *Heuchera × brizoides* and *Tiarella cordifolia*.

NAME CHANGES

The naming of plants using botanical nomenclature is an ongoing process. As botanists' knowledge increases, it sometimes becomes apparent that plants that appeared

---

similar at the outset are in fact sufficiently different to require separate classification, so it becomes necessary to make changes to nomenclature. Old names, when they are particularly well known, are often shown in parentheses after the new name. For example, *Leucanthemum × superbum* (*Chrysanthemum maximum*).

Plant nomenclature is controlled by two international codes. The botanical names (in other words, the generic and specific names) are covered by the International Code of Botanical Nomenclature. This is applied to wild and cultivated plants. The cultivar names, which are used in addition to the botanical name, are covered by the International Code of Nomenclature for Cultivated Plants. This relates only to garden plants.

PLANT NAMES ARE FUN!

Whether the gardener is a natural linguist or not, botanical Latin is a satisfying language. Just as a feel for plants grows the more you work with them, so a feel for plant names develops over time. Not only are the names in a language that can be used anywhere in the world, they also provide immediately accessible information about the plant to which they refer. A few examples:

Specific epithet	Meaning	Example
argenteus, -a, -um	silvery	*Salvia argentea*
bonariensis, -e	of Bonaria (Buenos Aires)	*Verbena bonariensis*
grandiflorus, -a, -um	large flowered	*Epimedium grandiflorum*
latifolius, -a, -um	broad leaved	*Campanula latifolia*
mollis, -e	soft	*Alchemilla mollis*
perennis, -e	perennial	*Linum perenne*
spinosus, -a, -um	spiny	*Acanthus spinosus*
spectabilis, -e	showy	*Dicentra spectabilis*
vulgaris, -e	common, familiar	*Pulsatilla vulgaris*

For a fuller exploration see Hillier's *Plant Names Explained*.

Buying perennials

Herbaceous perennials are available in a number of different forms, including seed, bare-root plants, young pot-grown plants, and larger, more mature specimens. All these have their advantages and disadvantages. Which form you choose depends to a large extent on how much money you want to spend – and how impatient you are to see results.

Many herbaceous perennials, such as delphiniums, are easily raised from seed.

SEED

For the admirably patient gardener who is prepared to start from scratch, seed is the ideal way of acquiring a number of plants at relatively little cost. Growing from seed is most attractive where a large area needs to be filled, or drifts of plants are required. Lupins, delphiniums and *Digitalis* (foxgloves) are all easily raised from seed, as is *Verbena bonariensis*♀; all these flower relatively quickly from seed. However, not all herbaceous perennials can be grown successfully in this way; named varieties, for example, do not come true from seed, while the seed of some others may be sparse or difficult to germinate.

Perennials with fleshy roots or rhizomes can be bought bare root in the dormant season.

BARE ROOTS

In the days before nurseries used pots for raising plants, perennials were grown in fields and then lifted, divided and sold as bare-root plants during the dormant season. Some are still sold in this way. While those with delicate roots must be protected in compost or moss in order to survive such treatment, there are many with tough swollen roots or underground stems that can live in a semi-dry state for several weeks out of the ground.

Buying bare-root plants can be an inexpensive way of acquiring perennials such as *Gypsophila* (baby's breath), *Incarvillea* or *Papaver orientale* (oriental poppy). They are often sold alongside summer-flowering bulbs in coloured packets. However, do not expect to acquire the choicest varieties in this way; plants are often sold by flower colour rather than by cultivar name. The divisions of more select plants such as peonies may be small and will take several years to flower and make a sizeable plant in the border.

Young pot-grown perennials planted in groups early in the season will make substantial clumps by midsummer.

SMALL POTS

To create an attractive effect, the majority of herbaceous perennials need to be planted in groups of three or five. To achieve this at a realistic price it is best to acquire young pot-grown plants in early spring. Because most perennials grow and establish quickly, these will soon catch up with larger, more mature specimens planted later in their life. It is important to buy and plant such

BUYING POT-GROWN PERENNIALS

Buying perennials grown in containers gives the gardener the flexibility to plant at any time of the year. Just as importantly, however, it avoids the check to growth that is caused when bare-root stock has to establish itself before it can begin to form new shoots. With herbaceous perennials it is the root system that is important, not what is above ground, since this growth is replaceable. When buying larger stock look for a good full pot, with plenty of healthy stems emerging from the compost. A small plant in the middle of a large pot of compost is usually not a good buy.

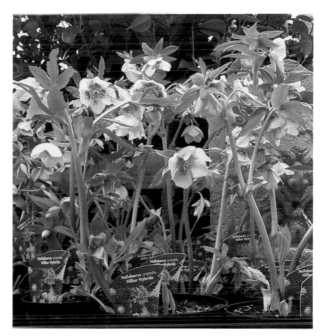

Buying choice perennials such as hellebores when they are in flower means you can see what you are getting, rather than relying on the label.

specimens early in the season: the amount of compost in the pots is small and the plants soon become starved. If they are not planted out, they may be stimulated to flower instead of producing good root systems and healthy foliage first.

LARGE POTS

Because of the modern trend towards 'instant' gardening specimen-sized container-grown plants have become very popular. This is one of the most expensive ways of buying plants, but may be worth it if the gardener wants a quick result.

Some plants are well worth the extra cost, because of the role they play in the garden. Architectural and statuesque perennials that will be used as features in planting schemes are examples: one good plant of *Cynara* (cardoon) or *Actaea* (*Cimicifuga*) will make an instant impact. In the case of *Actaea*, growth can be slow, so a large plant is a good investment. Large plants of easy-to-grow perennials such as *Alchemilla mollis* ♀ (lady's mantle) and most hardy geraniums really are an

extravagance; the money would be better spent elsewhere in the garden. The same is true of biennial plants and short-lived perennials such as foxglove; if you buy a mature foxglove it is often near the end of its lifespan.

THE PRICE OF PLANTS

The way that a herbaceous perennial is propagated usually has a major bearing on its price. Those raised from seed and fast-growing, clump-forming types that are easily divided are normally less expensive than those raised by root cuttings or shoot cuttings or those that are slow growing.

Named cultivars can only be propagated vegetatively, that is by taking part of the parent plant, not by using seed, so these cost more, particularly where propagation is slow and the availability of material limited.

MICROPROPAGATION

The availability of herbaceous perennials has increased in recent years due in part to the introduction of micropropagation, which enables a large number of plants to be propagated from a single individual in a relatively short space of time. Micropropagation is currently commercially satisfactory only for the propagation of herbaceous plants; it is rarely used for woody plants.

In laboratory conditions, the growing tip of a plant (the meristem) is removed and then cultivated in a sterile environment to produce more tissue, from which numerous tiny plantlets eventually form. These are gradually accustomed to normal growing conditions and are grown on until they reach saleable size.

The timescale of the operation varies according to plant type but in some circumstances a single plant can be multiplied into many thousands in only a couple of years. With the gardener's constant craving for something new, this is commercially very important. It has resulted in large numbers of new cultivars of genera such as *Hosta* and *Heuchera* becoming widely available in a short space of time.

Soil preparation and planting

Although some plants are very particular about the conditions in which they grow, most do best on neutral, fertile, well-drained soil that does not dry out. As perhaps only one in a hundred gardeners has these ideal conditions, the rest of us have to help our plants thrive through good cultivation techniques and adding nutrients to the soil.

Prepare the site well, mixing in compost and fertilizer. Dig a hole larger than the rootball.

Water the plant thoroughly, then carefully turn it out of its pot, without disturbing the roots.

Check the rootball surface is just below ground level. Replace soil, firm gently, then water well.

CULTIVATION

Thorough cultivation of flower beds is essential for good soil structure and healthy plant growth. Breaking up the soil with a fork will facilitate air and water penetration, which will help perennials develop a good root system. Prior to planting, digging should be deeper since this will encourage newly planted specimens to establish deep roots. Even apparently shallow-rooted perennials have fine roots that grow down into the soil in search of water. These roots are especially important for plants growing on soil that dries out in summer; they will be better able to withstand these conditions if their root systems are well developed.

Dig new beds in autumn, leaving the ground rough to allow the penetration of frost, which will continue the cultivation process through a freeze–thaw action. Using a fork or border spade rather than a traditional digging spade will make the task less arduous and will break up the soil more thoroughly. Where plants are being added to existing beds, cultivate the area deeply, adding compost or manure to the hole, along with a slow-release fertilizer; this will help to give the newcomers a head start over competing neighbours.

ORGANIC MATTER

Organic matter is good for just about all types of soil. Well-rotted manure or garden compost increases the soil's water-holding capacity and its potential to retain nutrients. By increasing the humus content it also improves the overall structure of the soil. For example, humus separates the fine particles of a clay soil, helping it towards a more open, crumbly texture, while in sandy soil it forms a gel-like layer around the large particles, helping in the retention of moisture and nutrients.

DRAINAGE

Some plants like wet conditions, but most appreciate good drainage, even if they do not like to dry out. Along with organic matter, sharp grit or gravel is useful to improve the drainage of heavy clay soils. Roughly dig a layer of sharp grit into the soil in the autumn; this will work in during winter as the ground freezes and thaws.

FEEDING

Most soils, especially clay, are adequately fertile for the majority of plants. Bulky organic manures add readily available nitrogen (for growth), but little else in the way of nutrition. Use a general slow-release fertilizer to ensure that plants receive all the main plant nutrients, and trace elements, if required.

PERENNIAL WEEDS

Perhaps the most important task when planting is to eradicate perennial weeds beforehand. Digging out is rarely entirely successful on the first attempt; fragments of root of weeds such as ground elder and bindweed quickly regrow. It is better to treat growing weeds with

Perennial weeds must be eradicated before any planting is undertaken.

a systemic herbicide, such as glyphosate, wait for any regrowth and re-treat before carrying out permanent planting. Bear in mind that perennial weeds themselves are herbaceous perennials, and herbicides are unable to distinguish between those that the gardener strives to cultivate and those that he or she wishes to eradicate. Remember, too, that systemic herbicides work only on actively growing weeds with plenty of top growth; they are inactivated by contact with bare soil.

Impatience to plant will not save time and effort in the long run. If perennial weeds persist in the flower beds, they will become a real problem to eradicate as the planting becomes established.

PLANTING

The majority of herbaceous perennials establish quickly and easily. The ideal time to plant is early spring, just as the plants are starting into growth. Those planted as bare roots will quickly start to produce leaf and stem growth and develop root systems to support it. Container-grown stock planted at this time behaves in just the same way. Whenever you plant, be sure to water well immediately afterwards and until the plant is established.

Some gardeners favour autumn planting. However, roots move hardly at all in winter, so there is little chance for plants to establish themselves. It is also more difficult to get the planting level right when there is nothing above ground. More tender subjects, and those that require good drainage, are best given the growing season to settle in before being faced with winter conditions.

When planting pot-grown specimens, aim to get the potting compost surface just below the soil surface. It is very easy to plant too deeply and this can affect performance in some subjects. For example, plants with rhizomes that need ripening by the sun, such as *Iris germanica*, will grow miserably and flower poorly, if at all, if the rhizomes are covered by soil. Similarly, peonies fail to flower if their crowns are covered by more than 2cm (about 1in) of soil. Planting depth is difficult to judge when soil is wet and sticky, another sound reason for good preparation and spring planting.

Maintenance

Herbaceous perennials are generally easy to cultivate and maintain, with one of the most important jobs being to ensure that those that need support are well staked before flowering time. Most perennials grow quickly and fill space effectively so may need control in future years, but there is less mystique attached to their pruning than with woody plants, and most can be increased through simple propagation methods.

DIVIDING AND REPLANTING

Most herbaceous perennials eventually become over-crowded and the clumps they form grow too large for their position in the flower bed. When this happens it is necessary to lift the clumps, divide them and replant some of the divisions, allowing space for them to develop. The frequency of this operation depends on the growth habit, rate and vigour of the individual plant. Some, including *Hemerocallis* (daylily) and *Helenium*, may benefit from this treatment every three to five years, while others such as peonies will live for many years without attention. There is no hard and fast rule; it is up to the discretion of the gardener.

Where winters are mild and wet, as in Britain, divide plants in early spring. Because of the lack of growth over the winter, autumn transplanting brings the risk of any damaged roots rotting in wet soil. In drier climates transplanting in the autumn is preferable as the plant then has the maximum time to re-establish before it is faced with summer drought.

Lift clump-forming perennials using a fork: work around the plant, carefully prising it from the soil and

A large clump of hemerocallis is split into smaller pieces.

Three of the divisions are replanted, allowing 30cm (12in) between them.

DIVIDING BEARDED IRISES

Some perennials are best divided and replanted after flowering. The most important example is the bearded iris: its clumps gradually become overcrowded, which reduces vigour and flowering. Take young pieces of rhizome from the outside of the clump, shorten the leaves to one third of their height to avoid wind disturbance, and replant the divisions, anchoring them onto the soil using wire pegs or hoops if necessary.

TAKING ROOT CUTTINGS

Root cuttings can be used to renew and propagate perennials with thick fleshy roots: *Pulmonaria* (lungwort), *Papaver* (poppy), *Anemone × hybrida* (Japanese anemone) and *Acanthus* (bear's breeches), for example. Use pots of general-purpose compost with added sand and insert pieces of root 2cm (about 1in) long so that the top cut end is just below the surface. Stand the pots in a frame or a sheltered, shaded corner of the garden and keep the compost moist.

Perennials such as hemerocallis need dividing every three to five years.

keeping the clump intact if possible. Then simply pull the clump apart by hand. With a stubborn clump, plunge two forks back to back into the clump and work them outwards to prise it apart. If all else fails chop the clump into divisions using a spade. For replanting, choose divisions from around the edge of the original clump as these will be the youngest and most vigorous, and they will not have suffered from overcrowding. Pot up some spare divisions to fill gaps or in case any of the planted ones fail.

Herbaceous perennials with deep, fleshy roots, such as poppies and peonies, are more difficult to divide as it is virtually impossible to keep the rootballs intact (see Moving peonies, below). In the case of oriental poppies, any pieces of root that break off in the process may be used as root cuttings. This type of perennial is the sort that grows like a weed in one garden and fails in another.

Some herbaceous perennials are woody at the base and more shrub-like in habit. These usually deteriorate with age so propagation is necessary for replacement of the plant as well as increasing your stock. Woody-based perennials are not usually suitable for division and are best propagated by stem cuttings. *Dianthus* (pinks) and

Penstemon are good examples of plants that are easy to propagate from cuttings but never seem to recover after division. Take cuttings in summer from non-flowering shoots and overwinter them in pots, under protection, before planting out the following spring.

COPING WITH RAMPANT VARIETIES

Some plants, such as those that spread by underground stems or long thin rhizomes, may need containing to prevent them taking over the border. *Macleaya* (plume poppy), for example, has long rhizomes that quickly find any available space and then send towering stems of jigsaw-puzzle leaves rocketing skywards. This can be overpowering for less robust shrubs and perennials growing in the area. Mint is often grown in a bottomless bucket plunged into the herb bed, and other plants of a similar habit can be grown in the same way. Inexpensive plastic pots are readily available from garden centres; choose ones at least 45cm (18in) across and of similar depth, in black or brown in case the rim becomes visible in the border. Either remove the bottom or drill plenty of large holes in it to prevent the container from becoming waterlogged.

Less invasive perennials with rhizomes near the soil surface, such as hardy geraniums, can be contained by inserting terracotta roofing tiles vertically into the ground to form a box around the plant. *Aegopodium podagraria* 'Variegatum' (variegated ground elder) makes a very attractive edging plant when grown in this way sandwiched between two rows of tiles.

Some vigorous perennials can be contained using a physical barrier in the soil. Here, *Aegopodium podagraria* 'Variegatum' is held back by roof tiles.

MOVING PEONIES

The peony has a reputation for being the most difficult herbaceous perennial to move successfully. Peonies have a tuberous root and little in the way of fibrous roots. Lift them just as the new red shoots are about to break through the soil surface in late winter or early spring. Replant immediately to the same depth as before. No more than 2cm (about 1in) of soil should cover the crown of the plant: deep planting will result in lack of flowers.

If lupins are cut back to ground level immediately after flowering, they will produce a second crop of flowers later in the season.

TIDYING AND CUTTING BACK

Since most gardeners were born to prune, herbaceous perennials will be their targets at some point in the year. Tidying up and cutting back at the right time can enhance the performance and appearance of most perennials. For inexperienced gardeners, there is little risk of inflicting a permanently damaging cut because the underground part of the plant will generate new stems next season.

Although tidying has its place in late summer, take care not to remove stems that still have decorative potential. While hardy geraniums and *Alchemilla mollis* ♀ (lady's mantle) will produce a new low mat of foliage if cut back after the main summer flowering, similar treatment of plants that colour well in autumn will rob you of a season of glory. Autumn colour is

After flowering, cut back *Alchemilla mollis* (left), but leave *Euphorbia griffithii* 'Fireglow' (right) so as to enjoy the autumn colour of its foliage.

mainly a feature of deciduous shrubs and trees, but some herbaceous perennials also play their part. *Euphorbia griffithii* 'Fireglow' is a good example. After its spectacular spring display of glowing bracts on upright shoots, 'Fireglow' grows branches and can become a rather untidy mass of stems and narrow green leaves. The temptation to cut it back at this point is strong, but to do this would be to sacrifice a superb show of orange and red shades that lasts for several weeks in autumn.

In addition, some herbaceous perennials have stems and seedheads that remain decorative late into the year. Although dead, and usually devoid of leaves, these stems and seedheads stand proud in the winter garden, making an eye-catching feature, especially when etched with frost; many are also appreciated by birds, which search out their ripe seeds. *Rudbeckia* and *Echinacea* are two that retain straight stems with cone-shaped seedheads, particularly attractive against the fine waving leaves of parchment-yellow winter grasses. The dark purple-pink flowers of *Sedum spectabile* ♀ (ice plant) become more sophisticated as they fade to chestnut on their fleshy stems.

Those perennials with soft, non-persistent stems and leaves, such as hostas, are the easiest to deal with. They quickly collapse and decay with the first frosts and the onset of winter. Tidy gardeners remove the leaf waste and commit it to the compost heap at any time between late autumn and early spring. In cold areas there may be an advantage in delaying this because the leaf waste provides an extra layer of protection on the soil surface. Take into account early-flowering bulbs planted among the perennials – late clearing may be made difficult by their emerging shoots.

DEADHEADING AND REMOVING FLOWERS

Some early-flowering perennials will produce a second crop of blooms if cut back immediately after flowering. Delphiniums and lupins are the most notable examples. When the first main spike fades, it is tempting to trim this back and preserve the weedy lateral flowers until

Penstemons will bloom throughout the season if regularly deadheaded. This keep the plants in trim without the need for hard pruning.

Verbena bonariensis self-seeds prolifically. To prevent unwanted spread cut back the flower stems as soon as the blooms have faded.

the very last bloom has faded. A positive approach is needed: once the main blooms have faded, cut the stems right back to ground level. Water plants well and apply a general-purpose fertilizer, in liquid form if conditions are dry. New foliage will quickly appear, followed by a further crop of flowers in early autumn. These colourful summer beauties are particularly welcome alongside autumn favourites such as *Crocosmia* and *Rudbeckia*.

Some herbaceous perennials can become pests if allowed to set seed, especially in light, sandy soil where seed germination is particularly good. If lady's mantle is not prevented from getting a hold, it will produce seedlings in profusion and can become too successful as a ground-cover plant. To prevent such spread, cut off the flowers as soon as the lime colour of the blooms starts to yellow. Alternatively, stems can be pulled off established plants by tugging firmly. Where the foliage has flopped and become untidy, the whole plant can be sheared off to ground level and allowed to regrow: a fresh crop of leaves and a few late flowers will result. Also consider removing the faded flowers of *Knautia macedonica*, *Verbena bonariensis* ♀ and *Verbascum* before seed is sprinkled liberally all over the border.

Some plants are mainly grown for foliage effect and these also benefit from the removal of the flower stems before seed is set. Flowering and seed production is part of a plant's life cycle; when seed is produced, the plant

knows that its job is done for the season. If the cycle is not completed, because seed is not allowed to set, there is more chance of the foliage staying in good condition. In other cases, the faded flower stems simply detract from the beauty of the leaves and for that reason should be removed.

Stachys byzantina is wonderfully silver as the new 'lamb's ear' leaves appear in spring. The plant becomes more noticeable as the flowering stems rise from the silver felted mat beneath. Once the lilac flowers open, however, these stems become untidy and the foliage starts to deteriorate. Cutting it back at this point will encourage the plant to produce new silver foliage, which will look good throughout the autumn. Statuesque *Cynara cardunculus* ♀ (cardoon) is a magnificent plant,

Stachys byzantina (left) looks better if flower stems are removed. Cut back *Cynara cardunculus* (right) after flowering and new leaves will appear.

but it declines after the flowers have produced their thistle-like mauve stamens in late summer. Cut the plant to ground level now and new silver leaves will emerge; these remain on the plant throughout winter, surviving all but the most severe weather.

Several hostas retain their leaf variegation better if the flower stems are removed as they appear. Hosta flowers are not unattractive, so it is up to the gardener to decide whether the flowers or the variegated leaves are preferable. The foliage of rheums also remains more attractive if the flower stems are removed at an early stage: allow them to develop but not to set seed. Keep pulmonarias looking better and encourage them to produce their new foliage more quickly by removing flower stems as the blooms fade in late spring. Do this to brunneras, too, especially the lovely silver-variegated *Brunnera macrophylla* 'Jack Frost'.

The foliage of variegated hostas (left) is preserved by removing flowers as they appear. The lovely *Brunnera macrophylla* 'Jack Frost' (right) remains in good condition if the flowers are removed as they begin to fade.

PROVIDING SUPPORT

Support in some form or other can make or break perennial planting, whether the subjects form part of a classic herbaceous border or are contributing to a mixed scheme. In mixed borders shrubs lend some support and shelter to their herbaceous companions. In prairie-style planting grasses may perform a similar function, filtering the wind and so reducing its impact. In traditional herbaceous borders, however, artificial support will always be necessary for the taller-growing perennials, whatever the situation.

Birch twigs put in position during early spring are natural supports for herbaceous perennials; they are hidden as the plants grow.

Traditional birch and hazel twigs are ideal for use as grow-through supports for individual plants in the herbaceous border. If you have a good local supply, they are generally inexpensive and easy to tailor to the height of the plants. Put them in position in early spring, well ahead of the perennials' main growing season. They look

REDUCING STAKING PROBLEMS

Grow strong, wind-resistant varieties. Choose plants that require little or no support rather than those that need every shoot staked. For example, *Aconitum* (monkshood) varieties are more upright and reliable than delphiniums. You may like the delphiniums' colour and habit, but are you prepared for the amount of maintenance they need?

Herbaceous perennials whose stems have collapsed under the weight of flowers, foliage and summer rain – like the peonies shown here – are never a pretty sight. Stay ahead of the game. Remember that perennials grow quickly and introduce support when they are still in good condition – not when the stems are starting to fall into one another.

Linked green metal plant supports, through which the developing stems grow, are strong and unobtrusive.

natural and in any case quickly disappear from view as the border billows in midsummer.

A similar effect is achieved with grow-through metal supports, which are basically metal hoops supporting a wire grid. These are held above individual plants on three or four legs and their height can be adjusted. Put them in position when the plants are just showing above ground. The stems grow up through the grid, gradually concealing it. In some cases, grids can be left in position through the winter. Metal supports are comparatively expensive but good quality galvanized ones last for many years. As they give support only to the lower part of the stem, they are most suitable for stouter subjects.

In herbaceous borders that do not contain any woody plants, large-gauge netting can be used over the whole planting area. Put this in position at the beginning of the season; as the plants grow through it they will be held upright by the mesh. Netting is extremely effective where all the border plants peak at the same time. If any cutting back is required, however, it can only be done down to the level of the netting, which will otherwise be exposed. Gaps in the border are difficult to fill during the growing season if netting is used in this way.

Bamboo canes are popular for supporting plants with tall spikes, such as delphiniums. Put them in place when the plants are knee-high and tie the stems in with twine or raffia as they grow. Thin, strong canes are the most discreet. Various metal and wire stakes are available that can be put in place during the growing season. These are

Semi-circular metal hoops on legs can be put into position later in the season to support tall perennials such as heleniums.

designed to support individual stems or whole clumps. The best ones are fairly inconspicuous, and are useful to have on hand to overcome unexpected problems due to abnormally lush growth or wind and rain damage.

WATERING AND MULCHING

When herbaceous perennials are planted during the autumn or early spring, a thorough watering helps to settle the soil particles around the roots and ensure easy establishment as new roots develop. Additional watering is rarely required during the early stages of growth, as perennial roots grow vigorously to balance the developing stems and leaves. When growth above ground is at its maximum, some perennials are particularly sensitive to drought, responding by wilting of foliage and of developing flowers. If dry conditions persist, their performance can be severely impaired. If they are watered liberally at the first signs of stress they quickly recover.

Generous mulching around the plants with garden compost, composted bark or well-rotted farmyard manure at the start of the season helps to conserve moisture and prevent water loss from the soil surface; it also helps to suppress weeds and will benefit the plants throughout the growing season.

Where do herbaceous perennials fit in?

Herbaceous perennials are extremely versatile and are as useful in new gardens as they are in established ones. They grow quickly and most show results in their first season (perfect for the impatient gardener). Many are inexpensive and offer exceptional value for money. In addition, they can be moved around within the garden and respond well to being divided and replanted.

LAYERING, STRUCTURING AND DECORATING

Trees, tall shrubs and climbers provide height in our gardens – they make them three-dimensional. The plants at eye-level are the first that grab our attention, so are perhaps the most important. Woody shrubs play a leading role, as do taller perennials, particularly many favourites such as delphiniums, foxgloves, heleniums, lupins, phlox and asters. The lowest layer – below eye-level – is the detail. It is often the closest to us and has become even more important in small modern gardens. Dwarf shrubs and annuals, bulbs and container plants

Herbaceous perennials predominate in the lower layer of planting, below eye-level. Here they are used both in the open ground and in pots.

are found here, but herbaceous perennials predominate because of the variety they offer. They include corydalis, hellebores, geraniums, hostas and pulmonarias.

Trees and shrubs form the basic structure of a garden. However, the average plot only has space for a certain number of these, so there are few opportunities for planting more once the selection has been made. Dwarf shrubs and container plants can be added, as can climbers, which occupy little space horizontally but fill the vertical space above them. But the biggest scope for adding plants comes in the form of bulbs, annuals and herbaceous perennials. All these may be seen as short-term propositions. Just like the accessories in a room, they are easily changed to alter the look, colour scheme and mood of a garden, as the gardener chooses.

COVERING GROUND

As well as being useful in their own right, herbaceous perennials are excellent for planting between newly planted shrubs and trees, to fill space and provide colour until the woody plants become established. Many are well adapted to poor soil or otherwise difficult sites so can be left in such positions as ground cover or used in other unpromising areas of the garden.

The choice of suitable herbaceous perennials is vast, and with a little thought, areas of ground cover can be made interesting and varied. The pretty *Erodium pelargoniiflorum* is a spreading perennial that will soon colonize poor soil in sun or shade, seeding freely on sandy soil. It resembles a hardy geranium, but with

GOOD GROUND COVERERS

The following perennials are good for filling the space under shrubs and covering ground in shade and semi-shade.

Ajuga reptans 'Atropurpurea' (page 118)

Ajuga reptans 'Catlin's Giant' ♧ (page 119)

Alchemilla mollis ♧ (page 46)

Epimedium × *rubrum* ♧ (page 62)

Euphorbia amygdaloides var. *robbiae* ♧ (page 57)

Euphorbia cyparissias 'Fens Ruby' (page 117)

Galium odoratum

Lamium galeobdolon (left)

Lysimachia nummularia 'Aurea' ♧

stiffer foliage, rather like that of a zonal pelargonium, in greyish green. The rosettes of leaves give rise to soft pink flowers in early summer. *Geranium* 'Ann Folkard' ♧ is often described as compact, but in semi-shade it will spread vigorously, its creeping stems carrying lime-yellow leaves and vivid magenta flowers, like those of its parent *Geranium psilostemon* ♧. Spreading and twining, it makes very effective ground cover, particularly under shrubs with gold foliage such as *Philadelphus coronarius* 'Aureus' ♧. On really challenging sites, such as beneath the canopy of mature rhododendrons, the tough and vigorous *Symphytum ibericum* will quickly create a bold leafy layer, with the benefit of pretty, creamy-yellow flowers in spring.

EXTENDING THE SEASON

Our gardens contain a profusion of shrubs that flower through spring into early summer. There are fewer woody plants that flower in summer and herbaceous perennials are ideal for filling the colour gap. Where roses predominate in a garden, cottage-garden favourites such as *Phlox paniculata*, *Leucanthemum* × *superbum* (shasta daisy) and *Campanula persicifolia* perform as the first flush of rose blooms starts to fade. Not only do they provide colour in the garden, but they are also valuable for cut flowers. Before the roses bloom, some perennials

start the period of interest: early peonies, oriental poppies, lupins and aquilegias bloom in late spring as colour from spring-flowering bulbs and shrubs fades.

PROVIDING VARIETY IN FORM AND TEXTURE

Many herbaceous perennials are soft in form and this softness brings movement into the garden. Perennials also come in a variety of shapes from rounded to spiky, spreading to vertical, all forms that bring borders to life. There is such a world of contrast between, for example, the upright spires of flowers produced by delphiniums and lupins and the mounded domes of hardy geraniums and some asters, that gardeners are almost spoilt for choice. (For more information, see pages 28–33.)

BROADENING THE COLOUR PALETTE

Herbaceous perennials are unrivalled in both the range and the intensity of colour they provide in our gardens. Bright gems are fitted into a planting scheme with partners that either soften or accentuate their display. For example, the solid blaze of flowers produced by star performers such as heleniums, rudbeckias, gaillardias, phlox and crocosmias is most effective diluted by foliage plants and other gentler companions. Adventurous gardeners have experimented with such neutral partners as grasses; in such associations the grass provides the perfect foil for the strength of colour of the flowers.

MIDSUMMER GAP FILLERS

These perennials are a good choice to follow on from late spring flowering shrubs such as deutzia, lilac and philadelphus, and the first flush of the roses:

Achillea hybrids

Coreopsis verticillata (left)

Hemerocallis hybrids

Knautia macedonica

Kniphofia hybrids

Salvia × *superba* ♧

Verbascum hybrids

Plant shapes

Borders consist of plants of different shapes and colours that work together to create a picture. Each plant shape contributes to the character and texture of the border as a whole. Changing the relative proportion of each shape in the composition has as much of an effect on the border's appearance as changing the proportions of the constituent colours.

The look of a planting scheme alters all the time, not only according to what is in flower, but also depending on the stage of growth of the plants. A successful scheme is a continuously changing picture, with enough variety to maintain interest throughout the seasons. Although herbaceous perennials are considered here, the majority of successful plantings use a mixture of perennials, trees, shrubs, annuals and bulbs, each making a contribution in shape, colour and texture.

These herbaceous borders at Ilnacullin, Ireland, are a symphony of different plant shapes, colours and textures.

SPREADING MATS

Often associated with hostile conditions, such as exposed situations and dry soils, mat-forming perennials lie low to avoid desiccation. Examples include *Acaena microphylla* ♥, *Sedum aizoon* and *Euphorbia myrsinites* ♥. Instead of growing upwards, these plants hug the ground, spreading out on it so their leaves can soak up the maximum amount of sunlight. Some develop long stems that grow out on the surface of the soil; some have underground stems or rhizomes that throw up short vertical shoots. However they grow, the overall plant shape is similar. Use these plants at the front of the border, where they will provide a gentle foreground for the plants behind. They associate well with paving and with gravel and are ideal for softening the edges of hard landscaping. Alongside a lawn, however, they make mowing difficult, unless contained.

Euphorbia myrsinites (left) and *Acaena microphylla* (right) are both herbaceous perennials that form low, spreading mats.

SPACE AND SHAPE

The space around a plant affects its overall shape and appearance. For example, to produce the impression of one large soft mound of herbaceous geraniums, plant several close together, but for several individual mounds, increase the planting distance to allow each plant enough space to develop fully.

Many herbaceous geraniums (left) and *Alchemilla mollis* (right) are perennials that form soft mounds near the front of the border.

Penstemon heterophyllus 'Catherine de la Mare' (left) and *Paeonia lactiflora* 'Bowl of Beauty' (right) both form mounds of solid structure.

SOFT MOUNDS

Soft mounds of foliage and flowers that melt into one another and billow across the border epitomize English gardens. Geraniums, *Anthemis tinctoria,* fine-leaved artemisias and *Alchemilla mollis* ♀ belong in this category. These plants are good at filling space either under or beside other plants. They are excellent companions for taller perennials and shrubs in a mixed border, and perfect under hybrid tea roses. Plant them at the front of a border or further back, or alternate them with lower spreading plants. The latter scheme accentuates the forms of the individual plants and makes the planting more interesting. Soft mounds can be monotonous *en masse* – relieve them with spiky and architectural forms.

Plants with narrow strap-shaped leaves, such as *Hemerocallis* and *Agapanthus,* create a different type of

soft mound. Out of flower, these two plants are fairly discreet, but when they are in bloom their shape and presence change dramatically; their exotic flowers are produced on relatively tall spikes in midsummer.

SOLID DOMES

Some plants are generally mound shaped, but have a more solid form. Most penstemons and *Euphorbia characias* varieties are good examples, forming shrub-like plants with persistent stems. Penstemon flowers rise on spikes above the mounded plants, which provide structure even when out of flower. The foliage of herbaceous peonies is also in this category; their blooms are short-lived, though spectacular, so the plant shape plays an important part. The foliage is attractive and provides long-lasting, bold rounded structure.

BROAD COLUMNS

Common among herbaceous perennials is the short, stout column. Plants of this form have many stems growing close together, all to the same height. The effect is of a green cylinder rising as the season progresses, and usually culminating in a sheet of flowers at the top of the column. Heleniums bear masses of daisy-like flowers, which open from dark buds, creating a rich velvet tapestry in late summer. Other examples include *Monarda, Aster, Heliopsis* and *Leucanthemum.*

Often these plants originate from grassland habitats where they need to grow tall to survive among the

REPEATING SHAPES

In larger borders repeat plant shapes at intervals. This simple technique holds the scheme together, regardless of what is planted in between. It was often used by Gertrude Jekyll to give her planting structure. She used blocks of the same plant, but a similar effect can be achieved with different plants of the same shape: a more practical solution in smaller areas.

Clumps of *Helenium* 'The Bishop' (left) and *Helianthus* 'Lemon Queen' (right) both make broad columns consisting of many upright stems.

grasses. In borders, the size of their clumps may need reducing regularly to prevent them predominating, and being too large and solid in effect. The interesting part of this shape of plant is at the top of the stems; they need lower, softer forms in front of them.

LIGHT SPIKES

Light spikes are among the most valuable plant forms because they provide vertical interest that will lift any planting scheme, whatever its scale. Plants such as

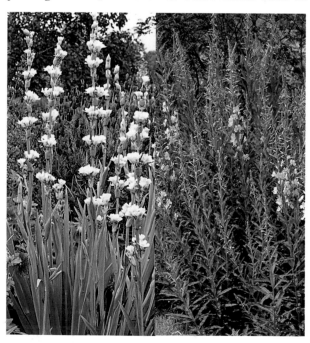

Sisyrinchium striatum (left) and *Chamerion angustifolium* 'Album' (right) have slender, upright flower stems that provide light spikes in the border.

Veronica spicata, *Digitalis lutea* and the familiar *Linaria purpurea* (toadflax) create gentle vertical brushstrokes in the border. They seed themselves freely on most soils, so increasing the sense of informality. *Sisyrinchium striatum* is a more definite spike and a wonderful cream colour. It has relatively few flowers but these, together with the grey-green sharp foliage, make it a good foil for frothy *Alchemilla mollis* ♀ or flowing *Nepeta* × *faassenii* ♀. On poor soils sisyrinchium seeds freely: thin as necessary.

The white form of the rosebay willowherb, *Chamerion angustifolium* 'Album', produces soft spikes

MAKING THE MOST OF BULBS

Bulbs are useful plants for prolonging the season of herbaceous perennials.

Alliums Ornamental onions naturally have poor foliage, so plant them where companions will hide this, such as beneath soft silver herbaceous plants. *Artemisia schmidtiana* ♀, with its finely cut foliage, is the perfect setting for *Allium cristophii* ♀, with its silvery lilac firework flowers.

Camassias For colour before many herbaceous perennials have got going, choose *Camassia leichtlinii*. Its spikes appear with the bluebells and the flowers are a similar colour. Plant it to grow through the emerging plumes of bronze fennel, *Foeniculum vulgare* 'Purpureum'.

Triteleias The long-lasting sapphire flowers of *Triteleia laxa* 'Koningin Fabiola' (QUEEN FABIOLA) are similar to agapanthus and add vibrant colour to mounds of soft lime-green *Alchemilla mollis* ♀. Both plants enjoy well-drained soil.

Tulips Create the effect of exotic poppies in the border by including well-spaced tulips among herbaceous perennials. The glorious simple dark flowers of *Tulipa* 'Queen of Night' are stunning above a lime-green carpet of *Euphorbia cyparissias* 'Fens Ruby'.

atop graceful stems clad with willow-like grey-green leaves. On a larger scale *Veronicastrum virginicum* is a taller, slimmer airy spike, reaching 2m (6ft) high. Where less height is required, the herbaceous salvias, such as *Salvia × superba*♀, contribute a mass of low spikes in glowing shades from midsummer onwards.

STATELY SPIRES

For a strong vertical statement, choose the stately spires of delphiniums, *Aconitum* (monkshood), lupins, *Alcea* (hollyhock) and *Digitalis purpurea* (common foxglove). These plants look spectacular, but no less impressive is their ability to achieve this height without producing permanent stems. The vegetative parts of the plant are not tall, only the flower stems, which thrust the flowers skywards to render them unavoidable to pollinators. Grandiose though these plants are in flower, their impact is lost at other times, so bear this in mind when planning their position. Also important are support, which needs to be in place before the flower stems arise, and access, which is necessary to allow them to be cut back after flowering to encourage a repeat performance.

In traditional herbaceous borders, spire-forming plants are placed at the back where their transient nature is disguised by more solid structures, such as a high wall or a yew hedge, perhaps with clipped hedges dividing the scheme into sections and providing height when the plants are not in full growth. This is rarely the way these plants are used in modern gardens. They need space but with their foundations screened behind more permanent subjects such as taller penstemons, whose main flowering season follows the peak of the lupins and delphiniums. Light foliage shrubs such as *Cornus alba* 'Sibirica Variegata' are another solution: they will grow on to fill the gaps created as the spires are removed. Alternatively, tall annuals such as the tobacco plant *Nicotiana sylvestris* may be planted alongside to take over the role of height provider, and make an equally arresting display later in the year.

Of all the plants in this group, *Acanthus spinosus*♀ (bear's breeches) is in a league of its own. It contributes

The stately spires of *Acanthus spinosus* (left) and *Digitalis purpurea* (right) create points of strong vertical interest in a planting scheme.

stately, self-supporting spires above a mound of bold architectural foliage. A favourite of Gertrude Jekyll, this is a plant that can be used nearer the front of a border to provide structure throughout the season.

BOLD BLOOMS

Some plants contribute little in terms of form, but their flowers can be used to make bold statements. Although the plants of *Papaver orientale* (oriental poppy) are of little substance in themselves and die down early in the

Achillea filipendulina 'Gold Plate' (left) and *Paeonia lactiflora* 'Lord Kitchener' (right) both provide bold flower forms of strong colour.

season, the flamboyant blooms are unmissable. Plant them beside more solid subjects that will hold the scheme together when the poppies have flowered and their foliage has faded. The larger achilleas, such as *Achillea filipendulina* 'Gold Plate' ♀ (see page 31), have an indistinct form with light fern-like foliage at the base of stiff stems. However, this is an advantage when they are in flower, as the bright flat blooms are solid shapes and seem to fly in loose formation above the border. The eye-catching flowers of tulips and alliums have a similar effect (see Making the most of bulbs, page 30).

Peonies, like acanthus, double up on effect. Their luxuriant floating blooms draw attention as they open (see page 31), and for the rest of the season the solid domes of strong green foliage contribute structure.

RISING CLOUDS AND DRIFTING MISTS

With their masses of tiny flowers or finely cut foliage, cloud-like plants add a magical lightness to planting schemes, softening the shapes and colours of their neighbours. Some grasses are particularly effective, the lovely *Stipa gigantea* ♀ (giant oat grass) for example. Its fine golden flowers reflect the light, especially in the low sun of evening. A smaller relative, *Stipa tenuissima*

The smoky foliage of purple fennel, *Foeniculum vulgare* 'Purpureum' (left), and the white cloud-like flowerheads of *Crambe cordifolia* (right) rise and drift above the border.

> ### HEIGHT IN THE FOREGROUND
>
> It is tempting to position tall plants at the back of a border and work forwards in order of decreasing height. Including some taller, lighter plants in the foreground makes the scheme more three-dimensional: this changes the perspective and the picture appears deeper and so more interesting.

produces a soft mist towards the front of a border and looks wonderful with short, smouldering *Crocosmia* (montbretia). The feathery foliage of bronze fennel, *Foeniculum vulgare* 'Purpureum', provides a drifting vapour throughout the season. Its soft colour is an excellent partner to most other perennials and it is especially useful to fill positions where seasonal interest is to follow: try it with *Dahlia* 'Bishop of Llandaff' ♀. However, *Crambe cordifolia* ♀ is the definitive cloud plant. Growing up to 2m (6ft) tall, it forms a billowing white cumulus above the border in early summer, the perfect setting for sapphire delphiniums or steel-blue monkshood. On chalk soils *Gypsophila paniculata* gives a similar effect, if lighter in quality. It is beautiful with scabious and other cottage-garden flowers.

SEE-THROUGH PLANTS

Plants that you can see through have two purposes in the border. In the foreground, they bring delicate height to the planting, something to look through, thereby increasing the perspective and depth of the scene.

> ### SUPPORT – THE SECRET OF SUCCESS
>
>
>
> Remember to provide support for plants before they need it. The beauty of a plant's shape is lost if it collapses just before it reaches its prime. Support is particularly important for plants with tall upright stems. Grow-through supports, put in place at an early stage of growth, are more satisfactory than trying to prop up fully grown stems. They also help to define the shape of a plant and the space it occupies.

Plants with tall, fine stems and small flowers such as *Verbena bonariensis* (left) and *Knautia macedonica* Melton pastels (right) can be used near the front of the border to add depth to the planting.

Further back, they can be drifted through the other plants: a thread holding them lightly together. *Verbena bonariensis*♀ is the ultimate see-through, drifting plant, hence its popularity. It has height without weight and its rich purple colour and deep green stems are good mixers with most. Other excellent qualities are a long flowering season and resistance to weather. *Valeriana phu* 'Aurea' possesses similar qualities, with tall, branched stems and small white flowers. It has the advantage of bright golden yellow young foliage, a cheerful addition to the border early in the year.

For temporary drifts through mixed planting, use hardy annuals. *Nigella* (love-in-a-mist), *Cosmos*, *Salvia viridis* var. *comata* and the annual grass *Briza maxima* are all easy to grow and associate well in informal schemes.

ADDING TO EXISTING PLANTING

Most herbaceous perennials arrive in the garden as additions to existing planting, rather than as part of a new scheme. When choosing a plant for a particular position, think about the shapes the scheme might lack, and at what time of the year. When positioning a new plant, think about the shape and texture of its potential neighbours, as much as their colour. A good combination of plant forms is just as important as a clever colour combination.

ACCENT ARCHITECTURALS

The shape of some perennials is unimportant compared to their bold distinctive stems and/or foliage. Use these plants as exclamation marks in mixed planting, giving them plenty of space to develop; if you do not, most will take it anyway, overwhelming weaker neighbours. With its huge steely leaves and statuesque stems, the cardoon *Cynara cardunculus*♀ will need more than a square metre (3ft sq) by midsummer. It is a good plant to take over where oriental poppies leave off as an accent point in the border. Its strong leaf form may fight with other bold subjects, so soften it with rounded mounds and light foliage. Another strong candidate is *Macleaya microcarpa* 'Kelway's Coral Plume'♀. Its jigsaw-puzzle blue-grey leaves on tall stems are more of a feature than the plumes of pinkish flowers. It is also an excellent choice for the back of a border against dark evergreens or growing through the soft fronds of bronze fennel. For an exotic touch use cannas with their fabulous foliage and brilliant flowers. As they are tender, they should be added seasonally in temperate regions.

Accent plants increase the sense of the exotic in a border and their effect can be stunning as long as they are appropriate to the style of the garden.

The bold foliage and flowers of *Cynara cardunculus* (left) and the tall stems and jigsaw-like leaves of *Macleaya microcarpa* 'Kelway's Coral Plume' (right) add dramatic effect to any planting scheme.

Colour: themes and continuity

In the planning stages, careful thought is often given to the colour scheme of a bed or border. Later, we tend to choose what appeals, often with little regard for perfect coordination. This is entirely acceptable. The most important rule of colour is to remember that it is a matter of personal taste. If you like a plant, and it looks good in your garden, then it is the right choice.

A yellow border at Hadspen Garden, Somerset, with a wonderful selection of soft yellow flowers set against an exuberant variety of foliage.

THEMING

Colour-themed planting is dependent upon what is in flower or otherwise performing at any one time. There are two ways to approach the planning: either go for a scheme that will look absolutely stunning over a few weeks at a certain time of the year by choosing plants that grow together and bloom together, or try to achieve continuity by choosing plants that reach their peak at different times so that the effect will last more than one season. The results will be quite different. The first will have a lively short-lived crescendo and the second will be quieter, gentler and longer lasting.

Foliage is the key to success in holding a colour scheme together, and can be provided by deciduous or

ADDING COLOUR WITH ANNUALS

Make full use of seasonal colour to ensure a continuity of interest in herbaceous borders. Annuals are excellent for providing high summer colour, often lacking in our gardens. Choose those with a tall loose habit, rather than compact bedding types, as these will sit more happily with the perennials. If annuals are to be a regular feature, keep spaces clear for them. The following annuals are all easy to grow and combine well with perennials. Some, such as the antirrhinum, are available in a variety of heights and colours.

Antirrhinum majus

Cleome hassleriana

Cosmos bipinnatus

Nicotiana alata

Nigella damascena 'Miss Jekyll' (left)

Salvia viridis var. *comata*

evergreen shrubs and trees or herbaceous perennials. Get the foliage plants right, and the flowers will act as seasonal highlights. For example, a yellow border might be based around shrubs such as the gold-variegated *Elaeagnus pungens* 'Dicksonii' and the yellow-leaved *Philadelphus coronarius* 'Aureus' ♥, with additional foliage interest being introduced by perennials such as *Hosta* 'Gold Standard' and the light, airy *Valeriana phu* 'Aurea'. To this add a long succession of perennials to continue the theme from early spring to late autumn: *Euphorbia polychroma* ♥ for early spring, *Ranunculus acris* 'Flore Pleno' ♥ for late spring, *Achillea filipendulina* 'Gold Plate' ♥ in early summer, followed later by *Helenium* 'The Bishop' and, finally, *Rudbeckia fulgida* var. *sullivantii* 'Goldsturm' ♥ in autumn.

FILLING GAPS

As borders grow and establish, they often need fine tuning. Gardeners usually choose plants that look good together, but this often means that they all flower together, too, leaving the garden dull at other times. In a large garden, this is not such a problem as the action can be concentrated in different areas, the various corners of the garden performing in rotation. It is less desirable in a small garden, where the interest is best distributed through as much of the year as possible. To ensure continuity of flower, go out when you spot a gap and deliberately obtain plants that are currently in bloom.

Whatever the scale of the planting there will always be peaks and troughs in performance; you may wish to plan for these. For example, there is little point having everything flowering in midsummer, if that is when you are normally away on holiday.

INTRODUCING NEW PLANTS

One of the great advantages of container-grown plants is being able to buy them in flower. Not only can you see what you are getting, but also you can experiment with the plant's position in the garden. Try the pot in different sites and see for yourself where the plant will fit best into a colour scheme and how it relates to its neighbours. If you find that the ideal site is already taken, leave the new plant in its pot until the autumn and then simply relocate the existing occupant. Herbaceous perennials are generally easy to transplant so do not be afraid to move things around if you can see a combination that can be improved by a little rearrangement.

LINK PLANTS

Colour-themed borders are most successful when some linking plants are incorporated. Select plants that do not need much space and that can be planted in subtle drifts among the other occupants. *Digitalis lutea* is useful to trail through yellow colour schemes. Its delicate spikes of creamy-yellow flowers are non-competitive but gently conspicuous. *Verbena bonariensis* ♥ is useful in pink, lilac and burgundy themes. The flowers are blue enough to be a good linking colour and the small blooms on tall stems create a wonderful see-through effect.

BLUE: THE PERFECT MIXER

Blue combines well with just about any other colour, so perennials such as nepetas and blue-flowered salvias and herbaceous geraniums are invaluable in any planting scheme where something is needed to unite two or more contrasting colours. Even clashing pinks and oranges will live together when blue is used to dilute and complement them.

SITUATIONS

All gardens have their different growing conditions. Most have places that get little or no direct sunlight; many have hot, dry areas with little moisture in the soil. Some have water or wet soil, a few trees or woodland, a little pasture or meadow. All these can support fascinating and desirable plants, and by choosing the right herbaceous perennials all can have colour and interest throughout the year. When it comes to perennials, no situation is a problem; all are an asset if the right selection of plants is made.

RIGHT: RHS Garden Rosemoor, Devon

The herbaceous border

A formal herbaceous border at its peak is one of the most spectacular sights in the English garden. An essential feature of Edwardian and Victorian gardens, it is rarely seen today, having largely been replaced by the mixed border and other, less formal styles of planting. Yet fresh ways of looking at the traditional herbaceous border can make it fitting for modern times while retaining the spirit of the original.

True herbaceous borders are long formal beds, often backed by yew hedges that provide shelter for the plants as well as serving as a backdrop to the display. Some borders are arranged as mirror images of one another; occasionally they are double-sided.

The herbaceous border can have up to eight months of interest in a year, but most have their moment of glory at one point during mid- to late summer; it is virtually impossible to achieve the same level of interest the whole year through. Even with careful planning, gaps will be left by early flowering plants (although these can be filled by annuals or tender perennials), and the ground is always left empty in the dormant season.

Traditional herbaceous borders are often said to be labour intensive. Undoubtedly plants require support, cutting back, weed control and periodic lifting and division. Whether this is more demanding than other styles of planting is debatable: perhaps it is the focus of these activities on one area of the garden, and on one group of plants, that has fostered the belief that the herbaceous border is hard work.

SELECTION AND PLANNING

The secret of success in any herbaceous border is the selection and placing of plants. Shape, height, flower colour and timing all have a contribution to make.

Mirrored herbaceous borders at Bramdean House, Hampshire.

Plants tend to be arranged with the tallest at the back and the shortest at the front, but the most successful schemes use variations on this pattern. Exclamation marks of tall, spiky plants and light, airy, see-through subjects increase depth and perspective as well as creating focal points in the long expanse of planting. Repetition of key plants is important to hold the scheme together, especially in double-sided or mirrored herbaceous borders.

EXOTICS IN THE BORDER

Tender, exotic perennials are often used in herbaceous borders to provide focal points and to fill the gaps left by early perennials such as oriental poppies (*Papaver orientale*). Cannas, with splendid foliage and brilliant flowers, are a natural choice, as are dahlias, particularly those with dark chocolate leaves. In warm, sheltered situations, dark-leaved aeoniums are stunning additions to hot colour schemes.

THE MAINTENANCE SCHEDULE

Work in the herbaceous border takes place mainly in the dormant season: soil cultivation, manuring, division and preparing supports. Once the border is in full growth, there is no stopping its progress, nor any room to manoeuvre between the plants. Selective cutting back and some watering during dry periods is all that is required.

Asters growing through twiggy supports.

Support is a vital element of any herbaceous border. The perennials grow in close proximity, particularly as clumps increase in size from year to year. There is a certain amount of competition between them and they are drawn upwards towards the light, increasing the need for support. This has to be in position before the plants require it; staking and tying once they have grown is difficult and results in an awkward, unnatural appearance.

Perennial weeds are perhaps the biggest problem in planting of this kind. They retreat below ground with the ornamentals, re-emerging as the young perennial shoots push through the soil in spring. Bindweed is a particular pest, using both perennials and their supports as a means to climb and smother the display. Using a herbicide is impossible without damaging the plants. The only solution is to save plants that are free of infestation by moving them to a nursery bed, then sacrificing the rest while dealing with the problem (see page 19).

HERBACEOUS PLANTING IN ISLAND BEDS

As gardens became smaller over the years, it became more difficult to find room for the traditional rectangular herbaceous border, and gardeners began to experiment with other styles of herbaceous planting. Alan Bloom at Bressingham Gardens in Norfolk pioneered the planting of perennials in informal island beds. Here the environment is less enclosed, promoting better air circulation and allowing more light to reach the plants from all sides; as a result, plants are sturdier, with a stockier habit, and the need to provide supports is often reduced. Because island beds are visible from all angles, they also allow more opportunity for variety and interest in the border: as one aspect is entering its quiet phase, another can be reaching its peak. In the average garden this style of bed is far easier to accommodate than the grand formal border.

HERBACEOUS BORDERS BASED ON FOLIAGE

Herbaceous perennials requiring no support or cutting back during the season are a much less demanding option. Beds of hostas, ferns, astilbes, aruncus, rodgersias and other lovers of semi-shade can be used to create a different type of herbaceous border that suits an informal garden with light tree cover. Using the effect of foliage more than the seasonal impact of flowers maintains interest over a long period. This can be further extended by planting bulbs that flower in early spring such as narcissi, camassias and leucojums, which perform before the perennial leaf cover is established. As the perennial growth develops, it hides the fading foliage of the bulbs.

Herbaceous borders based on foliage have a long season of interest.

CLASSIC HERBACEOUS BORDER PERENNIALS

Here is a selection of the key plants traditionally used in the herbaceous border. They have a variety of shapes, sizes and forms, and between them provide colour from early summer through to autumn.

The **asters** were adopted from the cottage garden because of their tall stems of colourful daisy-like flower-heads that are produced so reliably throughout late summer and autumn. Rich blue and purple asters contrast beautifully with the deep orange, yellow and flame shades of autumn, while pink and lilac varieties enliven the deepening burgundy heads of sedums and blend with the soft pink of anemones.

Aster novae-angliae 'Pink Victor'

Cultivars of **Aster novi-belgii**, or the Michaelmas daisy, mostly grow to about 1.2m (4ft). Strong stems and an upright habit lend them to a midway position in the border. Sadly their handsome, dark green foliage is often plagued with mildew, so they tend to be shunned by gardeners. Given good air circulation around the plants and regularly sprayed with a fungicide, they can be enjoyed in the border and make lovely cut flowers. **'Eventide'** is a glorious semi-double violet-blue, **'Marie Ballard'** a popular double light blue and **'Patricia Ballard'** a semi-double, vibrant pink.

Campanula glomerata 'Superba'

Aster novae-angliae, the New England aster, is woody stemmed with coarser, slightly hairy foliage that seems immune to mildew attack. It lacks the excellent blue shades of some *Aster novi-belgii* hybrids but has some good pink and red varieties. All grow to 1m (40in) or more. (See also page 174.) *Aster novae-angliae* **'Pink Victor'** has semi-double mid-pink flowers with golden yellow centres. Ruby-red **'Septemberrubin'** (SEPTEMBER RUBY) looks lovely behind the late flowers of wine-red penstemons and with the late indigo blooms of *Aconitum* 'Spark's Variety' (see page 46).

Campanulas come in many shapes and sizes, and both tall and shorter forms find their place in the herbaceous border. (See also pages 83 and 155–56.) *Campanula glomerata*, the clustered bellflower, produces rounded heads of upturned bell-shaped flowers on stout stems, 30cm (12in) high, and is useful to provide early colour at the front of the planting. The deep violet-blue blooms of *Campanula glomerata* 'Superba' ♥ are lovely with lime-green *Alchemilla mollis* ♥ (see page 46) and add depth and contrasting flower form to an edging of *Nepeta* × *faassenii* ♥.

Varieties of *Campanula persicifolia* (peach-leaved bellflower) mix easily with other plants. From rosettes of shiny, evergreen leaves arise slender stems, 90cm (3ft) tall, carrying nodding, cup-

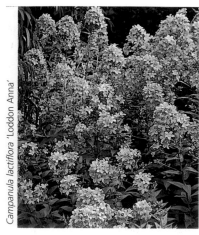

Campanula lactiflora 'Loddon Anna'

shaped flowers in early and midsummer. The single white blooms of *Campanula persicifolia* var. *alba* or the double white *Campanula persicifolia* 'Fleur de Neige'♥ look stunning with the bright indigo-blue *Baptisia australis*♥ (see page 132). **'Telham Beauty'** is a fresh, icy, light blue; **'Chettle Charm'**♥ is white with a pale blue frosting.

Campanula lactiflora, or the milky bellflower, finds its place further back in the border. Forming clumps of upright stems, 1.5m (5ft) high, with large heads of bell-shaped flowers, it needs support in most sites. It gives welcome colour from early to midsummer, its pastel shades mingling happily with stronger pinks and blues (see Good Companions, right). Its shape makes a good contrast to the upright spikes of delphiniums. Of the many named varieties, soft pink **'Loddon Anna'**♥ and deep lavender-blue **'Prichard's Variety'**♥ are two of the best. **'Alba'**♥ is pure white.

CUTTING BACK CAMPANULAS

When the flowers of campanulas have faded there is a temptation to cut them back immediately.
This is the right course of action with most varieties except for *Campanula persicifolia*. When the first flush of flowers is over, leave the stems in place: new flower buds will quickly appear.

Herbaceous borders always conjure images of the magnificent spires of **delphiniums** soaring above mounds of flowers in the foreground. Undoubtedly delphiniums are essential border plants, not only for their imposing stature but also for their brilliance of colour. No other plant delivers the intensity of blue in quite the same way, along with delightful pastel shades of pink, lilac, purple and white.

Delphinium **Pacific hybrids, New Century hybrids** and **Magic Fountains** series (see Good Companions, below right) are easily raised from seed sown in summer or early autumn, and young pot-grown stock grows quickly when planted in spring. All need deep, fertile soil with adequate moisture but resent being waterlogged, and are best in large, deep borders where they can be given space. The emerging shoots need early protection from slugs; and grow-through supports should be put into position before plants reach 30cm (12in) tall. After the first flowering in early summer, delphiniums must be cut back hard to encourage new shoots that will produce more flowers in autumn. Because of this they are best positioned behind later performers: phlox, asters, heleniums and kniphofias are all good choices. (See also pages 134–35.)

Heleniums have the ideal habit for the herbaceous border, the clumps growing to broad, stout columns topped with a brilliant display of long-lasting blooms from midsummer right through to autumn. Shades range from yellow to deepest red-brown, and they work well alongside subjects in the same colour spectrum, such as kniphofias (see page 42), crocosmias, dahlias and achilleas, as well as with rich blue asters. The shorter varieties such as *Helenium* **'Wyndley'**, with brown-eyed, yellow and copper flowers, can be planted in front of taller kniphofias to hide their untidy foliage. They are also

Tall spires of delphiniums provide impressive eye-level interest in early summer and again in autumn.

GOOD COMPANIONS

Campanula lactiflora (1) and *Phlox paniculata* (2) are similar in plant shape and flower form. The phlox follows on when the campanula flowers are fading.

The bold magenta-pink of *Geranium psilostemon* ♀ (3) gives strength of hue to the soft purple-pink blooms of *Delphinium* 'Magic Fountains Lilac Rose' (4).

Kniphofia 'Atlanta' with heleniums

Nepeta 'Six Hills Giant'

'Bressingham Comet' is at its peak in autumn, with spikes, over 1.5m (5ft) tall, of flame-red and yellow flowers. (See also pages 68 and 175.)

Nepeta 'Six Hills Giant' is one of the essential blues of the summer border. Reaching 1m (40in) high, this is not an edging plant but a definitive mixer, ideally planted between other subjects that will help to hold it up. It benefits greatly from a grow-through plant support or twiggy props of hazel or birch. The soft grey-green, aromatic leaves and lavender-blue flowers are a delightful combination that works with hot colours as well as soft shades and pastels. Plants can be cut back halfway through the season if they get too untidy, but left untouched will continue to flower through late summer. (See Good Companions, right.)

Peonies may have a relatively short flowering season, but when in bloom they steal the show. Most come into flower early on, making a spectacular start to summer. They are best near the front of the border where their beauty and fragrance can be admired; they also have the advantage of foliage that stays looking good throughout the season and provides some structure among less robust plants. Growing up to 1m (40in) tall, most benefit from some support in case heavy rain strikes when the plants are in bloom. Their colours are both subtle and vibrant. The popular *Paeonia lactiflora* 'Bowl of Beauty' ♥, with its soft pink and cream flowers, is essential in any border of warm summer colours.

an excellent choice behind the earlier-blooming hemerocallis, their colour taking over as the daylilies fade. (See also pages 52 and 159–60.)

Kniphofias (red hot poker or torch lily) are a must in any border using hot colours. Their upright spikes offer a strong contrast to the softer, rounded flowerheads of so many perennials. Enjoying an open, sunny position and adequate moisture, they do not like to be swamped by their neighbours; planted forward from the back of the border, their rising spikes provide relief from the contrived graded height from the back to the front of the planting. They are usually associated with late summer and autumn, but there are varieties that bloom in early, mid- and late summer. Careful selection will achieve continuity. Most early varieties are smaller than later ones. 'Atlanta' is early, with 1.2m (4ft) spikes of red and creamy-yellow flowers above blue-green evergreen foliage. 'Toffee Nosed' ♥ starts to bloom in midsummer; it has cream flowers ticked with brown in slightly shorter spikes, 1m (40in) high.

Paeonia lactiflora 'Bowl of Beauty'

OTHER PERENNIALS FOR THE HERBACEOUS BORDER *Agastache • Astrantia • Centaurea • Clematis recta •*

Phlox paniculata

Salvia × sylvestris 'Mainacht' (MAY NIGHT)

Paeonia lactiflora **'Lord Kitchener'** is upright in habit, with dark green leaves and gold-centred, bright scarlet flowers. (See Good Companions, right, and see pages 146–47.)

Peonies are especially useful planted in front of *Phlox paniculata*: their early flowers will hold the spotlight until the phlox is ready to produce its pretty heads of fragrant blooms, from mid-summer onwards. The phlox's sweetly spicy scent is as much a feature of the border as the fondant fancy shades of the flowers. (See Good Companions, page 41.) Most varieties grow to about 1m (40in) high, with light green foliage. *Phlox paniculata* **'Dodo Hanbury-Forbes'** has large heads of pure pink flowers. **'Prospero'** is lavender, with dark foliage. **'Starfire'** is deep red, **'Prince of Orange'** is salmon and **'Border Gem'** violet-blue. Phlox also offer some of the purest whites in the border: **'White Admiral'** and **'Mount Fuji'** are two of the best.

Phlox like a well-drained, fertile soil enriched with well-rotted manure. They need watering in dry spells, particularly

in the run-up to flowering. Where plants are not growing vigorously the foliage is prone to leaf spot and mildew. It is worth thinning mature plants in spring, removing weaker shoots to allow strong ones to develop. Dry weather can cause yellowing and browning of the foliage. If plants suffer from eelworm, causing poor growth and distorting leaves and stems, they should be disposed of, and new plants should be sited elsewhere in the border rather than in the same spot.

Herbaceous **salvias** provide some wonderful long-lasting, deep blue spikes that need little or no support and contribute superb depth of colour from midsummer to autumn (see also pages 166–67). *Salvia × superba* is an easy, very hardy plant with deep violet-blue flowers and red-purple bracts that persist long after the flowers have fallen. It grows to 90cm (3ft) high, so is perfect in the middle of the border with later perennials such as heleniums and

phlox. *Salvia × sylvestris* **'Mainacht'** (MAY NIGHT) is shorter and earlier but with the same colour intensity (see Good Companions, below). It makes a stunning combination with the pale yellow *Achillea* 'Moonshine', whose flat, plate-like flowerheads float above it on silver-green stems.

GOOD COMPANIONS

The frothy flowerheads of *Centranthus ruber* 'Albus' (1) provide the perfect background to the large, flamboyant blooms of *Paeonia lactiflora* 'Duchesse de Nemours' (2).

Salvia × sylvestris 'Mainacht' (MAY NIGHT) (3) strengthens the blue in the border and reaches the peak of condition when *Nepeta* 'Six Hills Giant' (4) may need a mid-season trim.

Helenium 'The Bishop' (5) and *Hemerocallis* 'Hyperion' (6): the sunny flowers of the helenium are at their best when those of the yellow daylily are fading.

Coreopsis verticillata • *Hemerocallis* • *Leucanthemum × superbum* • *Lupinus* • *Physostegia* • *Solidago* • *Veronicastrum* •

The mixed border

The mixed border is the most common planting ground for herbaceous perennials today. Here, trees and shrubs give structure, contribute foliage effect and in some cases offer seasonal flowers. Perennials provide colour from the ground to eye-level, mainly during the most important time of the year, from late spring through to autumn. Spring- and summer-flowering bulbs, annuals and climbers may also be used to add to the variety of colour and form.

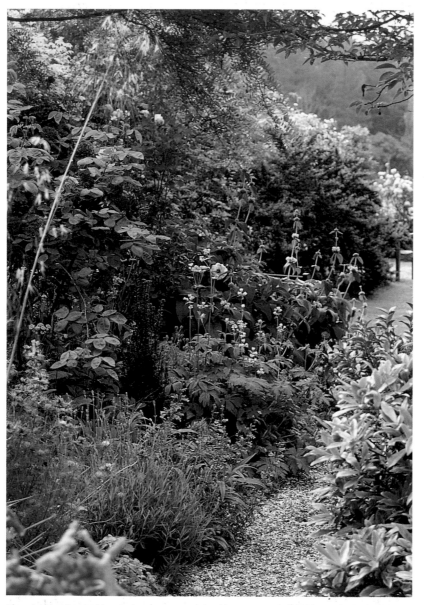

The mixed border combines herbaceous perennials with evergreen and deciduous shrubs and roses to provide interest all through the year.

A well-planned mixed border can be attractive throughout the year; unlike herbaceous borders (see pages 38–43), mixed borders have no empty, dormant season. Even in winter deciduous shrubs have branch framework and form, and evergreens come into their own when herbaceous perennials die down and deciduous shrubs lose their leaves.

Mixed borders are regarded as being less labour intensive than traditional herbaceous ones. While the herbaceous plants will require maintenance of one form or other every winter, the woody plants do not necessarily need annual attention; the decision as to when and how much to maintain is very much in the hands of the gardener.

THE IMPORTANCE OF FOLIAGE

The proportion and importance of foliage is greater in a mixed planting than it is in a truly herbaceous border, since foliage provides the setting for the blooms of both shrubs and perennial plants. Coloured foliage perennials and variegated shrubs and trees can form the basis of a colour scheme, with high-lights supplied by the perennial flowers.

Shrubs with purple or plum foliage work well with most flower shades and are especially useful to bring depth of colour to planting schemes.

Silver foliage helps to lighten mixed plantings, particularly those in full sun.

Papaver orientale 'Patty's Plum' seen against the subtle foliage of *Elaeagnus* 'Quicksilver'.

Silver shrubs or small trees are invaluable to plant with sun-loving perennials: they combine especially well with pink and blue shades and are sparkling with whites. The silver pear *Pyrus salicifolia* 'Pendula' ♥ is an excellent small tree for a border with roses, geraniums, nepetas and lavender. The large-growing shrub *Elaeagnus* 'Quicksilver' ♥ will create a silver-grey backdrop from late spring, just in time to show off the vibrant blooms of oriental poppies (*Papaver orientale*) planted in front; it makes a superb companion for *Papaver orientale* 'Patty's Plum'.

Shrubs with white-variegated foliage are good mixers in sun or shade. Those with yellow variegation need to be used more carefully, but can be stunning with yellow- and orange-flowered perennials. The ever popular *Helenium* 'The Bishop'

SHRUBS WITH PURPLE FOLIAGE TO MIX WITH PERENNIALS

Acer palmatum 'Bloodgood' ♥
Berberis thunbergii f. *atropurpurea* 'Rose Glow' ♥
Cotinus coggygria 'Royal Purple' ♥
Hebe 'Pascal' ♥
Physocarpus opulifolius 'Diabolo' ♥
Pittosporum tenuifolium 'Tom Thumb' ♥
Salvia officinalis 'Purpurascens' ♥
Weigela florida WINE AND ROSES ('Alexandra')

(see page 43) and *Rudbeckia fulgida* var. *sullivantii* 'Goldsturm' ♥ (see page 53) intensify the golden yellow variegation of *Elaeagnus pungens* 'Maculata' and *Euonymus fortunei* 'Emerald 'n' Gold' ♥.

ROSES IN MIXED BORDERS

When the herbaceous perennial was confined to the herbaceous border, the rose was at home in the rose bed surrounded by its own kind. The two have now forged a partnership in the mixed border, and it is a marriage made in heaven. The perennials extend the flowering season of the roses and complement their peak. Shrub roses, English roses and Floribundas are the types most frequently grown here, since their relaxed habit and soft colours allow them to mix well with a variety of perennials. Low-growing herbaceous geraniums, *Alchemilla mollis* ♥ (see page 46) and heucheras are excellent subjects for soft ground cover around

shrub roses. *Viola cornuta* ♥ (see page 49) will grow tall and twine through open-branched rose bushes, producing its delicate blue or white blooms from late spring through to autumn. The tall-growing *Geranium psilostemon* ♥, with black-eyed magenta flowers (see page 48), is stunning with pink and dark wine-coloured roses, especially in the presence of plum-coloured foliage.

EASY-CARE ROSES TO PLANT WITH PERENNIALS

Rosa AMBER QUEEN ('Harroony') ♥
Rosa 'Blanc Double de Coubert' ♥
Rosa BONICA ('Meidomonac') ♥
Rosa 'Cornelia' ♥
Rosa CROCUS ROSE ('Ausquest')
Rosa GOLDEN CELEBRATION ('Ausgold') ♥
Rosa 'Königin von Dänemark' (QUEEN OF DENMARK) ♥
Rosa RHAPSODY IN BLUE ('Frantasia') ♥
Rosa 'Roseraie de l'Haÿ' ♥
Rosa ROSEMOOR ('Austough')
Rosa VALENTINE HEART ('Dicogle') ♥

A mixed border with roses in the Jardin d'Angelique in Normandy, France.

PERENNIALS FOR MIXED PLANTINGS

Most of the commonly available garden perennials can, of course, be used in mixed plantings, but there are some that are particularly suitable. This may be because they have a long season of interest or because they are a useful colour to blend with most others. Some perennials are especially valuable for mixed borders because they add that certain something: an exclamation mark in the planting that is not contributed by other subjects.

Aconitum 'Spark's Variety'

Aconitum cultivars are a better choice than delphiniums in mixed borders. Also known as aconite, monkshood or wolfsbane, aconitums have more attractive, finely cut foliage and do not require the same degree of support as delphiniums (see pages 41 and 134–35). Because the plants stay in good condition after flowering, there is no immediate need to cut them back, so there are no large holes left in the border. *Aconitum* 'Spark's Variety' ♀ has tall, branching stems, 1.5m (5ft) high, of dark violet-blue flowers in late summer, associating well with the rich reds and golds of the season. The equally tall *Aconitum* 'Stainless Steel' is an exceptionally good mixer; with its straight spikes of steely blue-grey foliage and grey-blue flowers, it has an eryngium-like quality. The variety *Aconitum carmichaelii* var. *truppelianum* 'Kelmscott' ♀ is a real

Anemone × hybrida 'Honorine Jobert'

delphinium alternative with spikes reaching nearly 2m (6ft) and rich violet-blue flowers borne in early autumn.

Alchemilla mollis ♀ (lady's mantle) is an invaluable plant in the garden: useful at the front of the border, alongside paving, and as an edging plant, it is also excellent ground cover on any soil and in sun or shade. It has soft green foliage and, from early summer, clouds of lime-green flowers on stems 30cm (12in) high. The colour mixes superbly with any other (see Good Companions, right) and is especially lovely with soft blue. Its one failing is that it is perhaps too successful. It scatters its seeds very freely and if not controlled can become a pest. A few seedlings are useful to transplant elsewhere in the garden; to prevent it spreading further, cut off the flowers as they start to turn yellow.

On soils that are heavy and moist, the cultivars of *Anemone × hybrida* (Japanese anemone) will spread freely, throwing up their fine stems of perfect white or pink flowers, which enliven the border from late summer on (see pages 170–71). They mix well with strong-growing shrubs, which can cope with their interference. Japanese anemones are useful to plant behind and between shrub roses to lengthen the season of colour, particularly important with roses that flower only once in summer. The vigorous 'Honorine Jobert' ♀, with large, single white flowers, combines well with white-variegated shrubs such as *Cornus alba* 'Elegantissima' ♀. Pink cultivars such as 'Königin Charlotte' (QUEEN CHARLOTTE) ♀ are lovely against the purple foliage of *Cotinus coggygria* 'Royal Purple' ♀.

Alchemilla mollis

Digitalis, the foxgloves, are mostly biennial plants (see pages 56–57). This does not make them any less effective in the mixed border, it just means they need to be managed to ensure that some are in flower each year. There are also perennial species, their light spikes and subtly coloured flowers making them excellent mixers.

Digitalis grandiflora (which was formerly known as *Digitalis ambigua*) reaches only 45cm (18in) high, with narrow, hairy apple-green leaves and delicate spikes of soft primrose-yellow flowers, daintily curved at the top. It is easy to grow on well-drained soil and is a useful plant to bring light spikes to the foreground of the border in a subtle but uplifting colour. It looks very pretty in early summer against the emerging foliage of bronze fennel, *Foeniculum vulgare* 'Purpureum' (see page 90).

Digitalis lutea has darker green, narrow leaves in starry rosettes. The fine spikes of tiny, tubular greenish-yellow flowers are not spectacular but they do have wonderful shape and presence. Reaching 50cm (20in) in height, this is a superb plant to drift through the front of the border. After the flowers fade, the spikes remain attractive for several weeks. Leave a few in position for the seed to ripen; it sows itself freely and will provide ample young plants for use elsewhere in the garden.

Digitalis × *mertonensis* ♥ is reliably perennial, if often short-lived, especially on heavy, wet soils. It more closely resembles the native foxglove, *Digitalis purpurea*, which is one of its parents (the other is *Digitalis grandiflora*). Grey-green felty leaves in neat rosettes give rise to dumpy spikes of large strawberry-pink flowers in early summer, making it a good partner for summer-flowering shrubs such as deutzia and weigela. It looks pretty with silver foliage, such as that of *Artemisia ludoviciana* 'Valerie Finnis' ♥ (see page 51), and lovely with

Eremurus stenophyllus

the deep wine-red young foliage of *Lysimachia ciliata* 'Firecracker' ♥ (see Good Companions, below).

Eremurus (foxtail lily) have become increasingly popular in recent years, and few plants are as spectacular in bloom. Late spring sees the emergence of narrow grey-green leaves, which usually grow to a height of 30–40cm (12–16in). The flowering stem arises from the centre of the foliage rosette and grows quickly. In some species it can reach dramatic height, of up to 3m (10ft); in others it remains at around 1m (40in).

In midsummer a sparkling bottlebrush, 60–90cm (2–3ft) long, of starry flowers in pink, white or yellow is produced at the top of the stem; it opens from the bottom upwards, creating an attractive gradation of colour.

Foxtail lilies are planted in autumn as dry tubers; these are curious structures, like starfish, with one or two central 'eyes'. They should be given a sunny position, in a well-drained, fertile soil. Because of their height and stature, foxtail lilies suit planting with tall, upright perennials such as *Salvia* × *superba* ♥, a good solid companion above which the foxtail lily spikes can rise majestically. *Eremurus himalaicus* is the hardiest and reaches 1.2m (4ft). The flowers are pure white with orange stamens. The popular *Eremurus* × *isabellinus* Ruiter hybrids grow to 1.5m (5ft), with spikes of yellow, apricot- or peach-coloured blooms. *Eremurus robustus* ♥ is the tallest and can reach 3m (10ft). It has peach-pink flowers marked with brown and green. *Eremurus stenophyllus* ♥ is shorter at 1.5m (5ft), and has fine yellow flowers that look good with golden-variegated shrubs.

Herbaceous **geraniums** are a natural choice for mixed borders, especially the

GOOD COMPANIONS

The reddish-pink flowers of *Digitalis* × *mertonensis* (1) and the deep coppery purple foliage of *Lysimachia ciliata* 'Firecracker' ♥ (2) make a lovely partnership.

The burgundy blooms of *Penstemon* 'Port Wine' ♥ (3) combine beautifully with the frothy lime flowers of *Alchemilla mollis* ♥ (4).

larger-growing blue cultivars that mix so easily with roses and deciduous shrubs, silver foliage and lavenders. *Geranium* 'Johnson's Blue' ♥ is a real border basic. It is planted so widely because it takes some beating when it comes to reliability. It forms a clump up to 30cm (12in) high and 60cm (24in) across, so requires no support. The dark-veined lavender-blue flowers are produced over a long period in early to midsummer and it will usually perform again in autumn.

The cultivars of *Geranium pratense*, the meadow cranesbill, are also good mixers. Taller-growing, they reach 60cm (24in), with long-stalked, deeply divided leaves. Their flowers are smaller but have prettily veined, tissue-like petals. 'Plenum Caeruleum' is pale blue and double. 'Mrs Kendall Clark' ♥ is the loveliest of all, its pale blue-grey petals having a pink tint and delicate veining. (See also pages 91 and 164.)

Geranium psilostemon ♥ is not by any means a shrinking violet. Growing

Geranium 'Johnson's Blue'

Geranium psilostemon

Linaria purpurea

up to 1m (40in) high, it is a plant that can hold its own between medium-sized shrubs and taller perennials. The blooms are borne in long succession all through summer; vivid magenta-pink with black centres, they are striking and showy but mix surprisingly well with a wide range of colours. They look wonderful against plum-coloured foliage and with blue nepetas. Burgundy penstemons such as *Penstemon* 'Raven' ♥ and 'Port Wine' ♥ (see Good Companions, page 47) are its natural partners. Brave gardeners may like to try it with lavender-blue *Nepeta* 'Six Hills Giant' (see page 42) and soft orange hemerocallis (daylilies).

Linaria (toadflax) is one of those cottage-garden perennials that seems so familiar that no one ever bothers to find out what it is. *Linaria purpurea* is the commonest, with tall clumps of slender stems clothed all the way up with narrow blue-green leaves. At the top of each stem is a spike of tiny purple-blue flowers resembling those of a miniature antirrhinum. The spikes are often lightly branched, and the flowers fade to leave round seed capsules that distribute their contents liberally throughout the border. This is a plant to drift through the mixed border, its light height working well to make the planting three-dimensional.

Persicaria amplexicaulis 'Atrosanguinea'

Penstemon hybrids are some of the most valuable plants in the garden. These are evergreen perennials with a woody base, and are more like shrubs than herbaceous plants. Flowers vary from narrow tubes to broader foxglove-like trumpets, but all bloom for a remarkably long period starting in early summer and continuing until late autumn. Those with purple and ruby flowers are superb in mixed planting, their rich colouring blending beautifully with the pinks and blues of summer, as well as with the orange-flame shades of autumn (see pages 162–63).

The robust *Persicaria amplexicaulis* 'Atrosanguinea' is much underrated. Perhaps because the foliage is rather reminiscent of a coarse weed, some gardeners overlook its quality as a solid border plant that stays looking good from early summer through to late autumn. Healthy, dark green foliage and light spikes of red-brown flowers, 1.2m (4ft) high, are a good foil for showier subjects. It grows on just about any soil in sun or partial shade and thrives in wet sites. There are other varieties but this is the most versatile.

Thalictrums (meadow rue) are lovely foliage plants from the beginning of the season with their finely divided blue-

OTHER PLANTS FOR MIXED BORDERS *Chaenomeles* • *Foeniculum vulgare* 'Purpureum' • *Gaura lindheimeri* •

Thalictrum flavum subsp. glaucum

green leaves that resemble maidenhair fern (*Adiantum*). The foliage is a feature not only of the emerging plant but also of the rising flower stems later on. *Thalictrum aquilegiifolium* produces wide heads of fluffy mauve flowers during summer. There is also a white form, *Thalictrum aquilegiifolium* var. *album*. *Thalictrum delavayi*♀ has daintier foliage and more airy heads of

The perennial sweet pea *Lathyrus latifolius*♀ looks delightful threaded through with the delicate lilac-blue blooms of *Viola cornuta*♀.

lilac flowers with white stamens. Ideal with companions that offer some support, this is not a plant for an exposed position since the stems are liable to be blown over. It is good for cutting as an alternative to gypsophila. The cultivar *Thalictrum delavayi* 'Hewitt's Double'♀ bears tiny, very double lilac flowers, which are pretty but without the appealing soft fluffy stamens of the single form.

An excellent plant in any scheme, *Thalictrum flavum* subsp. *glaucum*♀ has particularly fine blue-green leaves and pale yellow flowers. The foliage stays in good condition throughout the season, after the blooms have faded.

PEAS AND VETCHES

Several members of the pea family are herbaceous climbers and scramblers that will use the branches of woody plants for support. They can add a new dimension to the border, and extend the season of interest, often by performing later in the year than their hosts. Some, like the everlasting peas (*Lathyrus*), use tendrils to help them climb over and through nearby plants; others, like goat's rue (*Galega*), simply drape their lax stems over their nearest neighbour, or anything else that will give them the support they need.

Galega officinalis (goat's rue) is a European native, often seen on roadside verges. A very lax plant, it depends on others to support its 1.5m (5ft) stems and fern-like foliage. Spikes of small pea flowers in shades of purple, pink and white appear in profusion from early summer to early autumn. It will grow happily in sun or partial shade.

Lathyrus latifolius♀, the perennial sweet pea, is a vigorous herbaceous climber, growing happily to 4m (12ft) in well-drained, fertile soil in full sun. It has flattened stems, fresh green foliage and flowers over a long period from early

Galega officinalis 'Alba'

summer to early autumn. The stout stems of silky, rounded blooms are weather-resistant and are excellent for cutting. The species often has vivid rose-purple flowers, which look stunning against the purple elder *Sambucus nigra* f. *porphyrophylla* 'Gerda'♀ (formerly called *Sambucus nigra* 'Black Beauty'). *Lathyrus latifolius* 'Rosa Perle'♀ has pale pink flowers while 'White Pearl'♀ gives pure white blooms in profusion. *Lathyrus latifolius* can be easily raised from seed or bought as container-grown stock and planted in spring. Named cultivars are propagated with difficulty from cuttings.

Lathyrus grandiflorus (everlasting pea) scrambles to 2m (6ft) or more. It has sparse, fine blue-green stems and leaves and large flowers produced in twos and threes throughout summer. Deep purple-pink with varying shades of maroon, the blooms have an old-fashioned character. This is a lovely plant that sits lightly on its host.

Lathyrus vernus♀ blooms in spring, forming clumps of 30cm (12in) stems with pretty fern-like foliage and heads of tiny pea flowers. There are several varieties, in purple, pink and pure white. All make delightful companions for spring-flowering bulbs.

Hemerocallis • Paeonia • Polemonium • Sedum 'Herbstfreude' (AUTUMN JOY) • Verbascum • Verbena bonariensis •

Prairie and meadow

Prairie planting and wildflower meadows both use plants hailing from grassland habitats to create a soothing, softly moving gardenscape that evolves and changes as the year progresses. Whether on a large scale or in a smaller bed, both planting styles can help to bring a real feeling of the countryside into the garden.

The Piet Oudolf prairie-style planting at RHS Garden Wisley, Surrey.

PRAIRIE PLANTING

In a natural prairie habitat, herbaceous perennials and grasses exist in harmony, the mix of species varying according to the conditions, wet or dry. In all cases a succession of flowers and seedheads punctuates a changing background of grasses from spring to late autumn. In most gardens the association of prairie plants and grasses can be used on a small scale to create a naturalistic effect that is at home in a rural environment or in an urban setting. Some of our most innovative gardeners on both sides of the Atlantic have used prairie-style planting for a number of years.

In cultivation prairie plants will require the minimum of maintenance and will tolerate quite hostile conditions. In their natural habitat, they need to cope with periods of drought, extreme heat and cold and heavy grazing by elk and bison. Unlike the flowers typically found in a meadow, many are robust plants able to compete with vigorous grasses growing in fertile soil. Bold and colourful, many are members of the daisy family, their individual flowers consisting of many small florets usually with a number of ray-like petals around a central disc. Rich in nectar and prolific in seed production, they are attractive to both insects and birds and perfect for wildlife gardens.

Agastache foeniculum 'Alabaster'

Agastache foeniculum (giant hyssop) is a deadnettle-like plant with square stems, reaching over 1m (40in) tall, and narrow, aromatic leaves. The spikes of bluish purple flowers appear at the top of the stems from early summer to early autumn. The whole plant smells of aniseed when touched. It suits a dry soil in full sun and is useful for its upright, spiky form and its blue colour, mixing well with prairie daisies. A number of cultivars exist, among them *Agastache foeniculum* 'Alabaster', which has white flowers. (See also page 153.)

Artemisia ludoviciana 'Valerie Finnis'

Artemisia ludoviciana will introduce softer foliage and subtle colour into prairie planting. The plant spreads to make loose patches of upright stems bearing willow-like silver leaves. The cultivars 'Silver Queen' ♀ and 'Valerie Finnis' ♀ are particularly fine and reach 75cm (30in). Greenish-yellow flowers appear in late summer, but the foliage is the feature of these plants.

The perennial **asters** (Michaelmas daisy) are a diverse group invaluable for their autumn pinks and purples. Sadly the susceptibility to mildew of some varieties has put many gardeners

A RARE NATURAL HABITAT

In North America, prairie plantings have been established by ecologists keen to preserve true prairie plants from extinction. Their natural environment was the vast grasslands that covered the Midwest 150 years ago. Today this is one of the rarest natural habitats in existence, most of it destroyed under a blanket of corn and wheat.

off these cottage-garden classics. The one aster that no garden should be without is *Aster* × *frikartii* 'Mönch' ♀. Raised in Switzerland in 1920, it is still considered the finest perennial aster, producing lavender-blue flowerheads 60–90cm (24–36in) high in late summer and autumn. It is not a true prairie plant, but can happily be used in this style of planting. (See also pages 40 and 171.)

The small-flowered asters are most effective mixed with bolder perennials. *Aster ericoides* 'Pink Cloud' ♀ has a light, airy habit and fine, starry, pale pink flowerheads over a long period in late summer and autumn. The stems are graceful and wiry and will reach 1m (40in) high. It combines well with the purple coneflower, *Echinacea purpurea* (see below).

Aster ericoides is a true prairie native, as is *Aster lateriflorus*. The cultivar *Aster lateriflorus* 'Horizontalis' ♀ has fine, spreading, stiffly branched stems, 80cm (32in) high, and clouds of tiny, starry, mauve-pink flowers with darker centres in late summer or autumn. This plant is quite different in habit from the other asters and it contrasts well with light grasses such as *Stipa tenuissima* (see page 73) and *Panicum virgatum* 'Heavy Metal'.

The purple coneflower, *Echinacea purpurea*, is another prairie native, perfect with spike-flowered plants such as verbascums or with grasses. Borne on stout, upright stems up to 1m (40in) high, the flowerheads are a wonderful combination of rich red-purple petals and chestnut-brown cones, laden with orange pollen when at their prime, in late summer. *Echinacea purpurea* 'Rubinstern' ♀ is especially pleasing, with glowing wine-red flowers on 60cm (24in) stems. *Echinacea purpurea* 'White Swan', also 60cm (24in) high, is elegantly beautiful with its greenish-cream blooms of reflexed petals. Plant it amid a cloud of smoky bronze fennel,

Echinacea purpurea 'Kim's Knee High'

Foeniculum vulgare 'Purpureum' (see Good Companions, page 52), or with the dancing butterfly-like blooms of gauras (see page 52). For exposed sites or the front of a planting scheme look out for *Echinacea purpurea* 'Kim's Knee High'. (See also page 175.)

Filipendula rubra 'Venusta' ♀ is a magnificent and stately prairie perennial reaching over 2m (6ft) tall. Both leaves and flowers resemble those of astilbe. The large, fluffy, bright pink flowerheads are produced over a long period from early summer right through to early autumn. (See Good Companions, page 52.) Just like the native British

MAINTAINING PRAIRIE PLANTING

Do not cut back prairie grasses and perennials after flowering. Leave the dry grasses and seedheads over winter and cut them back in early spring. With their dry parchment leaves and dark silhouettes, prairie plants look wonderful etched with frost and lit by the low winter sun.

Gaura lindheimeri

meadowsweet, *Filipendula ulmaria*, it likes a fair amount of moisture in the soil.

Gaura lindheimeri forms a low clump of narrow, dark green leaves, usually with chocolate spots. Upright, wiry stems, 1m (40in) tall, bear pointed pink buds that open into delicate white butterfly-like blooms from midsummer to late autumn. It is a very easy plant to grow in full sun and is particularly tolerant of hot, dry conditions.

The rich bronzes, oranges and reds of the **heleniums** have a wonderful period

character. Their silky petals and velvet button centres are like shreds of rich upholstery. Old cottage-garden plants, they are popular for their reliable late display, their disease-resistance and their tolerance of virtually any soil conditions other than very wet or very dry. Heleniums are commonly known as sneezeweed, a name that comes from the plants' use by the early American settlers to make snuff.

Most garden heleniums are hybrids of *Helenium autumnale* from North America, *Helenium flexuosum* from the Midwest USA, and *Helenium bigelovii* from California; they flower from mid-summer through autumn. *Helenium* 'Moerheim Beauty' bears bronze-crimson flowers and grows to 80cm (32in) tall. *Helenium* 'Wyndley', 60cm (24in) high, has yellow flowers marked with copper. *Helenium* 'Waldtraut', one of the loveliest, grows strong stems to 1.2m (4ft), carrying brown-flecked, rich orange blooms over a long period. *Helenium* 'The Bishop' is a strong-growing plant, to 90cm (3ft) high, and produces deep golden yellow flowers. (See also pages 159–60.)

Helenium 'Waldtraut'

Helianthus 'Lemon Queen'

Helianthus decapetalus, the wild sun-flower, is a very hardy plant, forming clumps of stems to 1.5m (5ft) tall and blooming in late summer and autumn. The flowerheads are yellow and dainty, only 6cm (2½in) across. There are several garden varieties with larger, showier flowers. *Helianthus salicifolius*, with finer foliage and prettier flowers, is a true prairie native with stems up to 2m (6ft) in height. The cultivar *Helianthus* 'Lemon Queen' is a softer yellow and is a better mixer. (See also page 160.)

The varieties of **heliopsis** are the more popular sunflowers for garden cultivation. *Heliopsis helianthoides* blooms through mid- and late summer and forms clumps of upright stems 1.5m (5ft) tall. *Heliopsis helianthoides* var. *scabra* 'Light of Loddon' has clear yellow single flowers, while those

GOOD COMPANIONS

The greenish-cream blooms of *Echinacea purpurea* 'White Swan' (1) are shown to perfection in a cloud of bronze fennel, *Foeniculum vulgare* 'Purpureum' (2), with its smoky foliage and ochre lace flowers.

The plume-like flowerheads of *Filipendula rubra* 'Venusta' (3) provide light contrast to the larger daisy blooms of *Echinacea purpurea* (purple coneflower) (4).

MORE PERENNIALS FOR PRAIRIES *Asclepias tuberosa* • *Camassia leichtlinii* • *Cirsium rivulare* 'Atropurpureum' •

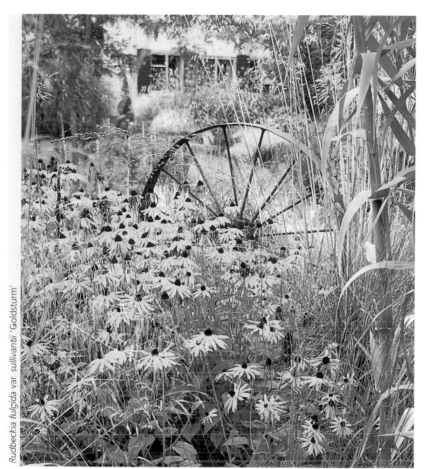

Rudbeckia fulgida var. sullivantii 'Goldsturm'

root divisions, resulting in their transfer from one cottage garden to another – either under or over the fence. As with other prairie plants, they are tough and tolerant. The originally cultivated species and hybrids tend to be rampant and invasive but there are more compact, better behaved alternatives. *Solidago canadensis*, with broad yellow plumes on stems up to 1m (40in) high, is well suited to a wild garden. *Solidago* **'Cloth of Gold'** and **'Crown of Rays'** are dwarf and compact but lack the grace of the tall varieties. *Solidago* **'Goldenmosa'** ♀ grows up to 1m (40in) high, with fluffy yellow flowerheads, and is one of the best. *Solidago* **'Golden Wings'** is a tall hybrid reaching 2m (6ft). *Solidago × hybrida*, now known as × *Solidaster luteus*, is a group of generally less invasive garden hybrids.

Solidago 'Goldenmosa'

of *Heliopsis helianthoides* var. *scabra* **'Spitzentänzerin'** (BALLERINA) ♀ are strong yellow and semi-double. There are double-flowered forms but these lack the charm of the single varieties and, like all double flowers, are useless at attracting pollinating insects.

The perennial **rudbeckias** start to come into their own in late summer, with a blaze of rich yellow that will brighten the dullest of days. *Rudbeckia fulgida* var. *sullivantii* **'Goldsturm'** ♀ never ceases to impress: a true black-eyed beauty, up to 90cm (3ft) tall, that will thrive in poor soil and the toughest of situations as long as it is not too dry. Leave the flower stems after the blooms have faded; the black, cone-shaped centres will make a stunning contrast to frost-traced grasses on a winter's morning. (See also page 177.)

Solidagos, or golden rod, are ancient garden plants hailing mostly from North America. They throw up fine stems that carry a shower of greenish-gold flowers in late summer and autumn. They seed themselves freely and grow readily from

GRASSES TO GROW WITH PRAIRIE PLANTS

Many true prairie grasses are large and vigorous and too big for smaller spaces. Several smaller grasses will give a prairie effect in mixed planting while allowing the flowering perennials to predominate.

Some of the best are:

Calamagrostis × acutiflora 'Karl Foerster'
Calamagrostis brachytricha (left)
Miscanthus sinensis 'Kleine Silberspinne' ♀
Panicum virgatum 'Heavy Metal'
Panicum virgatum 'Warrior'
Stipa calamagrostis
Stipa tenuissima (see page 73)

Eupatorium purpureum subsp. *maculatum* 'Atropurpureum' • *Oenothera speciosa* • *Veronicastrum virginicum* •

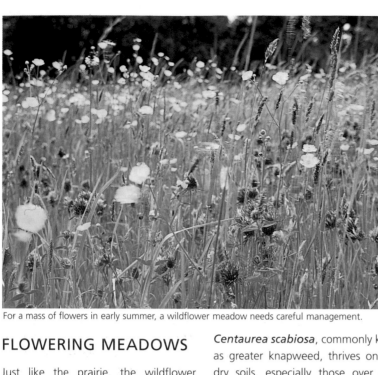

For a mass of flowers in early summer, a wildflower meadow needs careful management.

FLOWERING MEADOWS

Just like the prairie, the wildflower meadow is a mixture of herbaceous perennials, annuals and grasses that grow in harmony, adapted to the conditions of their natural environment.

The wildflower meadow features in gardens of all sizes but so often the results are disappointing after the first season: annuals die out, perennials fail to establish and grasses and coarse weeds take over. The secret of success is to emulate the natural environment as closely as possible. Soil type and fertility are primary considerations. Flowering meadows tend to do best on thinner, less fertile soils: grasses are not so dominant here, giving the flowers the chance to shine.

Wildflowers that succeed in meadow plantings are those that can coexist happily with grasses. Clovers, vetches, and buttercups, for example, reappear year after year with little problem. Plants such as annual poppies, on the other hand, quickly die out in grassland because their seed germinates best in broken soil, hence their prevalence in grain fields and on disturbed wasteland.

Centaurea scabiosa, commonly known as greater knapweed, thrives on poor, dry soils, especially those over chalk. With flowers like large purple cornflowers, borne on stems 60cm (24in) tall, it is attractive to butterflies and bees, and the ripe seeds are a favourite food of goldfinches.

Hardy orchids are an exciting addition to any wildflower meadow and plants are increasingly available through micropropagation. Thriving in damp as well as dry sites, *Dactylorhiza fuchsii* (common spotted orchid) bears its lilac

Dactylorhiza fuchsii

MAINTENANCE OF A FLOWERING MEADOW

Cutting is the key to a wildflower meadow. It needs to be treated like a field cut for hay, the environment where meadow flowers naturally thrive. Grass and flowers are allowed to grow through the spring and bloom through early summer. By midsummer their seed is set and ripe, at which point the meadow is cut and left to dry, and seed from flowers falls to the ground; all cuttings are then collected (as if hay is being made). The meadow is then cut again through autumn and early spring, as if grazed by animals; all clippings are removed each time. It is then left from early spring onwards to grow and to bloom.

Removing the plant cuttings is vital. Left on the meadow they feed the grass with nitrogen, making it lush and thick and more competitive with emerging wildflower seedlings.

Clearly, a wildflower meadow is not a low-maintenance option. You will also need to remove undesirables: docks, thistles, willow seedlings, and so on. You may need to thin areas to open up space for seedlings to develop; strew plant cuttings over the ground to help disperse seed; and reseed patches by hand, if you wish to introduce other varieties.

spotted flowers on 30cm (12in) stems in early summer. It is becoming more widespread in the woods and roadside verges of southern Britain, and may suddenly appear in a garden meadow once a balanced ecosystem is achieved.

Chalky soils with thin grass are ideal for *Geranium pratense*, the meadow cranesbill. This has been grown as a cottage-garden plant for many years on account of its large, bowl-shaped violet-blue flowers, carried on 30cm (12in) stems above aromatic, finely cut leaves. It is the parent of many garden cultivars (see pages 48 and 91).

MORE PLANTS FOR FLOWERING MEADOWS *Briza maxima* • *Centaurea montana* • *Fritillaria meleagris* •

Knautia arvensis (field scabious) is a beautiful perennial for late summer so does not fit into the same regime as most other meadow flowers (see left). Up to 40cm (16in) high, this plant can be grown in rough grass that is not mown; it too does well in poor, chalky soil. The pale mauve flowers look lovely with the pink musk mallow, *Malva moschata* (see below).

Leucanthemum vulgare, the white moon or ox-eye daisy of meadows and verges, is a short-lived perennial that requires thin grass and some space for the clumps of deep green, spoon-shaped leaves to become established. Where it is happy it will seed prolifically and can take over, dominating a meadow for a couple of years before eventually settling down to co-exist with its companions. Growing 60cm (24in) high and doing well in sun or partial shade, it is easily raised from seed.

The perennial flax, *Linum perenne*, is a less robust beauty with fine stems, to 40cm (16in) high, and shining blue flowers that open only in the morning. It must have very well-drained soil and little competition from other plants, so is often grown in gravel rather than in a meadow. This is a short-lived perennial, and it is worth collecting seed in late summer to sow the following spring.

Malva moschata, the musk mallow, tolerates fertile soils and grows well on chalk. Its large, open, shining pink blooms look far too exotic to be those of a wildflower. They are borne among deeply cut leaves on stems up to 60cm (24in) high, over a long period all through summer.

The bright red field poppy, *Papaver rhoeas*, is a much-loved native flower, but it will only seed itself in disturbed soil, and even then rarely performs the following season. *Papaver orientale* (oriental poppy) is a perennial and, although not a native plant, it offers a showy scarlet alternative for those who

Papaver orientale 'Beauty of Livermere'

are not purist about such matters. Fading foliage after flowering, deemed a failing in the herbaceous border, is an advantage in the meadow as it allows grasses to take over, and its tendency to collapse is somewhat overcome by the surrounding plants. Deep red *Papaver orientale* 'Beauty of Livermere' is a particularly good choice for its upright stems, 90cm (3ft) high, and glowing garnet blooms that are not too large. (See also page 148.)

The versatility of the cowslip, *Primula veris*, has led to its adoption as a garden plant for almost any situation. Growing in sun or shade and on dry or damp soils, it is also happy in grass and a wonderful late spring flower for the meadow. It carries its scented, pale yellow flowers well above the crinkled leaf rosettes, on stems to 25cm (10in) high. Even in the wild it will hybridize with the closely related *Primula vulgaris* (primrose) and *Primula elatior* (oxlip). Plants can be divided after flowering, or seed can be collected and sown in the autumn to overwinter outside.

Few flowers capture the spring and summer sunshine as effectively as the meadow buttercup, *Ranunculus acris*. It also grows well in light shade. Although it may be considered a weed in the flower border, it is an essential in the wildflower meadow.

Silene dioica (red campion) is also happy in either light shade or full sun. Reaching 60cm (24in) high, it has deep pink flowers that appear from mid-spring onwards; if stems are cut back after flowering it will produce another flush later on, in autumn.

The nectar-laden flowers of the clovers, species and varieties of **Trifolium**, are popular with bees and butterflies, and are a welcome addition to informal garden plantings. *Trifolium rubens*, a European native, is one of the largest: a clump-forming plant with many stems reaching 60cm (24in). The large, pink or white flowerheads appear in early summer. *Trifolium pratense* (common red clover) is easily grown from seed and is wonderful in a wild-flower meadow, or in rough grass in an orchard where the flowers will attract bees for pollination.

Trifolium pratense

GRASSES FOR WILDFLOWER MEADOWS

When starting a wildflower meadow from scratch, consult a reputable seed merchant and acquire a mixture of traditional meadow grasses, rather than using commercial lawn seed.

Galega officinalis • Lychnis flos-cuculi • Narcissus pseudonarcissus • Origanum vulgare • Saponaria officinalis •

Woodland settings

The dappled shade under the canopy of trees is the perfect setting for some of our loveliest herbaceous perennials. Enjoying the open soil beneath the leaf litter of the woodland floor, they emerge and bloom early, before the thickening leaf canopy steals the sunlight. In the garden, we can take advantage of the filtered light beneath trees and shrubs to create informal woodland plantings, using the charming unsophisticated species that originate in the natural habitat.

Digitalis purpurea is a wonderful plant for any natural setting in the garden.

The beautiful blue-flowered *Corydalis flexuosa* ♀ prefers neutral to acid soil rich in leaf mould, so is ideal for growing beneath deciduous trees. The plant becomes dormant in summer so will not suffer when the tree canopy deprives it of moisture. In late spring and early summer, tubular blue flowers are carried in graceful clusters above the fern-like foliage, which resembles that of *Dicentra*. About 30cm (12in) high, this is a lovely plant to grow with lime-green ferns under birch trees, where it can be left undisturbed to spread slowly. *Corydalis flexuosa* 'Purple Leaf' has purple foliage and sapphire-blue flowers (see Good Companions, page 59).

The foxglove *Digitalis purpurea* is really a biennial, forming a large rosette of broad oval, felted leaves in the first year and producing its majestic purplish-pink flower spike, 1.2m (4ft) tall, in early summer of the second. It seeds freely and is an excellent plant to encourage where deer and rabbits are a problem:

Corydalis flexuosa 'Purple Leaf'

these are well aware of the foxglove's toxic qualities and leave it untouched. The white-flowered *Digitalis purpurea* f. *albiflora* needs to be isolated from the purple species if white offspring are to be maintained. Although a garden cultivar, *Digitalis purpurea* 'Suttons Apricot' ♀ has all the grace and charm of the species but with flowers of soft apricot-pink; these look beautiful in a natural setting against the bark of trees.

Of the few evergreen woodland perennials, *Euphorbia amygdaloides* var. *robbiae* ♀ (Mrs Robb's bonnet) is one of the most useful. Spreading by underground stems, it produces heads of rounded leaves, crowned by lime-green flowers that appear in early spring and last until early summer. Up to 40cm (16in) high, this makes superb ground cover under large shrubs and tolerates sun as well as shade. In a woodland planting it provides evergreen interest at ground level throughout the year and can compete with the vigorous growth of both periwinkle and ivy. (See also page 113.)

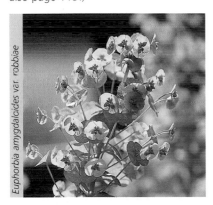
Euphorbia amygdaloides var. robbiae

Galium odoratum (sweet woodruff) is another delightful ground-cover plant for any shady spot under trees or shrubs. Its fine stems, 20cm (8in) tall, quickly emerge in spring, clothed in whorls of bright green, narrow leaves. In late spring, clouds of tiny white flowers appear across the mats of foliage. It is a delightfully aromatic plant, and can be gathered and used to flavour white

Lamium orvala

wine, or made into a refreshing cordial. Sweet woodruff looks lovely covering the ground around groups of the Lenten rose, *Helleborus × hybridus* (see pages 180–81), the fine foliage of the woodruff contrasting beautifully with the stiff, leathery hellebore leaves.

Lamium orvala, a member of the deadnettle family, has upright pinkish stems, 30cm (12in) or more high, with toothed, mid-green, slightly hairy leaves, well spaced in pairs; between them appear bruised pink, lipped flowers in mid- and late spring. These plants form wide mats and are valuable ground cover, retaining their foliage well into late summer. (See Good Companions, below.) *Lamium galeobdolon*, also known as yellow archangel, is similar, but more delicate in its habit, with silver-marked leaves and soft yellow flowers on fine stems. This is the perfect partner for bluebells.

For those blessed with sandy, peaty, acid soil that remains moist in summer the blue poppies are a must in the light shade of trees. *Meconopsis* are among the most desirable of flowers – simple

Lamium galeobdolon with bluebells

yet sophisticated, and heart-stoppingly beautiful. *Meconopsis betonicifolia* ♀ (Tibetan blue poppy) is perhaps the most widely cultivated. A native of Tibet, Yunnan and Burma, it grows in moist woods at high altitude so likes cool conditions. It is easily raised from seed, forming a rosette of hairy leaves in its first year. Flower buds appear in the second year, but ideally these should be removed to encourage the formation of basal shoots that will establish the plant as a short-lived perennial. If buds are allowed to develop, the plant usually dies after flowering. Planting in groups will mean that at least some plants can

---

PLANTING HERBACEOUS PERENNIALS UNDER TREES

Autumn is the best time to plant under deciduous trees. In winter and early spring, rain is able to penetrate and newly planted perennials have the opportunity to put down roots before the tree canopy thickens. If planted in spring, perennials will require regular and copious watering until their roots become established.

GOOD COMPANIONS

With its rich bronze metallic foliage, *Ajuga reptans* 'Atropurpurea' (1) complements the crushed strawberry-pink stems and flowers of *Lamium orvala* (2).

be left to flower while on others the buds are taken off. The flower stems rise to 1.5m (5ft) in summer, each with a number of buds that open to four-petalled flowers varying from purplish blue to clear azure with golden stamens. *Meconopsis grandis* (Himalayan blue poppy) is similar but with longer, lighter green leaves. In its native Sikkim it is cultivated around shepherds' huts where the seeds are used for oil. *Meconopsis* × *sheldonii*, a hybrid between these two species, is shorter, at only 1m (40in), and is easier to grow; it has given rise to some fine named cultivars, consistent in their colour.

Meconopsis × *sheldonii*

Meconopsis cambrica

Spigelia marlandica 'Wisley Jester'

SPRING BULBS

Bulbs that flower in early spring are natural planting partners for woodland perennials under trees. They too are well prepared to produce their display before the leaf canopy thickens. Natural species and graceful, small-flowered hybrids are always the best choice. Large-flowered garden hybrids and strong colours look out of place in a natural woodland setting.

Some of the best are:

Anemone blanda ♀
Cyclamen coum ♀
Cyclamen repandum
Erythronium dens-canis ♀
Erythronium californicum 'White Beauty' (and other erythroniums)
Galanthus nivalis ♀ (and other snowdrops)
Narcissus 'February Gold' ♀
Narcissus 'Hawera' ♀ (above)
Narcissus 'Peeping Tom' ♀

Not all meconopsis are shades of blue. *Meconopsis cambrica* (Welsh poppy) is normally yellow, and some orange forms occur, as do those with double flowers. It does not require acid soil but does prefer shade; thriving in conditions of low fertility, it does well naturalized in gravel, seeding itself freely. A long-lived plant with a deep, branched tap root, it has ferny foliage and upturned papery flowers, borne singly on fine 30cm (12in) stems throughout summer. The bright blooms sing out under the shade of trees.

The various species of *Polygonatum* (Solomon's seal) are native to European, Asian and American woodlands and hedgerows. They usually have gracefully arching stems of waxy foliage, which in late spring carry creamy, bell-shaped flowers tinged with green. After the flowers fade the foliage persists until late summer. Up to 90cm (3ft) high, they are effective plants to provide seasonal height among periwinkle and ivy, and follow on from the early spring display of snowdrops. (See also page 127.)

The British native primrose, *Primula vulgaris* ♀, is a charming wildflower, only 20cm (8in) high, that found its way from woodland edge to cottage garden many years ago. An easy plant to grow,

it thrives on both acid and chalky soils; where it is happy it seeds freely, forming large colonies. Fresh soft yellow blooms start to emerge from the rosette of bright green leaves in late winter and continue to a climax in late spring. Occasionally soft salmon forms occur. (See Good Companions, right.)

Spigelia marilandica is a hardy, clump-forming woodland plant from south-east USA, thriving in moist, fertile soil in semi-shade. Upright stems quickly rise to 30cm (12in), clad in narrow, fresh green leaves, and the flowers appear at

GROWING UNDER TREES

Growing conditions can be improved beneath trees by selective thinning of the canopy. This is particularly effective with light-headed trees such as birch; careful thinning of the branches will allow cultivation to within 1m (40in) or so of the trunks of mature trees. As an added bonus, thinning the lower branches makes attractive bark more visible in summer and winter.

OTHER PERENNIALS FOR WOODLAND *Actaea racemosa* • *Asarum europaeum* • *Campanula lactiflora* •

Toad lilies (Tricyrtis)

Toad lilies are interesting perennials originating from Japan, China and Taiwan. They need moist, shaded woodland conditions to grow well. They are attractive early in the year as the shoots unfurl glossy, sometimes spotted leaves. By early autumn the stems reach 0.5–1m (20–40in) tall, according to species. Flowers are produced singly or in clusters in the leaf axils or in clusters at the end of the stems: small and waxy, they are strikingly marked and spotted. Toad lilies form dense clumps and make effective ground cover. With their exotic appearance and subtle colouring, they are excellent for small, shaded gardens as well as for woodland settings. They associate well with ferns, hostas, heucheras and other foliage plants. In time, plants can become congested, particularly in heavier soils, and will need to be lifted and divided.

OTHER GOOD TOAD LILIES

Tricyrtis hirta More relaxed in habit than *Tricyrtis formosana*, with arching stems. Bears white purple-spotted flowers in late summer and autumn.

Tricyrtis 'Lilac Towers' Has stiff, upright stems and flowers similar to those of *Tricyrtis hirta*.

Tricyrtis formosana ♀ forms wide clumps of stems up to 80cm (32in) tall. The leaves are shining green with darker spots. Flowers are white with deep strawberry-pink markings, and are borne in open clusters at the end of the stems in early autumn. This is one of the easiest toad lilies to grow.

Uvularia grandiflora

the stem tips from late spring onwards. Long, pointed red buds open to reveal a creamy yellow interior to the petals; as these reflex the flowers resemble tiny jester's hats. The Hillier selection of this spigelia was named 'Wisley Jester' in celebration of the Royal Horticultural Society's bicentenary in 2004.

Uvularia grandiflora ♀ is another North American woodland native, also known as merrybells. Oval to lance-shaped leaves unfold in mid- to late spring, revealing pendent, bell-shaped, pale to mid-yellow flowers, sometimes with a hint of green, each one made up of clearly separate, gently twisted petals. Related to Solomon's seal (see left), this slowly spreading herbaceous plant will thrive in a rich, moist site and will deliver rare spring colour in deep or partial shade. Once established, it can reach 60cm (24in); its upright stems look stunning among ferns, *Tiarella* and the pendulous sedge, *Carex pendula*. *Uvularia perfoliata* has more rounded, lance-shaped leaves and pale yellow flowers that mix well with bluebells.

GOOD COMPANIONS

Lime-green fronds of the shuttlecock fern *Matteuccia struthiopteris* ♀ (1) will rise above the glowing sapphire flowers of *Corydalis flexuosa* 'Purple Leaf' (2).

The soft yellow of the primrose *Primula vulgaris* ♀ is the perfect partner for *Anemone blanda* blue shades. Truly the colours of spring, they are brighter and all the more welcome in the dappled shade of trees.

Campanula latifolia • Mertensia virginica • Phlox divaricata • Phlox stolonifera • Tiarella cordifolia • Trillium •

Shady sites

Nearly all gardens have some form of shade; it can be a problem or a blessing depending on what you plant. As a rule the showiest flowers are not found in shade, but you will find interesting foliage. The lower light conditions intensify colour and definition and plants are not scorched or bleached by high summer sunshine. Gardens with a high proportion of shade may not be the most colourful, but they can be stunningly effective in a quieter way.

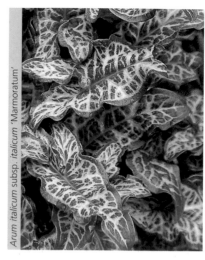

Arum italicum subsp. *italicum* 'Marmoratum'

A plant that is happy in partial shade or in sun, **Arum italicum** subsp. **italicum** **'Marmoratum'** (formerly *Arum italicum* 'Pictum') grows from tuberous roots and forms a clump of arrow-shaped leaves 40cm (16in) high. These are dark glossy green and attractively patterned with a tracery of silver veins. The plant is very early to emerge: it breaks through the soil in midwinter and the leaves persist until late spring. The greenish-white spathes often go unnoticed, but they are followed by spikes of orange berries that persist when the leaves die down. This is an excellent plant to combine with early spring bulbs and for early foliage interest among hostas.

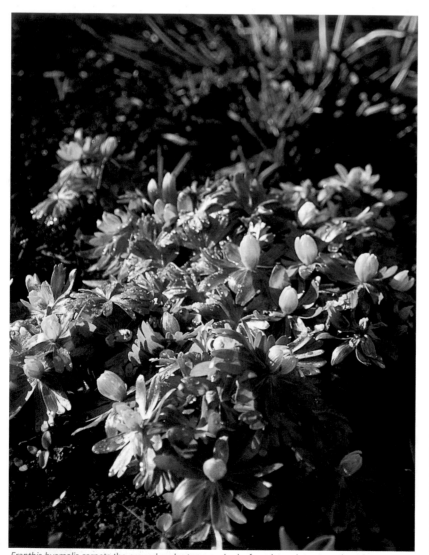

Eranthis hyemalis carpets the ground under trees or shrubs from late winter to early spring.

WHAT WILL GROW IN PARTIAL SHADE?

As a general rule, areas of the garden that get a few hours of sunshine in the course of the day will support most plants, apart from those requiring an open, sunny position. There is always a certain amount of trial and error here, but it is never worth persevering with perennials in shade if they become drawn and weak, struggling towards the light. Plants like this are not happy; move them and fill the gap with something else.

OTHER GOOD PERENNIALS FOR DRY SHADE *Ajuga reptans • Alchemilla mollis • Brunnera macrophylla •*

Convallaria majalis

Asarum europaeum

Asarums are low-growing woodland plants well adapted to deep shade. The Japanese species often have beautiful marbled leaves but are too delicate for garden cultivation. The European and American natives are hardy characters useful for foliage ground cover in shady spots. Their flowers are insignificant and usually hidden beneath the leaves.

They grow from aromatic rhizomes, hence the common name wild ginger. *Asarum caudatum*, a North American species, has heart-shaped, dark green leaves. *Asarum europaeum* has more rounded, glossy, bright green leaves.

With bold, leathery, evergreen foliage and early spring flowers in white to deepest purple, **bergenias** are excellent plants for shade or partial shade. They will not succeed in dry sites and want fairly fertile soil as well as adequate moisture. Most widely grown is pink-flowered *Bergenia corditolia*, to 40cm (16in) high; it has been in cultivation since the 17th century and is a very tolerant plant, surviving extremely cold conditions. (See also pages 110–11.)

Evoking memories of the cottage gardens of old, *Convallaria majalis* ♀ (lily of the valley) has earned its place among gardeners' favourites. It is found in much of the northern hemisphere, preferring deep to partial shade and happy in almost any soil, apart from heavy clay or marsh. The spreading rhizomes bear pairs of leathery, mid- to dark green leaves, from which 20cm (8in) stems of numerous pendent, waxy, white bell-shaped flowers arise in late spring. Sometimes flowers are followed by scarlet berries. Lily of the valley needs careful siting in the garden. It can be invasive, and will sometimes snub the original planting place, only to thrive elsewhere, in a site of its own choosing. It is useful to fill those narrow strips of redundant soil alongside paths and walls, and often thrives in full sun despite its preference for shade. Its dense foliage is very effective as weed control, perfect at the base of a shrubby border. Plants acquired as bare roots in the dormant season should be planted as soon as possible, with the rhizomes laid in shallow holes 4cm (1½in) below the surface.

Although *Convallaria majalis* is most commonly found, there are a number of variations of note. Most flower at about

61

Epimedium pinnatum • *Euphorbia amygdaloides* var. *robbiae* • *Linaria triornithophora* • *Vinca major* • *Vinca minor* •

Epimedium × rubrum

Geranium macrorrhizum

Lamium maculatum 'Beacon Silver'

and mature leaves, is one of the best ground-cover plants for partial shade.

Geraniums are normally associated with dry soil and a sunny position. *Geranium phaeum*, however, is often found naturalized in moist, shady sites. It has darkly marked foliage and long, fine stems, 60cm (24in) high, that bear small, dark plum-purple flowers in early summer. This is not an arresting plant, but interesting to lighten patches of heavy foliage and add detail. *Geranium macrorrhizum*, on the other hand, is good in dry shade and will form dense ground cover, 30cm (12in) high, under a tree or at the base of a wall. In such a position it holds its foliage for much of the year, but will not display the autumn colour that is a feature of the plant in full sun. Dainty pink or white flowers appear in late spring. The aromatic foliage is unattractive to animals so this plant is a good choice where deer and rabbits are a problem.

The various cultivars of *Lamium maculatum* are easy to grow in partial shade and make attractive low ground cover. These creeping members of the nettle family often have pleasing silver-marked leaves and white or pink flowers according to variety. **'White Nancy'**♀ has silver leaves and pure white flowers; **'Beacon Silver'** has silvery green leaves

and pink-purple flowers (see also page 106). They will withstand quite dry conditions once established.

With its leathery, grass-like foliage and dense spikes of lilac-blue flowers borne in late summer and autumn, *Liriope muscari*♀ (lilyturf) is a splendid evergreen for shade. It grows only to 30cm (12in) or so high, but eventually forms broad clumps and makes effective ground cover. A native of China and Japan, it is a woodland plant preferring soil rich in organic matter. Although hardy, it is not tolerant of the coldest conditions so the shelter of trees and shrubs is a blessing. (See Good Companions, right, and page 101).

Myrrhis odorata (sweet cicely) resembles the common cow parsley but with wonderful ferny foliage that smells sweetly of aniseed and lasts throughout the season. The white lace-like flowers are produced over a long period from late spring to midsummer. It will grow to 1.2m (4ft) tall and seeds itself where it is happy, but is never invasive. It likes a moist situation but will tolerate drier conditions, although growth is restricted here. This is a delightful plant to fill those shady gaps at the back of the border or to bring charm and interest to a neglected corner. It fits easily into any situation, rural or urban.

25cm (10in) but the large flowers of **'Fortin's Giant'** rise at least 30cm (12in) above broader leaves. **'Flore Pleno'** has double white flowers, while those of **var. *rosea*** are larger and lilac-pink. The more rounded foliage of **'Albostriata'** is finely striped with creamy gold along its length – simple yet stunning.

Epimediums, also known as bishop's mitre (see pages 112 and 114), are another excellent choice, requiring moist shade or partial shade with moderately fertile soil. Many are evergreen and make marvellous year-round ground cover with a carpet of richly hued foliage. *Epimedium × rubrum*♀, 30cm (12in) high, with red-tinted young

Myrrhis odorata

☉THER GOOD PERENNIALS FOR MOIST SHADE *Actaea simplex* • *Aspidistra elatior* 'Milky Way' •

There are few showy flowering perennials that succeed in shade. One of the loveliest is *Phlox stolonifera*, an American woodland native. It forms spreading mats of underground shoots that emerge from the soil in rosettes of leaves. In late spring and early summer, the scented flowers turn them into a colourful carpet. This is a hardy plant, 20–30cm (8–12in) high, excellent for ground cover beneath deciduous trees, or for a scree bed that gets only a few hours of sun each day. It prefers neutral to acid, well-drained soil. The cultivar 'Pink Ridge' is strong pink, and 'Blue Ridge' ♥ is ice blue. *Phlox divaricata* ♥ has pinky blue or white flowers; it will thrive in similar conditions but has a lighter, more sprawling habit and is better suited to woodland settings.

Pulmonarias or lungworts (see pages 106 and 115–16) bring interest to shady

Phlox stolonifera 'Pink Ridge'

sites with both their early spring flowers and their exotically spotted and marked foliage, which can stay looking good for most of the year and rivals that of many hostas. They prefer moist shade; in drier conditions the foliage will deteriorate. *Pulmonaria longifolia* 'Bertram Anderson', 30cm (12in) high, has long, narrow, well-spotted leaves and mauve-pink buds opening to rich blue flowers.

Pulmonaria 'Lewis Palmer'

Pulmonaria 'Lewis Palmer' ♥ is about the same height, with dark blue flowers held well above narrow, dark green leaves, heavily blotched greenish white.

Most **symphytums** (comfreys) are tough plants, native to shady places. With its cream variegated foliage and lilac-blue spring flowers, *Symphytum* × *uplandicum* 'Variegatum' ♥, up to 90cm (3ft) tall, is especially useful in moist shade. The green to gold markings on the dark green leaves of *Symphytum* 'Goldsmith' are brightest in early spring. Growing 25cm (10in) high, with pink to pale blue flowers, it looks lovely with blue-flowering bulbs (see Good Companions, left, and pages 116–17).

Many plants in the saxifrage family thrive in shade. *Tellima grandiflora* (fringe cups) is one of these – a rather unprepossessing perennial but valuable for its clumps of green foliage and spikes of lime-green flowers in late spring and early summer. It grows 60cm (24in) high, flourishing in both moist and quite dry conditions, and is useful ground cover over spring bulbs.

Tolmiea menziesii is similar but even less showy. Known as the pick-a-back plant, it produces offspring at the end of the leaf stalks, where they meet the leaves. Its indestructible nature has led to its adoption as a houseplant. *Tolmiea menziesii* 'Taff's Gold' ♥, with yellow-marked foliage, brings welcome colour to shady areas under shrubs and trees and among ferns. It grows 45cm (18in) tall.

GOOD COMPANIONS

The green and gold variegated foliage of *Symphytum* 'Goldsmith' (1) is beautiful with sapphire-blue *Muscari armeniacum* ♥ (2). Both will establish themselves firmly in a shady spot.

Phlox stolonifera 'Pink Ridge' (3) and *Ajuga reptans* 'Atropurpurea' (4): the vivid pink flowers of the phlox shine out against the bronze metallic foliage and deep blue flowers of the ajuga.

The deep green, strap-like leaves of *Liriope muscari* ♥ (5) contrast well with the soft silver-grey variegation of the ivy *Hedera helix* 'Glacier' ♥ (6).

Galium odoratum • *Hosta* • *Lamium galeobdolon* • *Ligularia* 'The Rocket' • *Petasites palmatus* • *Tiarella cordifolia* •

Sunny sites

Silver, spiky or aromatic foliage and bright flowers are often the livery of sun-loving plants. Natives of the Mediterranean, South Africa, California, Mexico and other warm, dry regions, these perennials luxuriate in sunny situations and shun the cold and damp.

Agapanthus Headbourne hybrids

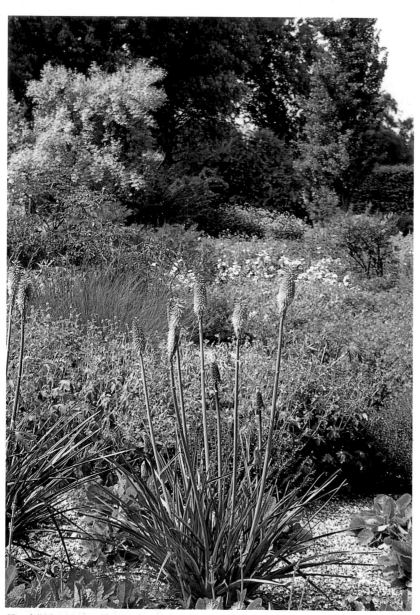

Silver foliage and aromatic shrubs combine with sun-loving perennials in an open gravel garden.

Many South African natives that enjoy full sun and good drainage must have plenty of moisture during the summer. **Agapanthus** (African blue lily) are classic examples. In their natural habitat these plants grow in moist, peaty soil, often in grassy and rocky sites. They have become naturalized in many places in the world, from the sand dunes of the Scilly Isles to the rocky terraces of Madeira. In gardens they fail to flower if given insufficient sun, or if their roots have too much freedom or the soil is too

PLANT ADAPTATIONS

Many herbaceous perennials are well adapted to dry, sunny situations where they get a good baking in summer and water is often scarce. Some have developed fleshy or woody roots that store food and water: when conditions become too difficult, the parts above ground simply fade away, and those below the surface keep things ticking over until the following season. Other perennials have modified their leaves and stems in order to prevent water loss, perhaps with an insulating layer of hairs, or have developed thick, fleshy leaves that store water. In some, the foliage is aromatic, because of the presence of oil, another way of preventing desiccation.

rich. Agapanthus produce bold clumps of grass-like leaves and, in the summer, rounded heads of trumpet or tubular flowers in shades of blue or white. The **Headbourne hybrids** are still the best for garden cultivation. These were raised in the 1940s by the Hon. Lewis Palmer at Headbourne Worthy near Winchester. Some were selected and named but they are usually offered as mixed shades of blue. They do not grow as tall as many agapanthus species and flower more freely in temperate climates. (See also pages 152–53.)

Silver foliage perennials are a natural choice for sunny situations. *Anaphalis triplinervis*♀ is a clump-forming, silver-leaved plant that bears flowers from late summer to early autumn. Clustered at the top of stems 30cm (12in) tall, these are small, white and everlasting, and can be cut and dried. Anaphalis relish full sun and good drainage, but do not like to be too dry in summer. (See page 102.)

Artemisias, too, are valued for their silver leaves, but their flowers tend to be of little interest. Some artemisias are truly herbaceous and deciduous, others are partly woody. The ever popular *Artemisia* 'Powis Castle'♀ can grow into a substantial shrub, 1m (40in) high, and lives longest in the poorest soil. *Artemisia pontica*, from northern Europe to central Asia, is one of the hardiest species. It forms clumps of fine stems with delicately cut silver foliage (see Good Companions, page 67). *Artemisia schmidtiana*♀, from Japan, is similar but more silvery with creeping stems, and forming a low mound of soft, hair-like foliage. *Artemisia alba* 'Canescens'♀ has wire-like stems and leaves that look good in contemporary schemes. While these three reach 60cm (24in) high, *Artemisia stelleriana* is much more prostrate, and has silver-white lobed foliage; it loves sandy soil so is particularly useful near the coast. (See also pages 51, 91 and 102–105.)

Centranthus ruber, the red valerian, is a native of the Mediterranean region, but is widely naturalized in northern Europe and is a familiar sight in Britain, especially by the coast. It produces a tough woody root and clings tenaciously in rocky crevices and gaps in paving, onto old walls, and on shingle banks and sand dunes. The hollow stems, up to 1m (40in) tall, carry light, evergreen leaves and clouds of red, pink ('Roseus') or white ('Albus') flowers from early summer onwards. In the garden it is a perfect choice for inhospitable sunny sites where other plants struggle. Remove flowerheads as they fade to prevent the downy willow-like seeds spreading, if you want to contain it.

Cosmos atrosanguineus, known as the chocolate plant, grows from a tuber like that of a dahlia, and indeed the flowers and foliage are not dissimilar, although this cosmos reaches only 60cm (24in) high when in flower, in mid- to

Cosmos atrosanguineus

late summer. The blooms, 4cm (1½in) across, are of the very darkest maroon-crimson, with a rich scent of chocolate. A warm, sunny spot is essential, and the plant needs protecting in winter with a generous mulch of straw or bracken. It is always late starting into growth so mark its position in the border carefully. It is a natural partner for warm pinks and also for oranges, reds and yellows.

Dictamnus albus, a member of the rue family, is a good example of a plant that survives dry conditions because of the presence of aromatic oils in its

CENTRANTHUS IN A BORDER

Although usually associated with the base of walls and gravel areas, *Centranthus ruber*, the red valerian, is a useful plant in the border. It looks especially attractive with peonies, its light flowerheads contrasting well with the heavy, flamboyant peony blooms. It is also a good companion for the oriental poppy, *Papaver orientale*: the valerian's strong stems and flowerheads conceal the fading foliage of the poppy once it has finished flowering.

foliage. A native of southern Europe, through Turkey into Asia, it grows wild in dry, rocky places. The erect stems, 80cm (32in) high, bear pretty, firefly-like flowers in pink or white in early summer. *Dictamnus albus* var. *purpureus*♀ has soft mauve-purple flowers with darker veining. On a hot, still evening the whole plant can be set alight because

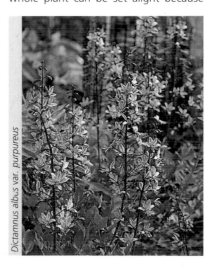

Dictamnus albus var. purpureus

of the oils vaporizing from the foliage. It will burn for a few seconds without sustaining harm. In the garden it is a lovely perennial for a sunny, sheltered position, perhaps at the base of a wall. Avoid touching the foliage in warm weather: like rue it is an irritant.

Echinops ritro

Echinops ritro ♀, the globe thistle, is a native of southern Europe to central Asia, where it is found in inhospitable stony places with little moisture. The spiny, thistle-like leaves are green above and white beneath. Stiff stems, 1m (40in) or more high, carry globe-shaped heads of steely blue flowers in late summer and autumn. This is a superb garden plant, striking with both grey foliage subjects and the hot oranges and reds of late summer flowers (see Good Companions, right). It survives anywhere, in shade as well as sun, and is excellent for a dry bed against a wall.

Erigeron karvinskianus ♀ is also a pioneer of dry, hostile places. Formerly known as *Erigeron mucronatus*, and originally from Mexico, it has become

Erigeron karvinskianus

naturalized in southern Europe and in parts of Britain. It colonizes similar places to valerian (see page 65), but is seen at its best hanging on in wall crevices, where the dainty, pink-tinged daisy flowers and wiry stems are the perfect contrast to the solidity of the stone. It is not a very hardy plant but regenerates freely from seed.

Erigeron glaucus has larger daisy flowers and makes a low, dense clump of soft, dull green leaves reaching 30cm (12in) in height. The flowers have bold centres and short ray-like petals, which are normally soft mauve in colour. They are produced over a long period from late spring to autumn. *Erigeron glaucus* is widely naturalized in coastal areas, where it thrives on cliffs and shingle.

Erigeron 'Dimity'

Erigeron 'Azurfee' (AZURE FAIRY)

A number of showier garden varieties are derived from it. *Erigeron* 'Dimity' is compact, with rich pink, gold-centred flowers, orange-tinged in bud.

The taller erigerons are often confused with asters, to which they are closely related. They have green foliage and bright flowers with orange-yellow centres. They bloom in midsummer and need full sun. *Erigeron* 'Dignity', 45cm (18in) high, has violet-blue flowers. 'Azurfee' (AZURE FAIRY) is lilac-blue, while 'Dunkelste Aller' (DARKEST OF ALL) ♀ is deep purple-blue; both grow to 60cm (24in) high.

The spiky metallic foliage and flowers of **eryngiums** tend to be associated with the seashore because of the species *Eryngium maritimum*, the sea holly. All eryngiums like full sun; some prefer dry conditions and some demand moisture at their roots in the growing season. *Eryngium agavifolium* is a succulent-looking plant with upright rosettes of fleshy, toothed, evergreen leaves, and tall, thick stems up to 1m (40in) high carrying greenish-brown flowers in midsummer. It works well planted in gravel but is out of place in a mixed border. This species does not like to be too dry. Nor does the widely available *Eryngium variifolium*, which produces leathery leaves and branching flower stems reaching 50cm (20in) in height. Its flowers are spiky and metallic and a good contrast to the evergreen, silver-veined leaves. The hardy species

DRYING ERYNGIUMS

Eryngiums make excellent dried flowers for winter decoration and lend themselves to contemporary designs as well as traditional arrangements. Cut the flowers in their prime and hang them upside down in a warm place with good air circulation until dry; this can take two or three weeks. Once dry, the flowers will last for several seasons.

OTHER PERENNIALS FOR SUNNY SITES *Acanthus spinosus* • *Anthemis tinctoria* • *Baptisia australis* •

Eryngium varifolium

Eryngium bourgatii 'Oxford Blue'

Eryngium bourgatii tolerates much drier conditions, and grows to 50cm (20in) when in flower in summer. The showy flowerheads vary in colour from that of stainless steel to rich blue. The flowers of the cultivar **'Oxford Blue'**♚ are particularly spectacular. **Eryngium alpinum**♚ is perhaps the most striking of all: large flowers with a broad spiky ruff are borne on stout stems, 1m (40in) high, in early summer. It looks stunning at the front of the border grouped with silver foliage plants such as lavender and artemisia. This species does not like to be too dry. (See also page 103.)

Most herbaceous **geraniums** enjoy a sunny site. *Geranium macrorrhizum* is the most reliable for a dry, sunny spot; it is also good in shade (see page 62). *Geranium × magnificum*, 60cm (24in) or so high, with large blue flowers, is an excellent plant, widely grown in cottage gardens. It likes good drainage and plenty of sunshine and will tolerate an exposed site. Its flowering season in early summer is short, but it is still well worth growing. *Geranium ibericum*

from Turkey is similar but blooms in mid- to late summer, so is good to plant with *Geranium × magnificum* for continuity of flower. *Geranium renardii*♚ is a lovely foliage plant, its sage-green leaves forming a neat, waved mound 30cm (12in) high. Prettily veined white flowers appear in midsummer, borne on dainty stems above the foliage. (See also pages 47–48, 91, 137 and 159.)

Limonium platyphyllum, the sea lavender, is popular in coastal gardens. A tough plant with leathery, evergreen leaves, it is able to withstand very dry conditions. In summer, wiry, branched stems, 60cm (24in) high, carry masses of starry, lavender-blue flowers that last for several weeks and can be cut for drying. **'Robert Butler'** and **'Violetta'** are two superior cultivars. All three are useful for gravel or scree, and combine very well with any silver foliage plant.

Another natural partner for silver-leaved plants, *Nepeta × faassenii*♚ makes a wonderful soft edging for hot, dry borders, particularly on chalky soils. Growing to 30cm (12in) in height, it has silvery leaves and stems and lilac-blue flowers throughout summer (see page 69). It flows over the edge of paving in a low cloud, and looks lovely with lime-green *Alchemilla mollis*♚ (see page 46).

(continued on page 69)

GOOD COMPANIONS

The soft grey leaves of *Artemisia pontica* (1) look lovely with *Allium cristophii*♚ (2) and will do an excellent job concealing the allium's unsightly fading foliage.

The steely blue globes of *Echinops ritro*♚ (3) contrast superbly with the fiery orange stars of *Crocosmia* 'Lucifer'♚ (4).

For a striking colour combination, try the bright blooms of *Verbena bonariensis*♚ (5) floating above the rising torches of *Kniphofia* 'Samuel's Sensation'♚ (6).

Eryngium planum • Papaver orientale • Romneya coulteri • Scabiosa caucasica • Sisyrinchium striatum •

Kniphofias

Commonly known as red hot pokers or torch lilies, kniphofias are not beautiful in isolation but when well planted can be some of the most striking subjects in the late summer and autumn garden. Towering above clumps of grass-like foliage, erect flower spikes provide strong vertical structure and contrast well with softer neighbours. They are useful to prolong interest in herbaceous plantings and look good with prairie plants and grasses. They are also eye-catching set against dark evergreens or against the shining bark of trees such as *Prunus serrula*♀. (See also pages 42 and 175.)

Natives of South Africa, kniphofias like fertile soil that does not dry out in summer; some simply will not flower if the soil is dry. They do, however, need a well-drained site, and loathe cold, wet winters. Clumps should be divided in early spring every few years.

Kniphofia 'Ice Queen' is a statuesque plant, with towering blooms 1.2m (4ft) high in mid- to late summer. The cool yellow flowers open from green buds and gradually fade to ivory as the season progresses.

Kniphofia 'Little Maid' One of the more diminutive varieties. Has delicate spikes of creamy-yellow flowers only 60cm (24in) high, in late summer and early autumn. Excellent for a scree garden.

Kniphofia 'Royal Standard'♀ is the classic red hot poker, with large, red and yellow flower spikes, 1m (40in) high, in mid- to late summer. Another classic is *Kniphofia rooperi*, a vigorous species that flowers in autumn.

Kniphofia 'Samuel's Sensation'♀ is an excellent plant producing tall, bold spikes of warm orange-red with a hint of yellow at the base. The flower stems can reach 1.5m (5ft) and appear from late summer onwards. (See also Good Companions, page 67.)

OTHER GOOD KNIPHOFIAS

Kniphofia 'Bees' Sunset'♀ Blooms in midsummer, with rich orange flowers carried on mahogany stems 80cm (32in) tall.

Kniphofia linearifolia Flowers in autumn, with characteristic orange and yellow spikes 1.5m (5ft) tall. The parent of many garden cultivars.

Kniphofia uvaria Grows 2m (6ft) high, with red flowers, fading to yellow at the base of the spike, in autumn. The coarse, spiky leaves form a dense clump and are evergreen.

Tulbaghia violacea

Verbena rigida

Zauschneria californica

Nepeta 'Six Hills Giant' is a much taller plant, reaching up to 1m (40in) high, with stronger stems and darker flowers. This is better placed further back in the border and grown with some support. (See also pages 42–43.)

Phlomis russeliana ♀ is a native of Turkey and is used to heat, but in its natural environment it often grows in woods or scrub so will tolerate partial shade in dry conditions as well as full sun. It has large, sage-like leaves and whorls of yellow deadnettle-like flowers borne on stiff, upright, square stems in summer. It is not wholly deciduous, retaining whorls of foliage in winter. The dead flowerheads are attractive if left on the plants during the early part of winter. *Phlomis samia*, with soft pink flowers, is similar and enjoys the same conditions. *Phlomis tuberosa* is a totally deciduous species, overwintering by means of root tubers. A tough, easy plant to grow, it has green leaves and pink flowers.

Tulbaghias look rather like miniature agapanthus with their slender grassy foliage and pretty lilac or white flowers on fine stems. Members of the lily family, they are strongly aromatic with a musty garlic-like odour. *Tulbaghia violacea* is reasonably hardy in a sunny, well-drained position. The variety 'Silver Lace' is particularly attractive with its silver- and sage-striped leaves and violet-pink flowers in early summer and autumn. Reaching only 50cm (20in)

high, it is a good choice for the front of the border or planted into gravel.

Verbena rigida ♀ is a stiff, wiry perennial with aromatic foliage. The purple-magenta flowers, produced from midsummer to late autumn, are striking and work well with silver foliage plants. (See page 152.) Growing from tuberous roots, it copes with dry soil and loves full sun. Only 50cm (20in) high, *Verbena rigida* offers a more compact alternative to ethereal *Verbena bonariensis* ♀, which can grow to 2m (6ft) in height (see Good Companions, page 67, and see page 169).

Watsonias are members of the iris family and hail from South Africa. They grow from corms and make dense clumps similar in habit to crocosmias. They are hardy in the mildest areas in full sun and moisture-retentive soil.

Watsonia pillansii grows to less than 1m (40in) tall, with spikes of funnel-shaped flowers in vibrant oranges, reds and pinks. *Watsonia borbonica* may reach 1.5m (5ft), and has clear pink flowers, arranged on only one side of the spike (not both as in *Watsonia pillansii*). *Watsonia borbonica* subsp. *borbonica* 'Arderne's White' is pure white and easier to accommodate. All of these flower in summer.

Zauschneria californica also likes a warm position in full sun but must have excellent drainage. It is a low, sprawling plant with many stems and usually narrow leaves. The brilliant orange flowers are borne freely in late summer and autumn. It will nestle at the base of a wall or soften the edge of paving or a raised bed. The cultivar 'Dublin' ♀ has excellent blazing orange-red flowers.

PLANTING PARTNERS

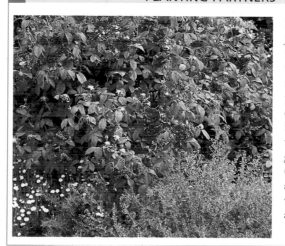

Dark lilac-blue *Nepeta* × *faassenii* ♀ complements the blooms of *Rosa gallica* var. *officinalis* ♀ (the red rose of Lancaster) at the peak of the season and extends it as the roses fade. Both *Rosa gallica* var. *officinalis* and *Rosa gallica* 'Versicolor' ♀ (known as Rosa mundi) are excellent choices where growing conditions are less than hospitable.

The scree garden

The scree or gravel garden is a new style of planting, particularly good for sun-lovers that like their feet in fast-draining soil. Growing plants in a bed or border topped with gravel shows them off beautifully. The effect can be that of a meadow, run through with sweeps of colour, but scree is also suitable for minimalistic schemes and provides the perfect setting for plants like phormiums, cistus, grasses, silver foliage subjects, alpines and dwarf bulbs.

Scree is ideal for an informal planting of grasses and sun-loving perennials.

ADVANTAGES OF GRAVEL

Scree is found naturally in many areas of the world, where rocks near the surface have shattered to create a layer of stony debris. In the garden, a sunny, well-drained scree or gravel bed gives plants from the Mediterranean, Australasia and South Africa the best chance of coping with the northern European climate. Alpines, low perennials and shrubs look better in this setting than in the false environment of a small rock garden.

Gravel shows off individual specimens to maximum advantage. It conserves moisture, but reflects light back onto the plants; and it prevents water splashes that spoil the lower foliage.

Gravel is low maintenance: there is no grass to cut. It is relatively inexpensive to install. A level site is not necessary: it is often more attractive if allowed to follow the natural contours of the land. A narrow scree bed alongside a path or a wall provides a pleasing solution to an awkward dry area.

Asphodeline lutea (yellow asphodel) has rosettes of blue-green, waved, grass-like leaves, from which the flower stems rise in spring, reaching 1.5m (5ft) by the time the starry yellow flowers open. These fade to leave round green seedpods on ragged spikes. Asphodel looks awkward mixed with other plants, but on well-drained scree in full sun it is striking. In larger sites it is the perfect

PLANT PROFILE

Diascias

Diascias have become popular plants for pots and hanging baskets. They grow quickly, flower profusely and are easy to propagate from cuttings. Many lovely hybrids have been raised in recent years. Diascias originate from South Africa, where they grow in moist sites by streams and other damp places, often in semi-shade. British gardeners think of them as sun-lovers because of how they grow them. Of course in baskets and containers they get regularly watered, and if overwintered in a greenhouse they are protected from the wet and cold of the British winter. When grown in scree beds with good, moisture-retentive soil under the gravel layer, they are rewarding plants with a very long flowering season.

Diascia rigescens ♀ has small spikes of strawberry-pink flowers on a flowing plant that forms a dense mat, about 30cm (12in) high. It normally flowers during late spring and early summer, but in the right conditions can be in bloom for much longer.

Diascia fetcaniensis is one of the hardiest and most reliable. Up to 30cm (12in) high, it has fine creeping stems of mid-green leaves and dainty spikes of pink flowers in summer.

Diascia barberae 'Ruby Field' ♀, loose in habit and only 20cm (8in) high, has plenty of large pretty, salmon-red flowers in summer.

partner for the bold emerging foliage of *Cynara cardunculus* ♀ (see page 102).

Many **dianthus** revel in dry scree, especially on alkaline soil (see also pages 81 and 136). *Dianthus deltoides* ♀ (maiden pink) forms low mats of fine blue-green leaves that are transformed from midsummer onwards with myriad bright perfect flowers, borne on upright stems 20cm (8in) high. It is a hardy plant and has given rise to many excellent varieties, from white to the most vivid cerise and dark red. Easy to grow, and perfect for scree, the similarly sized *Dianthus gratianopolitanus* ♀ bears deep pink flowers with cut petal edges

Dierama pulcherrimum

and a delightful clove scent. It is also known as the Cheddar pink.

Often plants grown in dry gardens prefer a moist soil but must have good drainage; this is particularly true of many South African natives such as dieramas. Grass-like perennials growing from bulbous bases, they are usually evergreen so are treated as herbaceous plants and are never sold as dry bulbs in Britain. *Dierama pulcherrimum* is the most spectacular, with upright foliage to 60cm (24in) long, and arching stems, more than 1.5m (5ft) tall, with large silky, bell-shaped flowers that are papery at the base. This is the lovely feature

THE GARDEN HOUSE

At The Garden House, Buckland Monachorum, in Devon, the traditional garden is integrated into the surrounding landscape using rolling scree beds planted in naturalistic styles. Here, drifts of *Dierama pulcherrimum* (angel's fishing rod) and *Campanula lactiflora* (milky bellflower) blur the boundaries of the scree. Both plants grow naturally in rather drier conditions, but scree planting provides excellent drainage at their feet, helping them to thrive even in the locally damp climate.

that gained dieramas the common name angel's fishing rod. As with all dieramas, flowers appear from early to midsummer, and colours range from white through shades of pink to dark purple. *Dierama dracomontanum* is a charming little plant for the smaller scree garden and dances happily above sedums, thymes and saxifrages. It grows to only 45cm (18in) tall and has flowers in various shades of dark pink. *Dierama floriferum* too grows only 45cm (18in) high and has fine foliage and narrow bells of blue-mauve. Often mistaken for a grass, it is fun to plant with fescues and stipas.

The whorlflower, *Morina longifolia*, is a native of the Himalayas, where it grows on moist but steep slopes. It has rosettes of aromatic, thistle-like foliage, 30cm (12in) long, and in summer these give rise to tall stems, up to 60cm (24in) high, of small white flowers that become pink with age. A scree bed with

Morina longifolia

good soil that does not get too dry is its best chance of survival in the garden.

Platycodon grandiflorus♀ (balloon flower), a member of the campanula family from Japan and China, enjoys similar conditions. Its thick roots are used to competing with grass on moist but well-drained slopes. The glaucous foliage, carried on wiry stems 60cm (24in) high, is particularly fine. Large, bell-shaped blue flowers top the stems in late summer. The species is rarely grown but a number of hybrids are widely available: **'Mariesii'**♀ is blue and early flowering; **'Albus'** is white; and **'Apoyama'**♀ is deep mauve. The beauty of the plant is lost when crowded among other perennials in a border; in a scree bed it can be shown off to advantage.

The lovely **roscoeas** also thrive in moist but well-drained soil, but these plants enjoy fairly cool conditions and will benefit from the shade cast by their neighbours. Rather orchid-like in flower, most are dwarf and upright in habit, producing succulent stems that emerge in spring from fleshy roots. *Roscoea cautleyoides*♀ has soft yellow flowers and *Roscoea purpurea* is rich purple. Both bloom in early summer.

ESTABLISHING A SCREE BED

An open, sunny site is best for a scree bed and allows cultivation of the widest range of plants. It is essential to rid the site of perennial weeds before establishing the bed.

Ensure good drainage by digging in coarse grit and improve water retention by adding plenty of well-rotted, organic manure or compost. On poorly drained sites raise planting areas into mounds.

Top the soil with at least 7cm (3in) of washed pea shingle. Larger stones, pebbles or slate scree can be added on the surface to enhance the scheme.

Roscoea purpurea

Sedums are versatile plants in spite of their succulent appearance. (See also pages 97 and 176.) The ice plant, *Sedum spectabile*♀, is widely grown in mixed plantings and is useful for its clumps of sea-green foliage, 45cm (18in) high, and its flattened heads of pink flowers in late summer. *Sedum spectabile* 'Iceberg' has large heads of white flowers and paler leaves. The large flowerheads of the slightly taller *Sedum* **'Herbstfreude'** (AUTUMN JOY)♀ turn from dark pink to chestnut as autumn moves into winter. They are a favourite haunt of butterflies in late summer. These sedums suit scree planting on sandy soil as long as they have adequate moisture in summer. They contribute bold form among grasses and softer

COLOUR WITH BULBS

Dwarf bulbs are shown at their best on scree, when they can get lost elsewhere in the garden. Choose those with fine leaves or those that die down quickly to prevent the fading foliage spoiling the effect.

A few of the best bulbs for scree:

Crocus chrysanthus 'Ladykiller'♀
Crocus tommasinianus 'Whitewell Purple'
Cyclamen coum♀ (above)
Iris reticulata♀
Narcissus 'Hawera'♀
Tulipa linifolia Batalinii Group 'Bright Gem'♀
Tulipa dasystemon♀

OTHER GOOD PERENNIALS FOR SCREE *Centranthus ruber* • *Crambe maritima* • *Erigeron karvinskianus* •

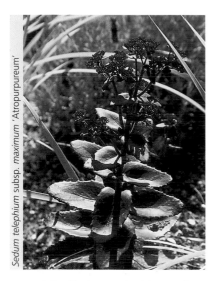

Sedum telephium subsp. _maximum_ 'Atropurpureum'

perennials. **Sedum telephium** subsp. **maximum** 'Atropurpureum'♔, a solid plant with a few erect stems up to 50cm (20in) tall, has pinkish-red flowerheads and deep wine-purple foliage; it makes a wonderful contrast to the fine foliage of _Festuca glauca_ (blue fescue). **Sedum 'Ruby Glow'**♔ is the perfect candidate for scree, with its sprawling stems of very grey, purple-flushed foliage and deep purple-red flowers in late summer.

More prostrate sedums are ideal for carpet planting with thymes in dry areas – a style of planting that brings a feeling of space, the equivalent of a lawn, to a larger scree bed. Especially worthy of note are **Sedum cauticola** 'Lidakense', forming a mat of blue-grey leaves on fine stems with deep pink flowers, and bright yellow **Sedum spathulifolium** 'Cape Blanco'♔, which has rounded, succulent grey leaves with a white bloom. Both flower in summer.

SCREE GARDENS ON WET SITES

Those gardening on wet sites or heavy clay are not precluded from enjoying this style of planting. Adding organic matter and sharp grit works wonders on even the heaviest soil. Raising the planting areas into mounds keeps the plants' feet out of the damp.

SELF-SEEDERS

Gravel provides the perfect medium for self-seeding subjects to germinate next year's plants. Grasses such as _Festuca glauca_ (blue fescue) and the feather grass _Stipa tenuissima_ seed themselves liberally. The gardener has only to carry out a little judicious thinning. Annuals like Californian poppy, _Eschscholzia_, with shimmering blooms in shades of glowing orange, create a sensational summer display and are often perennial in mild areas. Plant them with low silver foliage shrubs and early flowering helianthemums to prolong the season of interest. Or try them with purple-pink geraniums such as _Geranium cinereum_ 'Ballerina' (see page 137) or _Geranium sanguineum_ (see page 159).

Sisyrinchiums are excellent in scree and seed freely. _Sisyrinchium striatum_, with its summer spikes of pale creamy-yellow flowers 60cm (24in) high, can be overpowering in small areas but is valuable for the sharp lines of its grey-green, iris-like leaves. The cultivar **'Aunt May'** (see page 97) is less vigorous, to 45cm (18in) high, and has leaves striped cream and green, shown to good effect when planted in gravel. The smaller, grass-like species, to about 15cm (6in) high, provide strong tufts of foliage and brightly coloured flowers. _Sisyrinchium angustifolium_ (blue-eyed grass) will go

SCREE IN SMALL SPACES

Scree is a good alternative to a lawn in a small garden, where a patch of grass can be difficult to maintain and only rarely looks its best. A landscape of planting into gravel creates a soft sense of space that is easily cared for and can look attractive all year round.

on producing its violet flowers from late spring through to autumn. The cultivar _Sisyrinchium idahoense_ var. _bellum_ 'Rocky Point' is excellent, with large blue flowers borne over a long period in summer. _Sisyrinchium californicum_, the yellow-eyed grass, bears yellow flowers in late spring. These are useful perennials when allowed to seed and drift between other subjects, although some thinning of the seedlings may be required to prevent invasion.

Stipa tenuissima with red crocosmias and white achilleas, in a creative planting by Alan Bloom.

Wet conditions

Some of the most spectacular and arresting herbaceous plants are those that will grow on wet or waterlogged soil. All tend to have lush stems and foliage: with a plentiful supply of water at their feet they are able to grow to greater proportions than their cousins on dry ground. Whether you want to create a planting area around a pond or beside a stream, or turn a poorly drained patch of ground into a bog garden, there is a wealth of plant material from which to choose.

Aruncus dioicus

Aruncus dioicus ♀ (goatsbeard) is a handsome plant 2m (6ft) tall, with fern-like foliage and light, airy creamy-white blooms in early and midsummer. It likes moist, peaty soil and needs semi-shade, otherwise the flowers quickly fade to brown. It is often mistaken for astilbe, but the habit of its leaves and flowers is more open and wiry. It is perhaps better than astilbe in a naturalistic setting. (See Good Companions, page 79.)

Like goatsbeard, **astilbes** are plants for moist, peaty soil in semi-shade. Their fern-like foliage contrasts well with other heavier subjects and their feathery plumes of flowers appear as colourful see-through clouds when planted at the water's edge. They may be 60cm (24in) to over 1m (40in) in height, and they flower from late spring into midsummer, depending on variety. In shades from

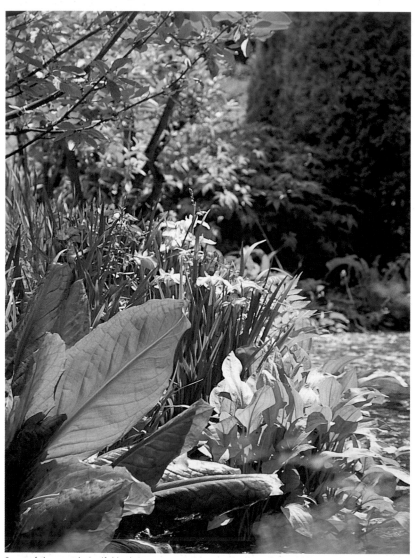

Some of the most beautiful herbaceous perennials grow in wet soil alongside water, as at Le Clos du Coudray, Normandy, France.

SUCCESS WITH ASTILBES

Astilbes need lifting and dividing every three to five years if they are to maintain vigour; otherwise the rhizomes become woody with age and the plants become overcrowded and deteriorate.

Buy astilbes as pot-grown plants and get them into the ground in early spring when the new foliage is emerging. Choose named varieties. Plants sold as dry rhizomes rarely give the best performance.

MARWOOD HILL GARDENS

The National Collections of astilbe and *Iris ensata* are held at Marwood Hill Gardens, Barnstaple, Devon. The work of the late Dr Jimmy Smart, the gardens are filled with an abundance of plant material in a beautiful naturalistic setting. The lakes and bog garden contain a wide range of perennials that enjoy wet conditions.

GOOD VARIETIES OF ASTILBE

Astilbe 'Bressingham Beauty' Grows to 1m (40in) and has broad, drooping panicles in deep pink.

Astilbe 'Cattleya' 90cm (3ft) tall, produces broad, angular plumes of orchid pink.

Astilbe chinensis var. *pumila* ♀ Only 40cm (16in) tall, with narrow, upright pink panicles.

Astilbe 'Deutschland' One of the most widely planted, grows 50cm (20in) tall, with white panicles.

Astilbe 'Fanal' ♀ 60cm (24in) high and early flowering, with dense, glowing red plumes.

Astilbe 'Jo Ophorst' 90cm (3ft) tall, has stiff, upright panicles of deep mauve-pink.

Astilbe 'Weisse Gloria' 60cm (24in) tall, produces early white flowers.

white through pink to deepest red, they associate well with white and purple irises. Astilbes are at their best planted in groups or drifts; they rarely look impressive as solitary plants. The dwarf varieties are useful to lighten the effect of hostas and bergenias.

Caltha palustris ♀, a native of Britain and other northern temperate regions, is commonly known as the kingcup or marsh marigold. It has dark, burnished stems, 45cm (18in) high, clad in kidney-shaped, toothed, mid-green leaves. Large, golden yellow, buttercup-like flowers appear in early spring. The double form *Caltha palustris* 'Flore Pleno' ♀ seldom exceeds 25cm (10in) high, the flowers made up of layer after layer of petals, ultimately resembling marigolds. It requires a rich, moist soil, preferably in full sun, and is often seen in boggy ground at the edge of a pond. Although it can be grown in water, in a planting container, it will not tolerate having its feet submerged for more than a month or two at a time.

A member of the saxifrage family, *Darmera peltata* ♀ has round, veined leaves up to 60cm (24in) across; these are the principal feature of the plant, rather than the pinkish flowerheads that emerge before them. It prefers moist conditions in semi-shade. The dwarf form *Darmera peltata* 'Nana' is useful beneath the vast leaves of gunnera (see Good Companions, page 79)

Houttuynia cordata is an excellent low ground-cover plant for wet sites in sun or shade. It spreads by creeping rhizomes that will happily wend their way between moisture-loving ferns and hostas. The stems grow to 30cm (12in) tall, usually less, and carry heart-shaped velvet-green leaves and white flowers at their tips in summer. The foliage smells unpleasant when disturbed. There is a double-flowered form, as well as various colourful variegated cultivars. The best known of these is *Houttuynia cordata*

Iris sibirica 'Flight of Butterflies'

'Chameleon': with leaves of gold, red, orange and green, it is striking when planted imaginatively with other boldly coloured foliage. (See also page 100.)

The most difficult sites are those that are wet in winter and dry in summer; here, few plants can thrive. *Iris spuria* is an exception, since it grows naturally in these conditions in full sun, which it needs to flower well. It is also tolerant of alkaline and saline conditions. It bears lilac-lavender flowers, on stems 90cm (3ft) tall, in early summer. Many superb cultivars have been raised in the USA.

Most irises fall into two groups: those that like an open, sunny site and good drainage and those that like their feet wet. *Iris sibirica* ♀ is one of the more adaptable; it relishes wet conditions, but is also content in normal soil as long as it does not dry out. It will grow and bloom happily in full sun or semi-shade. The fine vertical foliage stays looking good longer than that of its sun-loving relations, and the dainty blue flowers, carried high on slender stems, 1m (40in) tall, are a delight in early summer. The sapphire-blue *Iris sibirica* 'Flight of Butterflies' is particularly appealing when planted in drifts with moisture-loving ferns. (See also pages 140–41.)

75

The yellow flag, *Iris pseudacorus*♀, with its bright blooms in early spring, is too vigorous for most gardens, but *Iris pseudacorus* 'Variegata'♀ is well worth considering. Growing 1m (40in) tall in sun or semi-shade, it has creamy-yellow striped, sword-shaped foliage.

Iris setosa♀ likes wet, peaty soil; it has striking rich purple flowers in early summer, and grows 80cm (30in) high. *Iris laevigata*♀ has lovely bluish-purple blooms in early summer, on stems of a similar height. *Iris ensata*♀, from Japan (see Good Companions, below), is responsible for many beautiful cultivars, including the large-flowered **Kaempferi hybrids**, which sometimes involve hybridization with *Iris laevigata*. These are elegant plants with large, flattened blooms, in white, pink and lavender to deep purple, in early summer. They like wet soil, or shallow water, and prefer drier conditions in the winter. They can also be grown in planting containers in a pond, removed in winter and plunged into the ground, then returned to the pond in spring. They seem to survive happily in wet conditions whatever the time of year as long as they have full sun; they do not flower well in shade.

Liatris spicata

Liatris spicata is a tall, upright perennial that carries its vivid, light purple flowers in stiff bottlebrush spikes, which open from the top downwards. Flowers are produced from midsummer to autumn. The plant grows from curious corm-like rhizomes that look as if they would succeed in a dry situation; in fact, it suits waterside planting in a sunny spot, though it tends to rot if wet in winter.

Ligularias offer strikingly colourful flowers and fine foliage in mid- to late summer. They enjoy moist soil in sun or semi-shade. The various cultivars of *Ligularia dentata* have bold, rounded

Ligularia 'The Rocket'

Lobelia 'Queen Victoria'

leaves with dark stems and undersides. *Ligularia dentata* 'Desdemona'♀ produces strong stems carrying clusters of rich orange, daisy-like flowers in summer. The newer variety *Ligularia dentata* 'Britt-Marie Crawford' has superb dark wine-purple foliage (see page 87). These are not plants to grow where slugs and snails are a problem, since they will soon devour the young foliage. *Ligularia* 'The Rocket'♀ is very different in appearance. Its black stems, to 2m (6ft) tall, bear triangular, toothed leaves and slender spikes of tiny yellow flowers. A good see-through plant, it is well placed at the water's edge and offers strong but light vertical interest among hostas and rodgersias.

Lobelia 'Queen Victoria'♀ is a plant with a long season of interest.

GOOD COMPANIONS

With its upright shoots and glowing orange-red bracts, *Euphorbia griffithii* 'Fireglow' (1) is about 30cm (12in) high when *Iris sibirica* 'Ego' (2) blooms. The velvety, deep blue iris flowers flutter above the glowing heads of the euphorbia.

Rich blue *Iris ensata*♀ looks stunning when planted against the golden explosion of a clump of *Carex elata* 'Aurea'♀. When the iris flowers fade, the upright foliage still works well with the flowing leaves of the grass.

Clumps of rich red-purple leaves emerge in spring, contrasting well with fresh green ferns. As summer progresses the flower stems develop, reaching upwards to 1m (40in) or more. Finally the brilliant scarlet flowers open up against the dark plum-purple stems – a spectacular colour combination. It thrives in moist soil, in sun or semi-shade, but is not for the coldest sites. In more severe climates choose *Lobelia cardinalis* ♀, which has flowers of a similar colour but without the dark red foliage.

Lythrum salicaria (purple loosestrife) is an upright perennial, up to 1.5m (5ft) tall, with slender spikes of purple-pink flowers from early summer. The crepe-paper flowers are crowded in close whorls up the spikes. An easy plant to grow, in sun or partial shade, it provides useful continuity of colour, coming into its own just as the spring flowers fade. **'Blush'** ♀ has more subtle pale pink flowers; **'Feuerkerze'** (FIRECANDLE) ♀ is an iridescent pinkish red. *Lythrum virgatum* is more compact but equally stunning, with some distinctive named cultivars: **'Dropmore Purple'** and **'Rose Queen'** need no further description beyond 'vibrant'; **'The Rocket'** provides erect stems of deep pink flowers.

Many **primulas** enjoy a moist site, often originating from wet mountain meadows and streamsides in cool areas. They are mostly hardy plants, easy to grow in the right conditions. *Primula denticulata* ♀, also known as the drumstick primula, is among the most tolerant of drier soils. Its large drumstick-like flowerheads appear in spring, on stems up to 40cm (16in) tall, as the foliage is in its infancy: colours range from white through pink and mauve to deep red-purple. It grows in sun or semi-shade. *Primula vialii* ♀ is often mistaken for a hardy orchid, because of its narrow, pointed, mauve flowerheads showily tipped with crimson in late spring. Growing to about 60cm (24in)

Primula vialii

Primula pulverulenta

Primula florindae

Primula japonica varieties

tall, it prefers moist but well-drained soil in semi-shade. In boggy conditions it needs planting on a mound. The lovely *Primula alpicola* ♀ needs a wetter site and prefers shade. Its dropping clusters of creamy flowers, liberally dusted with a waxy, silver farina, appear at the top of elegant 60cm (24in) stems in spring. There are other pastel-coloured forms but this is the loveliest. *Primula florindae* ♀ is one of the largest primulas, with bold green foliage and tall stems up to 1m (40in) high topped, in spring to early summer, by a shower of bright yellow flowers trimmed with silver farina around the base. It is easy to grow in sun or semi-shade and mixes well with some of the heavier foliage plants of the bog garden.

The **Candelabra primulas** include many species and hybrids with whorls of flowers spaced at intervals up slender stems 30–75cm (12–30in) tall. They vary in origin, but generally they enjoy wet, peaty soil in semi-shade. These are truly the highlights of the late spring bog

garden, the brilliance and delicacy of their blooms being second to none. The flowers of *Primula bulleyana* ♀ are red in bud, opening to orange. *Primula beesiana* is carmine with yellow eyes; *Primula pulverulenta* ♀ is red with dark eyes. *Primula japonica* has given rise to many named hybrids including the wonderful **'Miller's Crimson'** ♀ and **'Postford White'** ♀. One of the easiest to grow is *Primula prolifera*, with

MAKING MORE OF CANDELABRA PRIMULAS

Candelabra primulas happily cross-pollinate and hybridize. They prefer a little space between the plants, which should be kept free from weeds. After flowering leave some of the seedheads to develop and ripen. Seed allowed to fall onto the moist ground between the plants usually germinates successfully to produce plenty more young plants. Leave these *in situ* and transplant them the following spring. The hybrids will be variable and exciting.

Trollius chinensis

Rheum palmatum 'Atrosanguineum'

white or yellow flowers. Candelabra primulas look their best planted in drifts of different colours; their clashing hues work together to create a shaft of shimmering coloured light against the lush foliage of their neighbours.

Candelabra primulas in orange and purple make good planting partners for *Trollius × cultorum* hybrids, moisture-loving plants that grow in sun or partial shade, producing luminous globe-like flowers resembling huge buttercups above attractive divided leaves. Flower colour varies, from the pale greenish yellow of 'Alabaster' and the lovely pale yellow 'Lemon Queen' to the rich orange of 'Feuertroll' (FIREGLOBE). Although the hybrids are striking, the wonderful *Trollius chinensis* from China is unsurpassed when it comes to colour. The upward-facing, open cups are brilliant orange-yellow, with upright, narrow petals that create an exotic horned effect in the centre. All these flower in late spring or early summer, on 70cm (30in) stems.

There is, however, no more exotically beautiful herbaceous perennial than *Zantedeschia aethiopica* ♀, familiar to most as the arum lily. Although often grown as a conservatory plant, it is reasonably hardy in open ground, in a sheltered position, or with the added insulation of shallow water. Given a moist site and fertile soil, it grows to 1m (40in) high, and produces glorious white blooms in spring and lush green foliage that stays looking good throughout the

season. It flowers best in full sun but tolerates semi-shade. It is an excellent choice for a sheltered courtyard garden. (See Good Companions, right.)

FOLIAGE DRAMA

Big, bold foliage is a feature of bog gardens, and *Gunnera manicata* ♀ has the biggest and boldest of all (see Good Companions, right). In rich, moist soil, in sun or shade, this Brazilian beauty will reach 3m (10ft) in height with leaves 2m (6ft) across. It is the ultimate in natural vegetable architecture. It is, however, not beyond cultivation in the smaller garden: it will survive successfully in a large barrel of wet soil, the restricted space naturally limiting its growth. In cold areas provide winter protection in the form of a frost cover or dry mulch; traditionally the leaves are cut in autumn and upturned on the crown of the plant.

Rheum palmatum provides the same foliage drama, but on a lesser scale and with more colour. This is the best choice for smaller gardens. Many of the rheums have wonderful reddish stems and veins in the foliage: *Rheum palmatum* 'Atrosanguineum' ♀ is one of the most colourful with deep red-purple emerging leaves and deep plum undersides to the mature foliage. The

stately rhubarb flower stems can reach 2–3m (6–10ft) tall, with myriad tiny flowers developing pinkish seeds. Removing these early on prevents the flowers and seeds dropping all over the foliage. Some claim that removing the flower spike prevents the early demise of the foliage; probably the most important factor is maintaining enough moisture at the roots. Rheums like plenty of well-rotted manure around the roots each year to maintain the richness of the soil. Enjoying sun or semi-shade, they are hardier than gunneras, and a better choice for colder areas.

On a still smaller scale, but no less impressive, *Rodgersia aesculifolia* ♀ offers the finest foliage in the bog garden, reaching a height of about 1m

Gunnera manicata

OTHER PERENNIALS FOR WET CONDITIONS *Cardamine pratensis* • *Euphorbia palustris* • *Mimulus ringens* •

Rodgersia aesculifolia

(40in). The dense, astilbe-like flower-heads are of secondary importance to the leaves, which are deep green-bronze and stiffly rigid, resembling those of horse-chestnut (*Aesculus*). They last well into the autumn, turning a richer red-bronze as the season progresses (see Good Companions, right). Rodgersias are hardy plants, so suitable for colder areas. They grow in sun or semi-shade

Lysichiton americanus

and prefer moist, peaty soil but are surprisingly tolerant of drier conditions.

By midsummer, the yellow skunk cabbage, **Lysichiton americanus** ♀, has leaves like a huge cos lettuce: great elliptical shields, up to 1.5m (5ft) tall, of fresh green that catch the light and contrast with heavier subjects such as gunnera and rheum. The flowers, waxy yellow and arum-like, with a musky smell, precede the leaves in early spring. A North American native, it is hardy and easy to grow in the bog garden. White-flowered **Lysichiton camtschatcensis** ♀ from Asia is smaller and smells sweeter, but is not so often seen in gardens.

GOOD COMPANIONS

The light, variegated foliage of *Cornus alba* 'Sibirica Variegata' (1) contrasts with the bold leaves of *Rodgersia aesculifolia* ♀ (2). Both take on reddish tones as autumn approaches.

Try setting the light, wiry form of goatsbeard, *Aruncus dioicus* ♀ (3), against the bold foliage and white flowers of the arum lily, *Zantedeschia aethiopica* ♀ (4).

The rounded leaves of *Darmera peltata* 'Nana' (5) reflect the vast umbrellas of *Gunnera manicata* ♀ (6) and provide low interest under its canopy.

GROWING MOISTURE-LOVERS IN DRY GARDENS

Those gardening on dry soil can achieve wet, boggy conditions by lining a shallow, basin-shaped hole, 60cm (24in) deep, with butyl pond liner, and filling it with rich loamy soil. It is essential to have an overflow pipe or drainage holes in the liner to prevent continual waterlogging in winter. Moisture-loving plants such as primulas, irises and other, not too vigorous perennials will grow happily in this mini bog garden. It is also an excellent way to give new purpose to a leaking pond.

Persicaria bistorta • *Pontederia cordata* • *Ranunculus aconitifolius* • *Sagittaria latifolia* • *Sarracenia* • *Thalictrum* •

Chalk and clay

Chalk and clay are invariably seen as problem soils by those who garden on them. Chalk is regarded as low in nutrients and impoverished; clay as wet, heavy and difficult to work. In fact, both soil types have their qualities and provide the perfect conditions for plants that are adapted to growing on them.

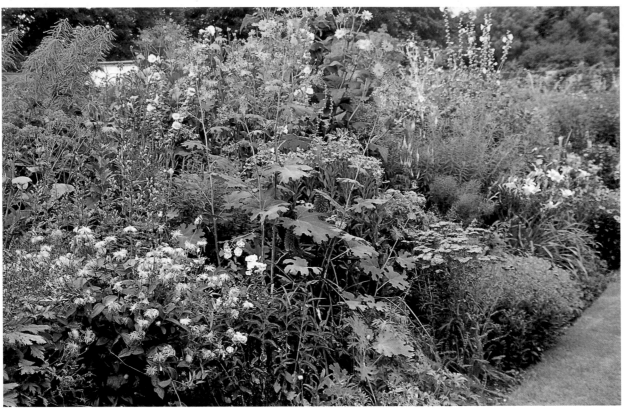

A herbaceous border on chalk, at Bramdean House, Hampshire.

PERENNIALS FOR CHALK

Most popular border perennials are unfussy when it comes to soil. The majority enjoy free-draining conditions and only moderate fertility; too much moisture and highly fertile soils can lead to soft, lush growth that will need some form of support and may be produced at the expense of flowers. For most perennials, therefore, chalk soils come close to the ideal, needing only the addition of organic material to help with retention of water and nutrients. Many plants, too, prefer alkaline conditions, and soils derived from chalk or limestone are by nature alkaline, to a greater or lesser degree (see page 19).

Clematis are usually thought of as climbers that retain flexible, woody stems during the dormant season. There are, however, several species that grow as herbaceous perennials, producing a clump of often lax stems and dying down to ground level in winter. Clematis prefer alkaline soils and thrive on chalk;

THE PROBLEM WITH CHALK

Summer drought is the main problem on chalk soils, hence the need for irrigation and the addition of organic matter to improve water retention. When plants are in maximum growth and flower, they are quickly put under stress if there is a lack of water at the roots. For example, although achilleas tolerate drought, they do not enjoy a sudden dry spell after a moist period, and respond with wilting foliage.

80

OTHER GOOD PERENNIALS FOR CHALK *Acanthus* • *Achillea* • *Asphodeline lutea* • *Campanula lactiflora* •

Clematis × diversifolia 'Hendersonii'

Dianthus 'Doris'

adding lime to the soil often helps them to succeed where conditions are acid.

Clematis tubulosa is shrub-like in growth with sprawling stems up to 1m (40in) high that need some support. *Clematis tubulosa* **'Wyevale'**♀ is the best cultivar, with starry bell-shaped flowers in late summer. These are a pretty shade of blue and delightfully scented. *Clematis integrifolia* is often shorter but more sprawling. The indigo-blue flowers are borne above the foliage on dainty crooked stems from early summer right through to autumn. They resemble those of *Clematis alpina*♀, but are narrower and more pointed, and are followed by attractive silky seedheads. A popular hybrid of *Clematis integrifolia* is **Clematis × diversifolia** 'Hendersonii', with deep blue flowers.

Clematis recta blooms in early to midsummer, producing a mass of starry cream flowers on a lax plant with fine stems 90cm (3ft) high. The flowers are fragrant and are lovely in semi-shade. *Clematis recta* **'Purpurea'** has the advantage of wine-coloured foliage, an attractive contrast to the silky seedheads that follow the flowers.

Dianthus are wonderful plants for alkaline soils and will grow happily on shallow chalk. They are very tolerant of drought, but deeply resent wet and soggy conditions. Cultivated since Roman times, there are myriad species and cultivars, from small alpine pinks to tall, large-flowered border carnations. (See also page 136.)

The old-fashioned garden pinks, with fine, greyish green evergreen foliage, flower early in summer and are often prized for their fragrance. *Dianthus* **'Mrs Sinkins'** is one of the best known, with very irregular white flowers that have a wonderful perfume. Growing 20cm (8in) high, it is commonly planted by the edge of a path and combines well with grey foliage plants.

The modern garden pinks, with blue-grey evergreen foliage, flower over a long period, from early summer through to early autumn, producing long-lasting, weather-resistant, scented blooms. Most grow to about 30cm (12in). Many are the result of crossing old-fashioned garden pinks with perpetual-flowering carnations, and are often known as hybrids of *Dianthus × allwoodii*, after the nursery where some of them were raised. *Dianthus* **'Doris'**♀, a lovely soft salmon with a deeper salmon eye, is one of the most popular. It is an excellent cut flower and an easy colour to mix with blue and silver partners. *Dianthus* **'Diane'**♀ is a deeper salmon-orange variety of similar quality.

Gypsophila paniculata (baby's breath) is one of our most familiar cut flowers. Its fine stems and clouds of tiny blooms are the perfect accompaniment to roses, sweet peas and other summer flowers. It grows from a large tuberous tap root and has traditionally been sold as a bare root in the dormant season. Gypsophilas are also valuable border plants: they rarely need support, and have a long flowering season from early to late summer. They are ideal to partner bold, large blooms such as those of poppy or peony and introduce a light ethereal look when combined with silver and blue subjects. Gypsophilas need alkaline soil if they are to thrive, and must have full sun; they do not enjoy wet conditions. *Gypsophila paniculata* **'Bristol Fairy'**♀ is the most reliable, producing a cloud of tiny, double white flowers on stems up to 1m (40in) high. *Gypsophila* **'Rosenschleier'**♀, which is also known as 'Rosy Veil', is a much more spreading plant, reaching up to

> ### MAKING MORE OF PINKS
>
> Garden pinks are easily propagated from cuttings, taken in summer. Root non-flowering side-shoots in loam-based compost with added sharp sand for good drainage, and keep them in a coldframe. Once rooted, they should be potted individually and left in the frame until spring, when they can be planted out. Pinks deteriorate after a few years so it is always worth having young stock coming on as replacements.

Centranthus • Euphorbia characias • Lychnis • Salvia × superba • Verbascum • Verbena bonariensis •

Potentilla 'Gibson's Scarlet'

Potentilla 'Gloire de Nancy'

1m (40in) across, but only 60cm (24in) high. The double white flowers turn pale pink with age.

Although gardeners are most familiar with the woody species of *Potentilla*, the herbaceous forms are some of our brightest and prettiest perennials, with an informal wildflower character. They are plants for sites in full sun and are useful at the front of a border with companions such as alchemilla (lady's mantle). The hybrids of *Potentilla atrosanguinea* are among the most vivid. Most grow to about 40cm (16in) high, with strawberry-like leaves and buttercup flowers all through summer. *Potentilla* 'Gibson's Scarlet'♔ has single, brilliant scarlet flowers with dark centres. 'William Rollison'♔ is semi-double with orange-red petals, gold on the reverse. 'Gloire de Nancy' is similar but orange-brown and red, rich and lovely. All these will mix beautifully with achilleas, dahlias and crocosmias in a border with a hot colour scheme.

Potentilla nepalensis offers some softer colours. The cultivars grow taller, often to 60cm (24in), with heavily toothed leaves and branched stems carrying profuse flowers throughout the summer. 'Miss Willmott'♔ is the most popular, with strawberry-pink flowers with darker centres.

Most species of **scabious** are native to chalk and limestone areas, flourishing in grassland, so they are not a good choice for heavy, wet clay. *Scabiosa atropurpurea* is regarded as an annual or biennial, although some cultivars can be grown as short-lived perennials on well-drained soil. Cultivars commonly sold as the Chile series have enjoyed recent popularity. These are tall plants with slender stems to 90cm (3ft) high, producing pincushion flowers with small outer petals throughout summer. 'Chile Black' is the deepest garnet, black and velvety; 'Chilli Pepper' has rather larger, flatter flowers of soft red; and 'Chilli Sauce' has ruffled purple flowers with a delicate white edge to the petals. These are wonderful plants to provide deep highlights in a border and they are excellent for cutting. In all cases some support will be needed.

Scabiosa caucasica cultivars are the familiar scabious of the cottage garden, in bloom from early summer onwards. Forming a low clump of divided leaves, the plants give rise to stems 60cm (24in) or more high, each of which carries a large round, frilled flower with a pin-cushion centre. Open and sparse in character, these are detail plants rather than ones to make a bold impact; they are, however, superb as cut flowers. 'Clive Greaves'♔ is a lovely shade of lavender-blue. 'Stäfa' is much darker with a central cluster of florets in inky blue, a colour more intense in the striking 'Blue Lace'. 'Miss Willmott'♔ has large, tissue-like white flowers.

Hybrids of *Scabiosa columbaria*, the small scabious, are more compact at 30cm (12in) high and flower more freely throughout the summer. *Scabiosa columbaria* subsp. *ochroleuca* is a charming plant, very tolerant of dry conditions. With grey-green leaves and small greenish-yellow flowers, it is a delightful companion to the pale yellow foxglove *Digitalis lutea*. *Scabiosa* 'Butterfly Blue' has been one of the most popular perennials of recent years. A compact plant with pretty cut foliage, it produces masses of lilac-blue flowers from late spring through to mid-autumn. 'Pink Mist' is similar in habit but has mauve-pink flowers.

Scabiosa atropurpurea 'Chile Black'

Scabiosa caucasica 'Clive Greaves'

OTHER GOOD PERENNIALS FOR CLAY *Astrantia major* • *Brunnera macrophylla* • *Campanula glomerata* •

PERENNIALS FOR CLAY

Most popular perennials grow well on clay soils, which are usually fertile and hold water well. However, they can be difficult and heavy to work and will bake hard in summer if water is short. They are often alkaline, as a result of being dressed regularly with lime, which helps to break up sticky clay.

Perennial weeds are near impossible to eradicate on clay soils, especially between herbaceous perennials. If you try to dig out ground elder, bindweed, docks and thistles, the fleshy roots quickly snap in the heavy clay, leaving numerous fragments to regrow.

Routine tasks like lifting and dividing clumps of perennials are more arduous on clay soils. Imagine lifting a large clump of hemerocallis (daylilies) from heavy clay in winter, then attempting to divide it and replant.

The planting of pot-grown subjects may be difficult, too. Sticky, wet clay soil is not easy to replace around the roots of a newly planted perennial without damaging emerging shoots; they are not as resilient as those of a woody shrub.

As a rule of thumb, plants with strong root systems and deep tap roots will do well on clay. Because clay soils are often wet, many perennials that thrive in boggy conditions succeed here,

A herbaceous border brimming with colour at Hadspen Garden, Somerset, a garden on alkaline clay.

providing there is adequate moisture in summer (see pages 74–79).

Many of the prairie subjects do well on clay as long as they do not become too dry in summer. *Aster* and *Solidago* are both certain winners on clay soils, hence their widespread use in gardens for many years. Another prairie native, *Filipendula rubra* 'Venusta' ♛ is an excellent choice, its statuesque form and astilbe-like flowerheads mixing well with shrubs and other robust perennials. (See also pages 50–53.)

Campanula latiloba, with its tall spikes of open bell-shaped flowers in late summer, is an easy perennial to grow on clay, in sun or partial shade. There are some lovely cultivars including the pale mauve 'Hidcote Amethyst' ♛, 'Alba' ♛, which has white flowers, and the blue 'Highcliffe Variety' ♛.

The early-flowering yellow daisy *Doronicum orientale* 'Magnificum' is also good on clay, but needs a partially shaded site. *Hemerocallis* (daylilies) are

at their best in sun, and they too do well on clay, enjoying its fertility and revelling in the damp conditions on wet sites (see pages 138–39).

With its pretty, fern-like leaves and mauve, gypsophila-like flowerheads, *Thalictrum aquilegiifolium* provides foliage interest throughout the summer as well as an impressive display of flowers. It is an easy perennial to grow in either full sun or partial shade, and usually succeeds in all but waterlogged ground. (See also page 49.)

Filipendula rubra 'Venusta'

> ### OVERCOMING THE PROBLEM OF CLAY SOIL
>
> Plants enjoying good drainage and dry conditions are not usually a natural choice for clay soils, although they may succeed if planted on top of the clay. Add sharp grit to the soil beforehand and plant on a mound rather than in a dip. This will prevent water collecting around the crown of the plant and causing it to rot.

Geranium himalayense • Lamium galeobdolon • Physostegia virginiana • Rudbeckia • Symphytum caucasicum •

FOLIAGE

Herbaceous perennials provide us with some of the most dramatic, colourful and textural foliage in the garden. From the large bold leaves of many waterside subjects to the soft silver of sun-lovers, long-lasting foliage effects come from perennials and grasses in the lower layers of the planting picture. Those that are grown especially for their coloured foliage have become some of the most popular plants in our gardens. The number of available hosta and heuchera cultivars increases every year, each new variety welcomed for its contribution to the leafy garden scene.

RIGHT: A variety of foliage forms: hostas, grasses and phormiums

Purple and plum foliage

Perennials blessed with purple and plum foliage are good mixers; they get along with their colourful neighbours and work with them to produce dramatic effect. Punctuating the mass of greenery, plants with warm wine tones in their leaves are striking alongside companions with silver or golden yellow foliage, while their rich notes bring flowers of many colours to life.

PURPLE AND PLUM FOLIAGE FOR SEMI-SHADE

Plants with purple foliage need good light to achieve the best leaf colour. In heavy shade plum tones can be muddy; dark green predominates and red-purple pigments fade. However, a number of purple-foliage subjects prefer a site in semi-shade rather than a dry position in full sun.

Actaea simplex Atropurpurea Group enjoy fertile, reasonably moist soil in partial shade. More familiar under their former name *Cimicifuga*, these are choice perennials that take a little time to become established and make an impact in the border. Container-grown plants can take a couple of seasons before their black stems reach over 1m (40in) high and the large elegant, fern-like leaves spread to 30cm (12in) or more in length. White bottlebrush flowerheads rise above the leaves in autumn. The cultivar **'Brunette'** ♀ has foliage of a wonderful burgundy-black colour: both sophisticated and dramatic. Although the plant grows tall, to 1.5m (5ft) or so, it rarely requires additional support. (See Good Companions, right.)

Ground-hugging **ajugas** (bugle) enjoy similar conditions. Purple-leaved forms are useful foliage plants that remain evergreen in all but the coldest areas. *Ajuga reptans* 'Atropurpurea' (see page 118) forms rosettes of shining

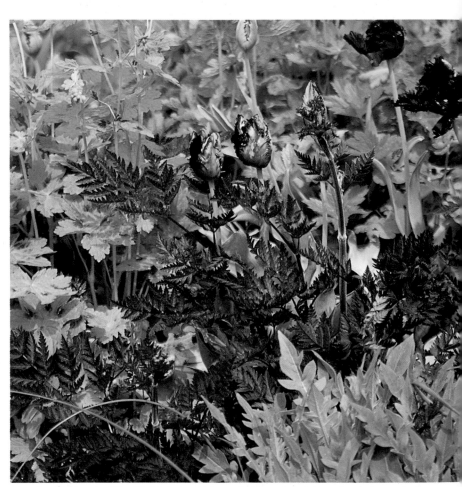

Fringed and feathered – *Tulipa* 'Black Parrot' amid the purple foliage of *Anthriscus sylvestris* 'Ravenswing'.

purple foliage, each strongly veined leaf up to 10cm (4in) long. *Ajuga reptans* **'Burgundy Glow'** ♀ is the darkest, with oblong-rounded leaves of rich wine red, deep green beneath. The much larger, dark, bronzed leaves of *Ajuga reptans* **'Catlin's Giant'** ♀ (see page 119) are excellent with golden hostas.

PURPLE GROUND COVER

Purple bugles make excellent ground cover. They are ideal on slopes and banks and are particularly effective in gravel. The shining purple plantlets are easily transplanted to bring evergreen interest to winter pots and containers.

Ligularia dentata 'Britt-Marie Crawford'

Persicaria microcephala 'Red Dragon'

For a selection of **heucheras** grown for their coloured foliage see pages 88–89.

Ligularias contribute to the garden with architectural structure and bold foliage as well as stunning flowers (see page 76). An old favourite is *Ligularia dentata* 'Desdemona' ♀, its rounded leaves of rich chocolate green making a perfect setting for the large orange, daisy flowers (see Good Companions, below right). *Ligularia dentata* 'Britt-Marie Crawford' is one of the finest for foliage. A hardy herbaceous perennial, it forms a robust clump of dark purple, glossy, rounded leaves 30cm (12in) or so across, with undersides of an equally gorgeous dark red. The 30cm (12in) leaf stalks are a similar colour. Flower stems over 1m (40in) high carry starry mid-yellow flowers in summer.

The dark reddish-brown, sprawling stems of *Persicaria microcephala* 'Red Dragon' are clothed in spectacular broad, oval leaves. Centred on the red spine of each leaf is a dark chocolate-brown heart marked with a silver flash against margins of purple-green. From midsummer each stem carries a spray of tiny white flowers, contrasting well against the foliage. On moist, fertile soil in semi-shade, the plant will grow more than 1m (40in) high by the end of the season. The stems and foliage are knocked to the ground by the first frost.

A number of **primulas** are blessed with bronze and chocolate foliage. The *Primula* **Wanda Group** are widely cultivated as spring bedding plants for their jewel-like flower colours and their rich, dark foliage. *Primula* **Cowichan** series, the winter-blooming polyanthus, have similar colouring (see page 182). *Primula* 'Guinevere' ♀ bears clusters of yellow-eyed purple-pink polyanthus flowers above an evergreen rosette of chocolate-red, bronzed leaves. All these primulas make delightful partners for the purple-leaved bugles, planted in partial shade.

Commonly called the bloody dock, *Rumex sanguineus* var. *sanguineus* is an attractive form of the pernicious weed. Very hardy and robust, it has a rosette of broad, lance-shaped, dark green leaves to 15cm (6in) long. Each leaf has a dark red midrib, which appears to bleed into the veins, forming an elaborate pattern. In summer, erect stems, to 90cm (3ft) high, bear many tiny, star-shaped green flowers with a delicate beauty as they mature through red-orange to light then dark brown. Like its relatives, this dock will grow anywhere; to prevent it spreading, cut and dispose of the flowering stems before the seeds fall.

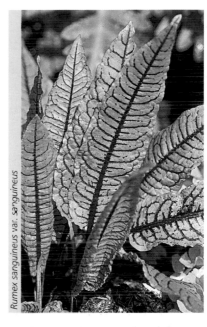
Rumex sanguineus var. sanguineus

GOOD COMPANIONS

Ligularia dentata 'Desdemona' ♀ (1) contrasts with the fresh yellow foliage of *Cornus alba* 'Aurea' ♀ (2). The cornus provides red stems when the ligularia dies down in winter.

Actaea simplex Atropurpurea Group 'Brunette' ♀ (3) with *Acer palmatum* 'Fireglow' (4): the deep dark leaves of the actaea are stunning against the acer's flame-red autumn shades.

Heucheras

Predominantly from North America, heucheras were originally cultivated for their flowers: showers of tiny blooms borne on fine, graceful stems for long periods in summer (see page 140). Today, few other plants have such popular appeal for the beauty of their foliage; and no other dark-leaved perennial delivers such a variety of tones. A steady stream of new selections reaches our gardens every year, and heucheras are now almost as common as hostas.

The rounded to heart-shaped, semi-evergreen or evergreen leaves are carried on either short and stocky or long and airy stalks, forming a clump of foliage 10–30cm (4–12in) high. The leaves vary in size and texture, and the colour ranges from handsome shades of green through red to deep burgundy; many exhibit fine variegation in white, silver or bronze. (For heucheras with golden yellow foliage, see page 93.)

Robust perennials and easy to grow, they thrive in moist, well-drained, neutral soil. Although extremely hardy, they resent waterlogged conditions, especially in the winter months. Heucheras with dark leaves excel in full sun, the strong light intensifying the colour of the foliage; in warmer climates, however, they appreciate a little shade. Even in the coldest areas, heucheras maintain a superb show of foliage throughout the year; regular feeding in the growing season enhances both quality and colour. Heucheras are also excellent for permanent or seasonal planting in pots and containers.

Mature plants develop thick, woody stems at the base and benefit from pruning. In late spring cut back old growth by half; this may appear extreme, but new stems soon appear. The removed shoots can be used as cuttings to produce more stock.

Seed can be collected in mid- to late summer. Sow immediately in a tray of moist seed compost; cover lightly and place in a cool, shady situation. The seed germinates in spring; the offspring are variable but may be uniquely different.

Heuchera 'Plum Pudding', with shiny plum-burgundy foliage, has become one of the most popular purple heucheras. Reaching 30cm (12in) tall, it is an essential in winter containers with *Primula* 'Wanda'♀ and early purple crocuses. As spring progresses, the deep purple leaves contrast with the sulphur-yellow bracts of *Euphorbia polychroma*♀, and later with the foamy lime-green flowers of *Alchemilla mollis*♀ (lady's mantle).

Heucheras are especially attractive to vine weevil, the larvae feeding voraciously on the roots through autumn and into spring. Biological control can be used in early autumn, or a suitable systemic insecticide applied in autumn or spring.

Heuchera 'Amethyst Myst' forms a clump of impressive dark purple, glossy foliage reaching 30cm (12in) in height. The waved, heart-shaped leaves are partially divided and burnished silver-pink. They look fantastic intermingled with the finely cut silver foliage of *Artemisia* 'Powis Castle'♔.

Heuchera micrantha var. *diversifolia* 'Palace Purple' was the original purple heuchera. A parent of many cultivars, it produces fine, dark stems up to 60cm (24in) tall, bearing large, glossy, dark red leaves with jagged margins. It is usually sold as a seed-raised selection, and the foliage colour is variable and can be muddy.

Heuchera 'Liquorice' has dark, ruffled leaves, which are outstanding planted with the golden yellow foliage of *Lysimachia nummularia* 'Aurea'♔. Height 30cm (12in).

OTHER GOOD HEUCHERAS

Heuchera 'Cascade Dawn' Dark leaves burnished with lavender-silver, and with rich purple veins. Height 30cm (12in).

Heuchera 'Chocolate Ruffles' Forms a tight clump of rich red-brown leaves with ruffled margins. Height 30cm (12in).

Heuchera 'Chocolate Veil'♔ Black-purple leaves, lightly marked with silver. Height 30cm (12in).

Heuchera 'Obsidian' A newcomer, with rounded, dark purple, almost black leaves; one of the darkest of all. Height 25cm (10in).

Heuchera 'Purple Petticoats'♔ A neat mound of dramatically ruffled, glossy, dark purple leaves. Height 30cm (12in).

Heuchera 'Velvet Night' Luxuriant leaves, 15cm (6in) across, slate black burnished silvery purple. Height 40cm (16in).

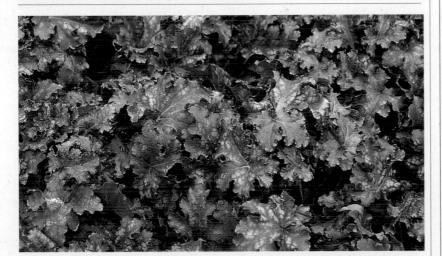

Heuchera 'Can-can'♔ has ruffled red-purple leaves, lightly burnished silver, forming a neat, tight clump of foliage 20cm (8in) high and 30cm (12in) across. It looks striking against the small silver-centred, nettle-like leaves of *Lamium maculatum* 'Album'.

PURPLE AND PLUM FOLIAGE FOR SUNNY POSITIONS

Purple foliage usually becomes richer and redder in full sun, the red pigments masking the underlying green of the leaves. Perennials with purple foliage are useful to bring depth and substance to bright summer-flowering plants. They mix particularly well with the pinks, mauves and blues of the midsummer border and provide the perfect foil for hot reds, oranges and yellows. They are successful partners for silver foliage plants that also favour sunny situations.

Anthriscus sylvestris 'Ravenswing'

Anthriscus sylvestris (cow parsley) is a common sight along hedgerows and verges in Britain in late spring. A froth of lacy white flowers that suddenly appear above the grass is a sign that summer is on the way. *Anthriscus sylvestris* 'Ravenswing' ♛ has burgundy-purple fern-like foliage and flower stems, and the same white filigree flowerheads. It does well on dry soil in full sun, reaching 90cm (3ft) tall. A short-lived perennial, it is easily raised from freshly sown seed; leave the seedlings to mature so that those with the best foliage colour can be selected. (See page 86.)

The imposing *Eupatorium rugosum* 'Chocolate' ♛ forms a clump of stiff brown stems to 1m (40in) high, clothed in deep chocolate-purple, nettle-like leaves, and produces insignificant heads of grey-white blooms in early autumn. It likes moist soil and will grow in semi-

Eupatorium rugosum 'Chocolate'

shade, although the colour is better in sun. It is notoriously slow to get going at the beginning of the season, not making any impact in the border before late summer. Plant it alongside early performing perennials such as achilleas.

The purple-leaved **euphorbias** are stunning when the lime-green flowers open in early spring and contrast with the velvety wine-coloured leaves. Sadly, these are often marred by mildew in damp, crowded conditions. To avoid problems give plants an open position and use a preventative fungicidal spray in dry weather in winter. *Euphorbia amygdaloides* 'Purpurea' grows 30cm (12in) tall, with red-purple foliage and lime-green flowers. *Euphorbia dulcis*

Foeniculum vulgare 'Purpureum'

'Chameleon' forms a clump of upright stems, 30cm (12in) high, clad in velvety purple leaves. The more recent cultivar *Euphorbia* 'Blackbird', up to 45cm (18in) high, is even darker and promises greater disease-resistance.

Foeniculum vulgare 'Purpureum' (bronze fennel) is an invaluable mixer and a wonderful see-through plant. Its feathery foliage is ornate and tactile, with a delicious aniseed aroma. Very hardy in all but the wettest soils, fennel emerges in early spring; by mid-spring its feathery bronze foliage is the perfect partner for tall, elegant tulips. Its new growth throughout spring and summer

CONTAINING FENNEL

The aromatic seeds of bronze fennel (*Foeniculum vulgare* 'Purpureum') are easily germinated and frequently come true to type. On light, sandy soils the plants seed profusely, and the deep-rooted seedlings can be troublesome. Remove the flowers as they fade to prevent seeds developing.

continues a rich, deep bronze before maturing to bronzed green. Over 1.5m (5ft) tall, it bears airy heads of modest, tiny yellow flowers in midsummer.

All **gauras** have curiously spotted foliage, their deep green leaves often blotched with chocolate. Some forms are blessed with red-purple foliage, particularly those with pink flowers. *Gaura lindheimeri* 'In the Pink' has a long flowering season from midsummer

Gaura lindheimeri 'In the Pink'

OTHER PERENNIALS WITH PURPLE AND PLUM FOLIAGE *Aster laterifolius* 'Prince' • *Canna* TROPICANNA • *Dahlia* 'Bishop of Llandaff' • *Heuchera* 'Regina' • *Lobelia cardinalis* • *Lobelia* 'Queen Victoria' •

to late autumn. It is an excellent choice for the front of a border or a container. If winter wet is avoided, this hardy perennial will produce a profusion of mid-pink, starry flowers above compact, bushy growth 30cm (12in) high. The foliage is dark green and bronzed; the new growth deep purple-red.

There is no denying the rich beauty of purple-leaved **geraniums**. *Geranium pratense*, the meadow cranesbill, has provided a number of desirable cultivars with the magical combination of divided purple-chocolate leaves and blue-purple flowers in early summer. *Geranium pratense* **Midnight Reiter strain** is a little gem of a plant, rarely growing to more than 20cm (8in) high. The foliage stays close to the ground so shows better against gravel than bare earth.

Geranium pratense Midnight Reiter strain

Other selections include **'Purple Heron'** and **Victor Reiter Junior strain**. These geraniums are certainly beautiful, but they are also a little temperamental. They enjoy sun but do not like to be baked dry, preferring reasonably moist soil that is moderately fertile. Detail plants rather than impact subjects, they need careful positioning, otherwise they are easily lost in the border.

Geranium phaeum **'Samobor'** is easier to grow, with mature plants attaining 60cm (24in) in height. The foliage is stunning: each leaf boasts a dark purple-black broken circle at its centre and can reach in excess of 10cm (4in) across. The deep violet-purple flowers are relatively insignificant.

Geranium phaeum 'Samobor'

Lychnis × *arkwrightii* **'Vesuvius'** boasts a divine combination of foliage and flower colour. Star-shaped flowers in vivid scarlet-orange are carried in small clusters above dark red-brown leaves, on similarly coloured, softly hairy stems, 45cm (18in) high.

Of all the purple-leaved perennials *Lysimachia ciliata* **'Firecracker'** ♀ is perhaps the most useful. Its new foliage is a sumptuous chocolate-brown and matures through shades of dark to wine red as its stems reach 1m (40in) or more. Growing in sun or light shade on any soil, this plant is an excellent mixer and is a natural addition to many plantings. (See Good Companions, below.)

Although *Sedum telephium* subsp. *maximum* **'Atropurpureum'** ♀ could never be described as a pretty plant, it is

Lysimachia ciliata 'Firecracker'

very handsome. Its stiff stems, clad in succulent, deep wine-purple leaves, form an upright clump to 50cm (20in) high. Loose heads of tiny pinkish-red flowers appear in late summer. (See Good Companions, below, and see page 73.) When fully grown, the plant may become top-heavy; to prevent this, cut stems back by half in early summer.

(See Good Companions, below, and see page 73.)

KEEPING 'FIRECRACKER' LOOKING GOOD

The starry yellow flowers of *Lysimachia ciliata* 'Firecracker' ♀ are stunning against the foliage but if they do not suit the colour scheme, cut the plant back to one third of its height in midsummer. New shoots will be produced and the purple foliage effect will be preserved.

GOOD COMPANIONS

The deep plum-coloured new shoots of *Lysimachia ciliata* 'Firecracker' ♀ (1) are stunning among the vivid lime-green spring flowers of *Euphorbia cyparissias* 'Fens Ruby' (2).

The heavy purple foliage of *Sedum telephium* subsp. *maximum* 'Atropurpureum' ♀ (3) provides a total contrast to the soft silver leaves of *Artemisia stelleriana* 'Boughton Silver' (4).

91

Ophiopogon planiscapus 'Nigrescens' • *Pennisetum setaceum* 'Rubrum' • *Penstemon digitalis* 'Husker Red' • *Ranunculus ficaria* 'Brazen Hussy' • *Rheum palmatum* 'Atrosanguineum' • *Tiarella* 'Spring Symphony' •

Yellow and gold foliage

Bright and sunny, demanding attention and attracting the eye, yellow can be a dominant colour; it can also be uplifting and invigorating to other colours. Yellow can be soft and soothing or acidic and aggressive. When it comes to foliage, gold and yellow fulfil all these roles in the garden. Yellow leaves glow brightly in sunshine and mellow to soft lime green in shade. Most gold-foliage plants are at their best in spring and early summer and again in late summer and autumn; the intense sunlight of midsummer can scorch and bleach some golden favourites.

Agastache rugosa 'Golden Jubilee'

Gold-foliage shrubs, both evergreen and deciduous, are plentiful and popular; while herbaceous plants offer fewer yellow-leaved options, those that exist provide bright relief to the predominant green in the border and the often drab leaves of many perennials.

A deadnettle-like plant that comes reliably true from seed, *Agastache rugosa* 'Golden Jubilee' emerges from a winter-dormant crown to form upright 70cm (28in) stems of golden yellow leaves; above these rise spires of tubular lavender-blue flowers from midsummer onwards. A sun-loving prairie native, it combines well with grasses, rudbeckias and echinaceas.

Some perennials with golden foliage display their most brilliant colour in early spring and summer when the new leaves unfurl. Few come close to the flaming orange-red of the emerging shoots of *Dicentra spectabilis* 'Gold Heart', with foliage that matures to

The striking form and foliage of *Dicentra spectabilis* 'Gold Heart' make a stunning setting for the heart-shaped, deep pink flowers, borne from late spring into early summer.

92

OTHER PERENNIALS WITH YELLOW AND GOLD FOLIAGE *Campanula garganica* 'Dickson's Gold' • *Carex elata* 'Aurea' • *Milium effusum* 'Aureum' • *Phormium* 'Yellow Wave' • *Physostegia virginiana* 'Olympic Gold' •

golden yellow. The arching pink-red stems, reaching 60cm (24in) high, carry both the golden leaves and the familiar deep pink 'bleeding heart' flowers (see Good Companions, page 95). A plant for fertile, moist, free-draining soil, this beauty dislikes the bright sun of mid-summer, which speeds it into early dormancy, a trait typical of the species.

In the shade, the unusual *Farfugium japonicum* 'Aureomaculatum' ♀ has distinctive glossy, dark green, kidney-shaped leaves generously splashed with irregular yellow spots. The leaves have an almost reptilian quality and make a dramatic contrast with the lighter foliage of shade-loving ferns. Borne on long, slender stalks, they form a loose clump above which yellow heads of flowers on stems 60cm (24in) high are borne from early to late autumn. In areas of penetrating frost, a dry winter mulch of bark or bracken is necessary to prevent damage.

Filipendula ulmaria 'Aurea', the golden meadowsweet, is happy in sun or partial shade and thrives in wetter soils. A hardy herbaceous perennial, 60cm (24in) high, it forms a clump of textured mid-yellow leaves that mature to creamy yellow then green as heads of tiny, fluffy, creamy-white flowers arrive in midsummer.

Geranium × *oxonianum* 'Spring Fling' stands out in the border in early spring: the newly emerging palmate leaves are bright yellow, flecked pinkish red. By midsummer the foliage matures to pale green, and is joined by white flowers with dark pink veining. Growing to 60cm (24in) high, it enjoys well-drained soil, in sun or semi-shade.

The ever popular *Geranium* 'Ann Folkard' ♀ combines magenta black-eyed blooms and lime-green foliage, which takes on stronger yellow tones in sun. A rampant grower, 60cm (24in) high, it makes marvellous ground cover in semi-shade.

Heucheras are usually associated with purple and plum foliage (see pages 88–89), but there is an increasing number of golden yellow varieties. More than mere novelties, these eye-catching foliage plants are particularly useful in pots and containers and to contrast with their purple cousins. The golden-leaved heucheras are more compact plants, with foliage mostly around 20cm (8in) high. First to arrive was the gorgeous *Heuchera* 'Amber Waves': its waved

Geranium 'Ann Folkard'

evergreen leaves are rich golden bronze with orange tones in spring, maturing to mid-ochre yellow as summer progresses. As a young plant 'Amber Waves' can be slow to get going, but once established it will thrive in moist soil shaded from midday sun.

A more uniform golden orange is found in the foliage of *Heuchera* 'Marmalade', with new growth and the undersides of the leaves flushed pink.

Heuchera 'Amber Waves'

Humulus lupulus 'Aureus'

Heuchera 'Crème Brûlée' is robust and compact in habit, with ruffled, creamy-gold foliage flushed orange. *Heuchera* 'Key Lime Pie' produces refreshing, shiny bright green leaves that become flushed with pale lemon in strong sun. The lovely × *Heucherella* 'Gold Strike' has reliably golden leaves with a distinct red-brown flush broadly colouring the centre of each leaf.

For a selection of **hostas** with yellow and gold foliage see page 94.

Herbaceous perennials come in many forms. *Humulus lupulus* 'Aureus' ♀ (golden hop) is grown for its rapidly climbing, twining stems of coarse, bright yellow leaves, which look even brighter in strong sun. It will put on 5m

(continued on page 95)

USING YELLOW LEAVES

Yellow foliage works best when combined with other yellow-leaved plants and yellow, white or blue flowers diluted with sufficient green. An occasional yellow plant in a border will always look out of place since it will attract the eye, often to the exclusion of all else. Yellow foliage is particularly useful when combined with yellow-variegated leaves to lighten semi-shade.

Pleioblastus viridistriatus • *Saxifraga* 'Cloth of Gold' • *Smyrnium perfoliatum* • *Symphytum* 'Goldsmith' •
Symphytum ibericum 'All Gold' • *Tanacetum parthenium* 'Aureum' • *Tradescantia* Andersoniana Group 'Sweet Kate' •

Yellow and gold hostas

Of all perennials, hostas provide the greatest variety of yellow leaves, offering shades of creamy yellow and pale lemon-gold in the form of both solid colours and attractive variegation. Most excel in semi-shade, and especially enjoy the dappled shade from trees; in full sun the foliage can become bleached and lacklustre.

The original hosta species reached cultivation in the late 18th century from their native habitats in Korea, China, Japan and eastern Russia. Virtually unrivalled success in hybridization has brought us the range we know today.

In fertile, moist, free-draining soil these hardy herbaceous perennials form neat clumps of rounded, oval or heart-shaped leaves, which vary from 10cm (4in) to more than 50cm (20in) in length. Attractive tubular, lily-like flowers of white and shades of pink to lilac grace upright stems from early to late summer.

Slugs and snails are the major problem but they can be kept at bay with barriers, baits and cultivation techniques. Grow hostas away from damaging winds, which scorch and break the succulent leaves.

Hosta fortunei var. *albopicta* ♥ is one of the most popular hostas, with soft golden yellow leaves irregularly margined in green. In early spring the colour is strong and eye-catching, fading as the season progresses and as stems of mauve-white flowers appear above the foliage in midsummer. Best in semi-shade, it grows 45cm (18in) high and 60cm (24in) across.

OTHER YELLOW AND GOLD HOSTAS

Hosta 'Golden Prayers' Bright golden yellow leaves, with lavender-blue flowers just above the foliage in midsummer. Grows 45cm (18in) high, 60cm (24in) across.

Hosta 'Piedmont Gold' Grows 50cm (20in) high, 1m (40in) wide. Deeply veined blue-green leaves flushed sulphur yellow. Pale lavender flowers above the foliage in midsummer.

Hosta 'Zounds' Large, veined and puckered leaves of soft gold tinged blue-green. Grows 40cm (16in) high and 90cm (3ft) across. Pale lavender flowers rise above the foliage in late summer.

Hosta 'August Moon' grows to 50cm (20in) high and 70cm (28in) across. Its gently cupped leaves are initially pale green, maturing to soft golden yellow. Stems of lilac-white flowers rise above the foliage in midsummer. Tough and reliable, it produces the best leaf colour when grown in full sun.

Hosta 'Sum and Substance' ♥ is the biggest and boldest of hostas, 80cm (32in) high with a spread of 1.5m (5ft). Massive heart-shaped leaves are glossy, yellow-green, gently puckered with age. Bears flowers of palest lavender just above the foliage in late summer.

(15ft) of growth in a season before dying back to the ground in autumn. Care should be taken in positioning such a vigorous plant; it will soon sprawl over its neighbours, adventurous shoots emerging far from the main plant. In the right place, it will create dramatic effect.

Lysimachia nummularia (creeping Jenny) forms a carpet of stems with rounded leaves, excellent for evergreen ground cover. *Lysimachia nummularia* 'Aurea' ♟ has bright golden yellow foliage in sun, more lime yellow in shade. It is delightful trailing over the edge of a pot or in a hanging basket.

GOLDEN COVER

Lysimachia nummularia 'Aurea' ♟ is useful to bring the effect of golden foliage to ground level. Try planting it beneath a gold-leaved tree or shrub such as *Catalpa bignonioides* 'Aurea' ♟ or *Ptelea trifoliata* 'Aurea' ♟ for a carpet of summer sunshine.

Favoured by butterflies, ***Origanum vulgare* 'Aureum'** ♟, the golden wild marjoram, is a wonderful all-rounder. Stems 60cm (24in) high bear rounded, pale to golden yellow, aromatic leaves, which can be used for cooking in the same way as those of the green species. Clusters of rosy pink, tubular flowers are produced in late summer. Extremely hot sunshine may scorch the foliage; if this occurs cut the plant back and it will produce another flush of growth. When the flowers have faded in late autumn, cut the plant back to the ground to leave a mat of golden foliage that will persist through the winter. Origanum thrives on poor soil in a sunny position and is successful on chalk.

Commonly known as lamb's ears, ***Stachys byzantina*** has long been a garden favourite (see page 105). The cultivar ***Stachys byzantina* 'Primrose Heron'** has silver-felted leaves flushed lemon yellow, the colour becoming more prevalent in full sun (see Good

Stachys byzantina 'Primrose Heron'

Valeriana phu 'Aurea'

Companions, below). Above the leaves, woolly stems 45cm (18in) high carry small pink-purple flowers; these are best removed to preserve the effect of the foliage. Like the species, 'Primrose Heron' must have free-draining soil, but with adequate moisture. Drought can reduce the vigour of the plant and increase its susceptibility to mildew.

The foliage of the golden valerian, *Valeriana phu* 'Aurea', is full of spring-time promise. It appears above ground early in the season and is the brightest of yellows. The leaves, 20cm (8in) long, are divided into well-defined leaflets

that age from yellow through lime green to mid-green. Airy heads of tiny white flowers form on slender stems over 1m (40in) high; although not showy, these bring light relief to the border and offer a white alternative to rich lilac-purple *Verbena bonariensis* ♟. Golden valerian is easy to grow, thriving on most soils.

***Veronica prostrata* 'Trehane'** is a low-growing, mat-forming plant. The foliage is lime yellow in shade and a bright golden yellow in full sun, and it creates a striking background for the 15cm (6in) spikes of inky-blue flowers appearing in early summer.

GOOD COMPANIONS

Stachys byzantina 'Primrose Heron' (1) with *Heuchera* 'Can-can' ♟ (2): with its soft, silvery lemon foliage, the stachys contrasts in colour and texture with the waved, red-purple heuchera.

The pink and green blooms of *Tulipa* 'Fantasy' ♟ (3) pick up on the pink stems and flowers of *Dicentra spectabilis* 'Gold Heart' (4) and contrast with its golden foliage.

Variegated foliage

Plants with variegated foliage have a special appeal; perhaps because they rarely occur in nature, gardeners identify them as theirs to cultivate. They are easy to accommodate as most have some green in the leaves, providing a link with surrounding plants. Variegated shrubs are some of the most popular garden essentials; variegated perennials are fewer in number but no less valuable.

The architectural form of the species *Euphorbia characias* is further accentuated in the cream-variegated foliage of *Euphorbia characias* SILVER SWAN ('Wilcott').

Erysimum linifolium 'Variegatum'

VARIEGATED PERENNIALS FOR DRY, SUNNY SITES

Erysimum linifolium 'Variegatum' is a form of perennial wallflower. A bushy, woody-based plant, it grows to 60cm (24in) high, with pale stems clothed in narrow evergreen leaves conspicuously margined in creamy white. These are a striking contrast to the purple-pink flowers in late spring and summer. Like the other perennial wallflowers, it is short-lived and new plants should be started from cuttings every couple of years. These are usually taken in late summer and rooted in a coldframe; take plenty, since they are not so easy to root as the green-leaved varieties.

There have been several variegated forms of *Euphorbia characias* introduced over the years; often sulky plants, they are slow-growing and unreliable. Not so *Euphorbia characias* SILVER SWAN ('Wilcott'): a magnificent evergreen, it has stout stems forming an elegant, upright bush to 90cm (3ft) high, with eye-catching foliage. The narrow leaves

are blue-green broadly edged in creamy white, presenting a vivid picture all through the year in a sunny position on well-drained soil. The late spring flowers are creamy white and usually go unseen against the foliage. Prune out flowered stems to ground level in summer to allow new stems to develop. This is a wonderful plant in the winter garden, especially when it is set close to the white stems of birch (*Betula*), the white-suffused leaves of *Prunus laurocerasus* 'Castlewellan', or the silver foliage of *Pittosporum* 'Garnettii' ♥.

There are variegated forms of iris for wet and dry conditions. *Iris pallida*, from rocky limestone hills around the Adriatic, forms spreading clumps of pale grey-blue leaves that remain in good condition throughout the season, even after the fragrant, pale lilac-blue flowers have faded. Variegated forms are more often seen than the species, with fans of sword-shaped leaves up to 60cm (24in) high. The variegation is bold: broad creamy-white stripes in the case of *Iris*

OTHER VARIEGATED PERENNIALS FOR DRY, SUNNY SITES *Arabis alpina* subsp. *caucasica* 'Variegata' •

Iris pallida 'Variegata'

pallida 'Variegata' ✿, the most widely grown form (see also page 152.)

Although they are really sub-shrubs, the variegated forms of common sage, *Salvia officinalis*, are often sold alongside herbaceous perennials (see page 166). *Salvia officinalis* 'Icterina', with golden-variegated foliage, and *Salvia officinalis* 'Tricolor', with white- and purple-variegated leaves, are much less vigorous than the green and purple sages and need full sun and good drainage to succeed.

Sedum erythrostictum has upright stems of grey-green foliage, with heads of green-white flowers in late summer

and autumn. The variegated forms include 'Mediovariegatum', which has bold creamy-yellow centres to the leaves, and 'Frosty Morn', with clear white markings (see page 176). *Sedum sieboldii* 'Mediovariegatum' ✿ has trailing stems 15cm (6in) long bearing blue-green, coin-like leaves, creamy yellow in the centre and often flushed bright pink; heads of pink flowers form at the stem tips in late summer.

The fans of soft, sword-like leaves of *Sisyrinchium striatum* are hardy and evergreen in free-draining ground. The variegated form *Sisyrinchium striatum* 'Aunt May' has creamy-white striped leaves in fans reaching 40cm (16in); the stems of pale lemon flowers rise just above the leaves in early summer. The variegated form is more compact and less invasive than the green form, but is perhaps a little less hardy.

Tulbaghia violacea 'Silver Lace' forms expanding clumps of grey-green, narrow, fleshy, grass-like leaves, striped silver-white. From early summer, slender 50cm (20in) stems are each topped in a cluster of lilac-pink flowers, which open to six-pointed stars; these have a gentle, sweet fragrance best enjoyed at dusk. The foliage has a less pleasant aroma when disturbed, hence the colloquial

name 'society garlic'. The aromatic foliage has its uses, some species being cultivated as snake repellents. Dry soil in winter is essential, so a position at the foot of a sunny wall or in a well-drained scree bed is ideal.

VARIEGATED PERENNIALS FOR MOISTER SOIL

Few plants will grow in any soil in both sun and full shade. *Aegopodium podagraria* 'Variegatum', however, is an exception and thrives on neglect, providing valuable ground cover in otherwise barren areas of the garden. Up to 30cm (12in) high, it has leaves made up of three or more toothed leaflets, which are olive-green margined and splashed in creamy white. In early summer lacy heads of white flowers (continued on page 100)

PATHS AND POTS

Aegopodium podagraria 'Variegatum' makes an attractive path edging if contained by tiles pushed vertically into the ground to create a narrow border along the path. It also looks good in a pot. It will quickly fill a container, producing a mass of bright, pest-proof foliage that will stay looking good throughout the season, especially if flower stems are removed.

WHAT IS VARIEGATION?

Variegation is often caused by mutation: a change to the genetic information in the plant's growing point. The pigments of variegated leaves are unevenly dispersed, resulting in white, cream or yellow spots, splashes, streaks, stripes and, most commonly, leaf centres or margins, against the original green leaf colour. The areas of the leaf that are not green lack chlorophyll, which the plant uses to manufacture food for growth. Variegated plants are therefore often less vigorous than their green counterparts.

Sisyrinchium striatum 'Aunt May'

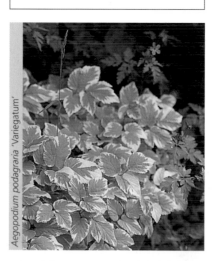

Aegopodium podagraria 'Variegatum'

Aubrieta 'Argenteovariegata' • *Iris foetidissima* 'Variegata' • *Ophiopogon jaburan* 'Vittatus' •

Variegated hostas

Hostas offer an outstanding range of variegated leaves: every possible combination of silver and green, blue and yellow has been selected and developed by the hybridists to create a phenomenal choice of cultivars.

Rounded, oval or heart-shaped leaves range from less than 10cm (4in) long to 50cm (20in) or more, ample surface to show off the variegation. The smaller, delicate varieties are more for the collector and the enthusiast; all gardeners can grow and appreciate the more substantial cultivars. Tubular flowers in white or shades of pink to lilac are borne in early to late summer.

Hostas thrive in fertile, moist, free-draining soil. They are often thought of as plants for shade, but many do best in a sunny spot. While too much shade may limit colour development, strong sun can damage some variegation. As a rule, shadier positions result in larger leaves and fewer flowers; sunnier sites produce more compact plants with small leaves and more flowers.

Variegated hostas have many uses. In mixed borders their foliage colour helps to reinforce a colour scheme

Hosta 'Patriot' is perhaps the boldest and showiest of the variegated hostas. Strong, narrow, heart-shaped leaves form large open rosettes up to 45cm (18in) high and 75cm (30in) across. The leaves are rich dark green, with broad white margins overlapping the green and streaking the centre with grey-green. Stems of lilac flowers stand well above the foliage in mid-summer. A superb variety for a pot and outstanding in the border, it is normally recommended for light shade but will withstand a reasonable amount of full sun.

and their bold leaves provide contrast and a focal point in the planting. They are useful in shady situations to lighten the dark green of shade-loving subjects. They make excellent planting partners for early-flowering bulbs, their lush foliage covering the ground when the spring display of the bulbs is over.

Hostas are also stunning subjects for pots, the ideal place to grow them in gardens plagued by slugs and snails. Copper tape placed around the pot or a copper-impregnated mat beneath it will help defend emerging shoots and succulent leaves from attack.

Hosta 'June' ♀ has elegant leaves, broad and lance-shaped, forming a fairly upright clump 50cm (20in) high and the same across. Each leaf is soft yellow with an irregular blue-green margin, suffusing the centre with soft blue-green and yellow. Lilac flowers appear in mid- to late summer on tall stems, above the foliage. Excellent for a pot and for cutting. It succeeds in light shade but needs a reasonable amount of sun to develop the best colour.

OTHER VARIEGATED HOSTAS

Hosta 'Cherry Berry' Very compact, at 25cm (10in) high and 40cm (16in) wide. Narrow, dark, glossy green leaves with a cream centre. Red-flushed stems carry violet-mauve flowers above the foliage.

Hosta fortunei var. *aureomarginata* ♀ Large, deeply veined, dark green leaves with golden yellow margins ageing to cream. Reaches 45cm (18in) high and 60cm (24in) across. Pale lavender flowers, well above the foliage.

Hosta 'Francee' ♀ Large, spreading and 60cm (24in) high and 90cm (3ft) across. Foliage is late to emerge but matures to narrow, heart-shaped leaves of rich green with white margins. Bears lavender flowers well above the foliage.

Hosta 'Revolution' Medium-sized, 30cm (12in) high and 60cm (24in) wide. Dark green leaves with white markings. Pale lilac flowers well above the foliage.

Hosta 'Wide Brim' ♀ grows 60cm (24in) high and 90cm (3ft) across. Its large, puckered, heart-shaped leaves are rich green with an irregular creamy margin overlapping the green, resulting in green-yellow shades towards the centre. White flowers in midsummer rise above the foliage on sleek stems. Excellent for large containers, for borders in light shade and for cutting.

Hosta 'Gold Standard' ♀ is one of the most popular hostas. It emerges in late spring, the leaves unfurling sage-green, becoming light yellow as they mature, and fading to cream with a dark green margin. It is a large spreading plant, 50cm (20in) high by 90cm (3ft) across. Lilac flowers are borne in midsummer, held well above the leaves. Despite its popularity, it is not the easiest to grow; dappled shade is ideal, allowing the gold colour to develop, without the leaves becoming scorched.

Hosta 'Frances Williams' ♀ is very large, reaching 60cm (24in) high and 1m (40in) across. The large thick, puckered leaves are rounded and gently cupped and of a dusky blue-green with pale creamy-yellow margins. Lavender flowers appear in midsummer on thick leafy stems the same height as the leaves. Does best in shade.

Armoracia rusticana 'Variegata'

appear on tall green stems. This is the variegated form of ground elder, a weed cursed by many gardeners, but it is far less invasive and is a very useful plant.

Armoracia rusticana 'Variegata', the variegated horseradish, is an under-used perennial with lush green foliage stunningly marked in cream and white. It forms a vigorous clump of leaves to a height of 60cm (24in) and multiplies readily. It grows anywhere but gives its best performance in an open position on deep, moist, fertile soil. It is a good plant to bring interest to the edge of the vegetable garden; the long tap root can be used for culinary purposes in the same way as that of the green form.

Striking in spring, *Astrantia major* 'Sunningdale Variegated' ♥ forms a rounded clump, 20cm (8in) high, of large, deeply divided, dark green leaves,

striped and mottled in creamy white. The variegation ages to pale green in summer, as the delicate, pincushion-like flowerheads, framed in pale pink bracts, appear on 40cm (16in) stems.

Houttuynia cordata 'Chameleon' is a robust, spreading ground-cover plant with brightly variegated foliage. It has numerous red stems, to 30cm (12in) high, and heart-shaped leaves of green, flame and gold. Small white flowers in summer are of secondary importance. This houttuynia likes moist soil and will grow happily in partial shade, although full sun brings the most intense leaf colour. It makes a colourful subject for a

container. The stems and leaves are knocked back to the ground with the first frost. The plant's worst quality is an unpleasant aroma given off when the foliage is disturbed. A number of other selections are available, among them **'Pied Piper'** and **'Flame'**, both of which have brighter foliage of red and orange with green and cream variegation (see Good Companions, below).

Iris ensata **'Variegata'** ♥ must have constant moisture. The narrow, upright sword-like leaves, 90cm (3ft) high, are striped in white or creamy yellow. Large purple blooms are a stunning contrast to the bright foliage in early summer. *Iris pseudacorus* **'Variegata'** ♥ is more tolerant of drier situations. Its creamy-

Houttuynia cordata 'Flame'

Astrantia major 'Sunningdale Variegated'

GOOD COMPANIONS

The bright colours of candelabra primulas (1) are striking with the emerging flame-coloured shoots of *Houttuynia cordata* 'Flame' (2).

The striped, grass-like foliage of *Liriope muscari* 'John Burch' (3) combines well with the similarly variegated but differently shaped leaves of *Euonymus fortunei* 'Silver Queen' (4).

OTHER GOOD VARIEGATED PERENNIALS FOR MOISTER SOIL *Oenanthe javanica* 'Flamingo' •

yellow striped leaves usually fade to green from midsummer onwards. Small yellow flowers are produced in spring.

Growing 50cm (20in) high, *Kalimeris yomena* 'Shogun' is ideal mid-border, usefully covering the unsightly stems of taller herbaceous perennials. It emerges from the ground with creamy shoots in late spring. The blue-mauve flowers in midsummer resemble those of aster, a close relative, yet its dark green and cream foliage is refreshingly unique.

Liriope muscari ♀ (lilyturf) forms a clump of broad, grassy, dark green leaves from which appear short, dense spikes of small lilac-blue flowers in late summer and autumn. Variegated forms are good in the shade of trees, offering light foliage interest at ground level. *Liriope muscari* 'John Burch' (see Good Companions, left) has creamy-yellow striped leaves, 30cm (12in) long. Although it tolerates drought, it grows best on fairly moist, slightly acid soil.

Moist soil and light shade are ideal conditions for the variegated forms of the loosestrife *Lysimachia punctata*. The cultivar 'Alexander' has upright stems 75cm (30in) high, densely clothed in green leaves edged with creamy white. 'Golden Alexander' has leaves with margins of golden yellow. Both have the starry yellow flowers of the species in early summer (see page 144), although both are at their best before the flowers, when the leafy, upright shoots provide a wonderful contrast to the bold fresh foliage of hostas.

The variegated **mints** are not only ornamental but deliciously aromatic culinary herbs of popular appeal. They are happy in poor, moist soils and are easy to grow. They are propagated by root cuttings, usually taken in autumn, or by layering the stems in summer.

Mentha × *gracilis* 'Variegata', the ginger mint, has upright, spreading red-tinted stems, up to 30cm (12in) high, bearing oval, mid-green leaves striped

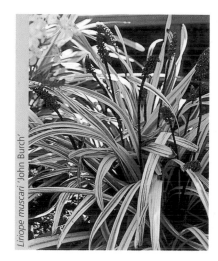

Liriope muscari 'John Burch'

and speckled with bright yellow. The stems are topped with clusters of small tubular lilac flowers in summer.

Mentha suaveolens 'Variegata' (pineapple mint) is distinctly pineapple in fragrance. Its vigorous stems are clothed in small, oval to rounded, softly hairy grey-green leaves, with irregular creamy streaks, tips and margins. Very small, tubular pink or white flowers form short, densely packed spires on 50cm (20in) stems.

Persicaria virginiana 'Painter's Palette' is a hardy perennial preferring moist soil in semi-shade and a sheltered position where wind will not damage the intricately patterned foliage. It forms stems 60cm (24in) high of green leaves splashed and striped with cream, each with a brown central zone and flushes of salmon pink.

Persicaria virginiana 'Painter's Palette'

A native of England and parts of western Europe, *Scrophularia auriculata* is found in woods, meadows and along river banks, where it thrives in rich, moist soil. With small brown flowers, the species is not worth growing in the garden, but the variegated form *Scrophularia auriculata* 'Variegata' certainly deserves a place. A good companion for hostas, ligularias and sedges, it has tall, square red stems, nearly 1m (40in) high, carrying toothed, wrinkled mid-green leaves, boldly edged and splashed in creamy white.

Symphytums grow well on any soil and make excellent ground cover (see pages 116–17). The variegated forms are tough plants that will often succeed where choicer subjects may struggle. *Symphytum* 'Goldsmith' successfully colonizes moist shade: its carpet of tumbling, early spring foliage illuminates the ground, despite the thickening tree canopy. A hardy perennial growing from rhizomes, it produces crinkled, coarse, lance-shaped leaves of dark green with thick, irregular variegation of lime green to bright gold. Foliage-clad stems, 25cm (10in) high, bear clusters of pendent tubular, pink to pale blue flowers in mid-spring. *Symphytum* × *uplandicum* 'Variegatum' ♀, up to 90cm (3ft) tall, is popular for the distinct creamy-white margins of its leaves. Unfortunately it is prone to revert to plain green unless happy in its situation.

CONTROLLING MINT

Variegated mints can be as invasive as the culinary types grown in the herb garden. Although their habit of running between other plants, throwing up random stems in the border, can be attractive, it may become overpowering. Contain clumps by planting in large pots sunk into the soil. The mints will also enjoy any additional moisture trapped by the containers.

Phlox paniculata 'Norah Leigh' • *Polemonium* BRISE D'ANJOU ('Blanjou') • *Pulmonaria rubra* 'David Ward' •

Silver and blue foliage

Grey and blue are marvellous foils for other colours. Light, ethereal silver is a natural choice with the blue, pink and purple flowers of sun-loving plants. It is also a ravishing contrast with deep red blooms. Blue-green foliage works as a bond between other colours, in the same way that blue flowers can provide that all-important link. As a contrast to the predominant green of most gardens, silver or blue foliage attracts the eye and draws attention to highlights in the border.

Anaphalis triplinervis

The dramatic silver foliage of *Cynara cardunculus* adds architectural impact to any border.

Most silver-leaved perennials and shrubs are plants for sunny sites and soils with good drainage. They often hail from dry Mediterranean climates, the silver of their leaves a means of reflecting light and preventing water loss. Most silver shrubs have finely cut foliage; for broader silver leaves the gardener needs to look to herbaceous perennials. Some have adapted to climatic conditions by covering their foliage with fine silver hairs that create a microclimate over the surface, thereby preventing desiccation. Others have developed thick, leathery leaves with a reflective surface. These crave lots of light, and sit well among the reflective stones of scree or alongside walls and paved areas.

SILVER AND BLUE SUN-LOVERS

Anaphalis triplinervis ♀ thrives in full sun, as long as it has adequate moisture in summer. A clump-forming plant, it is grown both for its neat, narrow silver leaves and for its tiny white, papery, everlasting flowers, carried in clusters at the end of the stems.

Many sun-loving sub-shrubs native to Mediterranean regions have silvery foliage: *Lotus hirsutus* ♀, *Helichrysum italicum* ♀, *Convolvulus cneorum* ♀, *Santolina chamaecyparissus* ♀ and many lavenders for example. These are often offered alongside herbaceous perennials and have as much in common with them as they do with woody shrubs. *Artemisia* 'Powis Castle' ♀, with fine filigree silver leaves, is classified both as a shrub and as a herbaceous perennial.

Although partly woody, it is often knocked back by half in winter, then sprouts from the woody base of the plant the following spring. (See Good Companions, below, and see page 65.)

Eryngiums (see pages 66–67) are prized for the silver-blue metallic beauty of both their flowers and their foliage. Strikingly spiky plants, they radiate resistance to drought and contrast dramatically with the lush green foliage of their neighbours. Contemporary in character, they are favoured in modern garden design and floral art. The species can vary considerably in their silver and blue colouring, which is also affected by light, moisture and soil.

The well-known biennial *Eryngium giganteum* ♀ (Miss Willmott's ghost) is reliable for the silver-white of its flowers

Eryngium giganteum

and foliage. Although the plant dies after flowering in summer, it readily self-seeds, especially on dry soils. The lovely *Eryngium* 'Jos Eijking' is of similar size, reaching 60cm (24in), but is a perennial, with silver-blue foliage and wonderful metallic-blue flowers from mid- to late summer. It looks superb with artemisias and santolinas, its blue stars shining out from a cloud of silver-grey.

Helleborus argutifolius 'Silver Lace' is more compact than the species. It grows to 30cm (12in), and has bold ice-green foliage with a silvery sheen. By late winter the domed plant is crowned with lime-green flowers held in a loose head. It prefers an open position on well-drained soil and is a handsome companion to the exquisite flowers of *Fritillaria meleagris*.

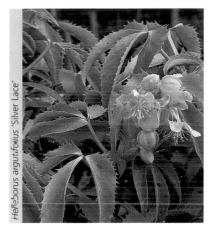

Helleborus argutifolius 'Silver Lace'

Lychnis coronaria ♀ produces splendid white rosettes of soft, felted leaves and white-woolly flower stems, 50cm (20in) high, carrying vivid magenta blooms in summer – a wonderful contrast, but not ideal as a silver foliage plant because the flowers will always steal the show. *Lychnis coronaria* 'Alba' ♀, with white flowers, is a superb mixer and will excel in white or silver schemes.

Salvia argentea ♀ is sought after for its large white-woolly leaves. These are produced in a basal clump in the first season, before being overpowered in the second summer by the candelabra-like flower stem, which can reach 1m (40in) high. The flowers are grey-white, sadly not a pretty combination with the white-woolly stems. This is a plant for a dry, well-drained position in full sun. A wet summer can reduce the leaves to a soggy mess on the soil surface.

SEASONAL SILVER PLANTS

Some herbaceous perennials are treated as annuals and used to contribute silver-grey foliage to seasonal planting schemes in the border and in containers. *Senecio cineraria* 'Silver Dust' ♀ is the most widely planted of all, with attractively divided silver-grey leaves. *Tanacetum haradjanii* has curiously cut, fern-like leaves. *Tanacetum ptarmiciflorum* 'Silver Feather' is a useful, bushy plant with finely cut foliage. All grow to around 30cm (12in) if kept in trim by removing the unattractive yellow daisy flowers before they open. All will overwinter in a sheltered, dry situation, but the plants often lose vigour and are slow to recover the following year, so it is best to replace them with new stock.

GOOD COMPANIONS

The softly divided foliage of *Artemisia* 'Powis Castle' ♀ (1) forms the perfect backdrop for the shining metallic blue blooms of *Eryngium alpinum* ♀ (2).

Stachys byzantina 'Silver Carpet' (3) and *Acaena microphylla* 'Kupferteppich' (COPPER CARPET) (4) is an ideal combination for edging a path in a sunny position.

BOLD, DRAMATIC SILVER

Cynara cardunculus ♀, the cardoon, is one of the most dramatic herbaceous perennials. The leaves, up to 1m (40in) long, arch gracefully from the ground, dissected and sharply toothed, and silver-grey, especially when young (see page 102). Vast branched flower stems arise as summer progresses: silver-grey and also carrying foliage, they may grow 3m (10ft) high. The large, spiny, thistle-like flowerheads develop from buds at the top of the stems; as the heads mature they open to reveal purple-red bristly bracts. Once the flowers are at their peak in late summer, the plant starts to deteriorate. At this point the flowering stems should be cut to ground level. New leaves will quickly appear, developing rapidly to full size; they will normally persist without damage throughout the winter in all but the coldest conditions.

Cynara cardunculus **Scolymus Group** is the globe artichoke, prized for its edible flower parts. It varies in its foliage colour; some selections are quite blue and, just like the species, can be used for dramatic effect in the garden.

Cynaras like deep, well-drained soil in full sun. They make a bold statement in

Macleaya microcarpa 'Kelway's Coral Plume'

the border but will also stand alone as architectural specimens.

Few herbaceous perennials have the stature of *Macleaya cordata* ♀ (plume poppy) and *Macleaya microcarpa* **'Kelway's Coral Plume'** ♀. Spreading underground rhizomes throw up fleshy shoots that grow quickly to stems 2m (6ft) or more high. These carry large, lobed leaves, grey-green above and silver-grey beneath, that resemble the pieces of a jigsaw. When disturbed by the wind they flutter silver in the border.

Light airy heads of small, tubular, pale coral flowers are borne at the tops of the stems in late summer. Macleayas are easily grown in sun or partial shade and look dramatic against dark evergreens. They rarely stay in the original planting position, and can be invasive.

Many **verbascums** are similar to *Salvia argentea* ♀ (see page 103) in their life cycle. *Verbascum thapsus* (Aaron's rod) produces a felty rosette in the first year, then a strong spike, 1.5m (5ft) tall, of yellow flowers in the summer of the second, before the plant dies. It is, however, perennial in the garden because it so freely self-seeds, resulting in large numbers of seedlings in the following autumn and spring. Although impressive in flower, it is at its loveliest as a grey rosette, especially in winter when etched with frost.

Verbascum bombyciferum is an architectural plant, one of the most stunning in the border. In summer, its white-woolly 2m (6ft) stems emerge from a rosette of large, silvery-grey leaves and bear closely packed, bright yellow flowers. *Verbascum olympicum* is similarly handsome: a long-lived, imposing perennial with tall, branched stems of yellow summer flowers rising from silver-grey leaf rosettes.

LIGHT, ETHEREAL SILVER

Artemisia absinthium **'Lambrook Silver'** ♀ is a woody-based plant with finely cut foliage, somewhat broader and more parsley-like than the well-known *Artemisia* 'Powis Castle' ♀ (see Good Companions, page 103). The colour is clear silver-grey. In midsummer, 75cm (30in) stems develop, with a mass of creamy-yellow flowers. These tend to look dirty against the clean silver leaves and should be cut off. This preserves the quality of the foliage and encourages new growth, maintaining a bush of around 60cm (24in).

Verbascum bombyciferum

OTHER PERENNIALS WITH SILVER AND BLUE FOLIAGE *Achillea clypeolata* • *Asphodeline lutea* •

Artemisia ludoviciana is a useful plant to introduce shots of silver among other perennials and shrubs. The upright stems, 60cm (24in) high, of willow-like, toothed silver leaves are virtually self-supporting in sunny, dry sites, needing only a little help from neighbouring plants. The cultivars **'Silver Queen'**❦ and **'Valerie Finnis'**❦ (see page 51) are excellent, the latter increasingly used as a companion for summer-flowering annuals such as *Salvia farinacea* and *Salvia viridis* var. *comata*. Both artemisias are effective in herbaceous planting to add substance to *Nepeta* × *faassenii*❦ (see page 67).

For frothy effect *Artemisia pontica*, *Artemisia alba* **'Canescens'**❦ and *Artemisia schmidtiana*❦ are hard to beat. Reaching 60cm (24in) in height,

Artemisia ludoviciana 'Silver Queen'

these are the ultimate silver clouds for planting among alliums, to disguise their fading foliage. *Artemisia schmidtiana* **'Nana'**❦ is shorter, usually reaching only 20cm (8in). It is the finest, silkiest and most silver of them all.

GARDEN ARCHITECTURE

Bold silver and blue leaves are the perfect partners for architectural stone in the garden. Statues, urns, balustrades, steps and walls are a natural setting for the strong form and sympathetic tones of silver and blue, which can link the stone with the surrounding planting.

SILVER CARPETS

Artemisia stelleriana **'Boughton Silver'** is much heavier in character than other artemisias. It is a rosette-forming plant with divided, felted foliage, spreading by runners to form broad mats. It is not particularly elegant, but it

Artemisia stelleriana 'Boughton Silver'

is useful in a gravel area, and especially good in a coastal garden.

Stachys byzantina (*Stachys lanata*), or lamb's ears, is the ultimate evergreen, silver mat-forming plant. Producing a series of rosettes of oval, pointed, heavily felted leaves, it is commonly seen at the front of borders, especially alongside paving. Small purple flowers are carried in woolly 40cm (16in) spikes in summer. These can be cut back to preserve the quality of the foliage. *Stachys byzantina* was a favourite of

Gertrude Jekyll, who planted it widely. It associates well with old roses, dianthus and *Viola cornuta*❦.

There are several named cultivars, of which the best known and most useful is perhaps *Stachys byzantina* **'Silver Carpet'** (see Good Companions, page 103), which does not flower. *Stachys byzantina* **'Cotton Boll'** does produces flower spikes but with woolly bobbles up the stems rather than flowers: an attractive novelty and good for cutting.

In a sunny situation with well-drained soil, *Veronica spicata* subsp. *incana* forms a mat of silver foliage, and in summer produces 30cm (12in) spikes of sapphire-blue flowers that shine out against the grey of the leaves. There are a number of forms: **'Silver Carpet'** lives up to its name.

STACHYS BYZANTINA AND MILDEW

Mildew is the scourge of this excellent ground-cover plant, usually disfiguring the foliage in midsummer. The woolly leaves do not take kindly to being sprayed, so prevention is better than cure. The risk of infection is increased by drought and overcrowding. Keep plants free from competitive neighbours and water them regularly.

Stachys byzantina

Cerastium tomentosum • *Crambe maritima* • *Festuca glauca* • *Helichrysum petiolare* • *Leucophyta brownii* •

SILVER IN THE SHADOWS

Some silver-leaved plants will grow in full or partial shade. These provide shining relief from the heavy greens that also thrive in such conditions, and complement the white variegation of shrubs such as *Vinca minor* 'Argenteovariegata', *Euonymus fortunei* 'Emerald Gaiety' ♀ and *Osmanthus heterophyllus* 'Variegatus' ♀.

Shade-loving silver plants do not have woolly leaves; instead they have reflective markings or marbling on the leaf surface. In the case of *Brunnera macrophylla* 'Jack Frost' the foliage appears metallic silver, etched and veined in mid-green. Sprays of bright

Brunnera macrophylla 'Jack Frost'

blue forget-me-not flowers form in early spring. The plant is deciduous, but the heart-shaped leaves are still perfect at the onset of winter, forming a mound of bold silver 20cm (8in) high. They look dramatic beneath the deep plum foliage of *Acer palmatum* 'Bloodgood' ♀.

A number of the lower-growing **dicentras** have attractive blue-green leaves and create a silvery effect against deep green foliage. *Dicentra eximia* 'Snowdrift' has fine fern-like foliage of blue-green and numerous white flowers in late spring to early summer. It forms splendid light ground cover at a height of 25cm (10in). *Dicentra* 'Langtrees' ♀ is one of the most popular, with low

Dicentra 'Langtrees'

silver-grey leaves and dainty white flowers held well above the foliage.

Heuchera 'Mint Frost' makes a refreshing change from the popular purple heucheras. Its fresh green leaves are overlaid with silver, making a striking mound of foliage 20cm (8in) high. The colouring resembles that of *Lamium maculatum* 'Beacon Silver' but is softer. The deep red leaves of *Heuchera* 'Silver Scrolls' are similarly mottled silver (see Good Companions, below).

Lamiums often have silver markings on their foliage and are particularly useful on sites with poor soil. *Lamium maculatum* 'Beacon Silver' has superb silver-green foliage with just a narrow margin and veins of darker green. From a distance the overall effect is of a mat

of silver, studded in summer with pink-purple flowers. (See Good Companions, below, and see page 62.)

Mertensia virginica ♀, the Virginian cowslip, is a delightful woodland plant with smooth grey leaves and arching sprays of tubular violet-blue flowers in spring. Up to 40cm (16in) high, it mixes well with pulmonarias and dicentras.

Hosta-like, and no less impressive, are some of the **pulmonarias** (lungwort). Their silver-spotted foliage has earned them their names both botanical and colloquial. The wonderful *Pulmonaria* 'Margery Fish' ♀, 30cm (12in) tall, has leaves completely overlaid with silver-green, which look lovely with lilac-blue and mauve-pink spring flowers. (See also pages 63 and 115–16.)

Heuchera 'Mint Frost'

GOOD COMPANIONS

Plant *Hosta* 'Fragrant Blue' (1) with *Dicentra* 'Langtrees' ♀ (2): the large, bold leaves of the hosta set off the fern-like, silver-blue foliage of the dicentra and its pearly white flowers.

The silvery wine-red leaves of *Heuchera* 'Silver Scrolls' (3) contrast with the silver-green foliage of *Lamium maculatum* 'Beacon Silver' (4) and enhance its purple flowers.

Blue hostas

Hostas with blue leaves are mostly plants for semi-shade, where the sun cannot bleach or scorch the exquisite foliage. They offer some of the most stunning leaves in the garden: beautiful in their own right but also dramatic partners to other leaves and flowers. Many bloom in mid- to late summer, producing stems of tubular flowers in white and shades of pink to lilac.

They make excellent subjects for pots, their waxy blue-green hues associating well with both the matt earth tones of terracotta and the shinier oriental glazes. Although still at risk from slugs and snails, blue-leaved hostas seem to suffer less damage than other hostas.

When planting in groups, give each plant plenty of room to grow. Light foliage subjects such as dicentras are perfect partners, contrasting well with the boldness of the hosta leaves.

There are innumerable named hosta varieties, often having only minor differences between them. Such

Hosta 'Fragrant Blue', at 20cm (8in) high and 30cm (12in) across, is one of the smaller hostas, with small, smooth, heart-shaped leaves of blue-green. Fragrant, pale lavender flowers are carried above the foliage on leafy stems in midsummer.

subtleties are really of concern only to collectors: simply choose varieties of a good colour with a leaf shape that you find pleasing.

Hosta 'Blue Umbrellas' is the best blue variety for a sunny site, with plenty of moisture. The large leathery leaves are convexly curved on stiff stalks. Height 60cm (24in), spread 1m (40in). Very pale lilac flowers in midsummer.

OTHER BLUE HOSTAS

Hosta 'Blue Angel' ♥ Faster-growing than *Hosta sieboldiana* var. *elegans* and has better flowers.

Hosta 'Blue Moon' Slender heart-shaped leaves of a wonderful blue. Height and spread 25cm (10in).

Hosta 'Silvery Slugproof' One of the most resistant to slugs and snails. Grows 40cm (16in) high, 1m (40in) across.

Hosta 'Halcyon' ♥ has elegant blue leaves and greyish-lavender flowers rising above them in mid-summer. The blue is most intense in shade where, in moist soil, the plant will reach 50cm (20in) high, 1m (40in) across. The pointed leaves are narrow on young plants, wider on more mature specimens. Excellent for a pot.

Hosta 'Blue Wedgwood' is a smaller hosta reaching 30cm (12in) in height by 60cm (24in) across. The wavy-edged, pointed leaves are intense blue-green. Pale lavender flowers are carried on straight stems above the foliage in midsummer.

Hosta sieboldiana var. *elegans* ♥ is the classic big blue hosta, with large, cupped, corrugated, silver-blue leaves. In midsummer, pale lilac flowers are borne in silver-blue spikes, rarely higher than the leaves. Height is 60cm (24in), spread 1m (40in). *Hosta* 'Big Daddy' is similar but with rounded, more cupped leaves.

SEASONS

Summer is the season for herbaceous perennials: as the flowering shrubs complete their spring display, perennials take on the star role. Making the most of the leafy backdrop of their woody neighbours, they fill the garden with a pageant of colour. As the heat of summer dies away, autumn flowers begin to shine in the warm light. Later on their faded remains are decorated with frost and snow, an effect surpassed only by the clear beauty of delicate winter flowers – until the ground awakens in a carpet of fresh spring foliage and bright new blooms.

RIGHT: Penstemons, bronze fennel and lilies in a summer garden

Early spring

As winter releases its grip, the garden becomes a place full of promise, with fresh shoots, unfurling leaves and jewel-like flowers. Early spring is a time for preparation: soil conditioning, planting and division are just some of the early annual tasks. Plans for a new or refurbished border can now take the first steps towards becoming reality. Any committed gardener will agree: the anticipation and creation of a new garden feature is one of the greatest of pleasures.

The fresh green shoots of herbaceous perennials appear among the fading foliage and flowers of spring bulbs at East Lambrook Manor, Somerset.

Bergenias (elephant's ears) produce evergreen rosettes of large rounded, leathery, glossy leaves. The foliage of most varieties takes on some kind of winter colouring, from subtle bronzing and reddening on the upper surface, to bold ruby red on the underside. As spring approaches, stems in shades of light green to dark red carry clusters of bell- or funnel-shaped flowers, which may be white, pale pink, rose-pink, salmon pink or almost red.

Originating from central and eastern Asia, bergenias are found in moist woods, meadows and moorland. They are hardy perennials, most tough enough to endure the Siberian winters. The plants spread slowly to form dense ground cover that suppresses all but the most determined weeds. They are truly useful garden plants, thriving in both sun and shade, although a site in full sun certainly improves flower quantity and quality. (See also page 61.)

Bergenia ciliata, a distinctive Himalayan beauty, has large, rounded, densely hairy leaves, 35cm (14in) long, and short red stems, 25cm (10in) high, bearing tight clusters of white or sometimes pink-blushed flowers in spring. Although very hardy, it behaves as a deciduous plant in exposed areas, and a sheltered position brings the bonus of glorious burnished winter foliage.

Bergenia cordifolia 'Purpurea' ♥ was praised by Gertrude Jekyll for its

Bergenia purpurascens

Bergenia 'Silberlicht' (SILVERLIGHT)

Brunnera macrophylla

Brunnera macrophylla 'Dawson's White'

beauty in both winter and summer. Its rounded to heart-shaped, thick, fleshy, deep green leaves, to 30cm (12in) long, are gently puckered, with purple tints in autumn and winter. Magenta flowers on

A SELECTION OF GOOD BERGENIA HYBRIDS

All do well in moist soil in sun or shade. Flowers are produced from early to late spring.

Bergenia 'Abendglocken' (EVENING BELLS) Large, glossy green leaves, reddening in autumn, and semi-double crimson flowers.

Bergenia 'Abendglut' (EVENING GLOW) Mid- to dark green leaves, ruby red beneath, turning maroon in winter, with semi-double magenta-crimson flowers.

Bergenia 'Bressingham White' ♥ Broad, deep green leaves and pure white flowers.

Bergenia 'Bressingham Ruby' Foliage colours in winter to glowing red-purple with copper tints. Red-purple flowers.

Bergenia 'Morgenröte' (MORNING RED) ♥ Deep green leaves and deep carmine-pink flowers; often blooms again in midsummer.

Bergenia 'Silberlicht' (SILVERLIGHT) ♥ (above centre) Rounded, gently scalloped mid-green leaves. White flowers age to pink.

Bergenia 'Wintermärchen' (WINTER FAIRY TALES) Deep green leaves with red undersides, bronzed in winter. Dark pink-red flowers.

tall red stems, up to 60cm (24in) high, appear in late winter to early spring. (See Good Companions, page 117.)

Bergenia purpurascens ♥ produces narrow leaves, 10–25cm (4–10in) long, which are held more upright than most; they are deep green above and purple-red on the undersides. In autumn the upper surface becomes dark beetroot red, the underside rich mahogany. In mid- and late spring, rich brown-red stems, 45cm (18in) high, bear nodding purple-red flowers.

Brunneras, members of the borage family, are native to eastern Europe, where they grow in light woodland and scrub. In the garden they are excellent at the edge of a border or as ground cover; they are also useful in containers in shade, perhaps at the base of a Japanese maple (*Acer*). The pretty blue flowers offer a perennial alternative to the much-loved biennial forget-me-nots (*Myosotis*). They look wonderful against a backdrop of dark foliage such as a

PROTECTING BERGENIAS FROM VINE-WEEVIL

Bergenias can be prone to attack by vine-weevil. Problems are indicated by notching around the leaf edge, and eventually the plant collapses as the roots are destroyed by vine-weevil larvae. Treat in autumn and early spring with a suitable systemic insecticide or use a biological control.

privet or laurel hedge and are delightful beneath shrubs with silver foliage such as *Elaeagnus* 'Quicksilver' ♥.

Brunneras prefer moist but well-drained soil, and will tolerate full sun as long as air movement is good. The variegated forms dislike being baked: the leaf margins are prone to browning when plants are dry.

Brunnera macrophylla ♥ has dark green foliage and a profusion of bright blue flowers, on stems 45cm (18in) high, from early spring onwards. It is a tougher character than the variegated forms. 'Dawson's White' brightens the spring garden with its heart-shaped mid-green leaves, generously edged with white. Delicate stems of sky-blue flowers contrast with the foliage. 'Hadspen Cream' ♥ is similar but widely thought superior. 'Jack Frost' has become the brunnera of choice for designers and gardeners alike. Its large heart-shaped leaves look metallic silver with a network of mid-green veins, and they make a stunning canvas for its sky-blue flowers (see page 106). **'Langtrees'** is an exceptionally good ground-cover plant for shade. It has dark green leaves, generously spotted silver-grey, and the same sky-blue flowers.

MAINTENANCE OF BRUNNERAS

Shoots of some variegated varieties may occasionally revert to green; these should be removed by cutting them off at the base. With brunneras grown for their foliage, remove the flower stems as they fade. This presents a sharper foliage effect that will stay looking good throughout summer and well into autumn.

The cheerful daisy flowers of leopard's bane or **doronicums** are a delight in the spring garden, rivalling the display of many summer-flowering daisy-like plants. Native to Europe, south-west Asia and Siberia, they are found in woodland, scrub, meadows, heathlands and rocky habitats; in the garden they do best in moist, well-drained, humus-rich soil, in sun or partial shade. Slowly spreading or clump-forming plants growing from rhizomes or tubers, they have mid-green, oval, pointed leaves, often toothed and heart-shaped at the base. The yellow flowers with slightly darker centres are carried on branched stems, either singly or in clustered heads. They last well as cut flowers.

Doronicum 'Miss Mason' � is the best single-flowered cultivar, producing golden yellow blooms on 45cm (18in) stems with bright green leaves. This is a good choice to set against the shiny copper bark of *Prunus serrula* ♈. A much taller cultivar, growing to 90cm (3ft) high, *Doronicum* × *excelsum* 'Harpur Crewe' puts on an outstanding display, with large yellow flowers borne three or more on a stem. *Doronicum plantagineum*, a native of Europe, also produces a wonderful show of large,

Doronicum plantagineum

Epimedium × versicolor 'Sulphureum'

golden yellow flowerheads, on stems up to 80cm (32in) high. The foliage dies back soon after flowering, making this a good species for naturalizing in grass. A dwarf cultivar, popular for its tidy, compact habit, *Doronicum* 'Little Leo' is less than 30cm (12in) tall; it is ideal to plant with forget-me-nots (*Myosotis*) and dwarf spring bulbs. *Doronicum orientale* 'Frühlingspracht' (SPRING BEAUTY) reaches 60cm (24in); its double flowers are bright and sunny, but it lacks the charm of the single varieties.

Epimediums (also known as bishop's mitre and barrenwort) are not widely cultivated, but these are undemanding treasures and deserve more attention. Clump-forming, hardy perennials, no more than 30cm (12in) in height, they may be deciduous, semi-evergreen or fully evergreen. Their pointed, heart-shaped, fresh green leaves mature to bronzed leathery shields with gently spined margins. Early spring sees the arrival of slender stems of pendulous, star-like flowers in white, lilac, pink, red, purple or yellow. The flowers clearly resemble those of berberis, which belong to the same family.

Their native habitat is the scrub and woodland of East Asia and parts of the Mediterranean. In the garden they thrive in rich, moist, well-drained soil, enjoying the dappled shade of shrubs or trees. Plant container-grown plants in spring; they quickly become established and soon spread, forming excellent ground cover. Seedlings often arise in the most unlikely of places, flourishing in small *(continued on page 114)*

GOOD COMPANIONS

The evergreen *Epimedium* × *versicolor* 'Sulphureum' ♈ (1), with its copper-bronzed foliage, mingles happily with grasses and spring bulbs such as bluebells (*Hyacinthoides non-scripta*) and *Anemone blanda* ♈ (2), and is especially effective beneath trees with attractive bark such as the black birch, *Betula nigra* (3).

Euphorbias

Euphorbia is a fascinating genus, containing a variety of plants ranging from cacti and poinsettias to some favourite hardy perennials. Herbaceous euphorbias are often thought of as plants for shade but most prefer an open site and a reasonable amount of sun. Many hail from Mediterranean regions, so they enjoy good drainage and resent being waterlogged.

At home in traditional planting schemes as well as in contemporary settings, euphorbias work well with other bold foliage plants such as phormiums and look good in gravel and among paving. Some of the smaller forms make excellent ground cover; larger evergreen varieties are excellent for providing structure in a planting and can fulfil the role played by evergreen shrubs. All contribute to the spring garden with their fresh green-yellow flowerheads, which last until early summer. (See also pages 57, 90, 96 and 122.)

All euphorbias contain a milky sap that can irritate the skin and eyes. Take great care when handling the plant, particularly when cutting the stems.

Euphorbia characias subsp. *wulfenii* 'Lambrook Gold' ♀ (above left) and 'John Tomlinson' ♀ (above right) are large, evergreen, yellow-flowered forms, 1.2m (4ft) high.

Euphorbia polychroma ♀ is lower growing than most, at 45cm (18in), and makes a stunning rounded plant with fresh green leaves and a profusion of bright yellow flowerheads. Deciduous.

Euphorbia characias has a neat, shrub-like habit up to 1.2m (4ft) high, its many stout stems clothed with narrow, grey-green, often bluish, evergreen leaves. In early spring large bold flowerheads appear, made up of cup-like bracts in varying shades of yellow-green, with purple-brown or black nectar glands at the centre.

Euphorbia palustris ♀ has tall, slender stems, 1m (40in) or more high, clad in deciduous, oblong-lance-shaped pale green leaves and bearing striking heads of golden yellow flowers. It likes a moist site.

OTHER GOOD EUPHORBIAS

Euphorbia characias subsp. *characias* 'Humpty Dumpty' Very compact and dense, only 45cm (18in) tall.

Euphorbia characias subsp. *wulfenii* ♀ Often confused with the species (see below left), but supposedly is taller, with larger flowerheads of a more reliable yellow-green.

Euphorbia cyparissias 'Fens Ruby' Fine stems of feathery, needle-like, glaucous purple deciduous foliage and green-yellow flowers. Only 20cm (8in) high. (See page 117.)

Euphorbia × *martini* ♀ Pretty yellow-green flowers and evergreen purple-tinged foliage. Compact in habit, and 60–75cm (24–30in) high; good for small gardens.

Euphorbia myrsinites ♀ Prostrate species, with evergreen succulent blue-green leaves on sprawling stems. Bright yellow-green flowerheads. Must have sun and good drainage.

Helleborus argutifolius

Helleborus foetidus

SOME GOOD EPIMEDIUMS

Epimedium grandiflorum 'Crimson Beauty' Deep red buds opening to crimson flowers. Deciduous, fresh green foliage.

Epimedium grandiflorum 'Rose Queen' ♀ Large pink flowers. Deciduous green foliage.

Epimedium × *rubrum* ♀ (see page 62) Semi-evergreen leaves are red when young and old; tiny crimson and yellow flowers. One of the best foliage plants for ground cover.

Epimedium × *versicolor* 'Sulphureum' ♀ (see page 112) Yellow flowers and copper-red evergreen foliage.

Epimedium × *versicolor* 'Versicolor' Light to dark pink flowers with yellow centres and coppery evergreen foliage.

Epimedium × *youngianum* 'Niveum' ♀ Pendent, pure white flowers. Bronzed deciduous foliage.

Epimedium × *youngianum* 'Yenomoto' Similar to 'Niveum' but has larger flowers and green deciduous leaves.

pockets of soil in paving and at the foot of a wall or steps. (See also page 62.)

Hellebores do much to lift our spirits in the darkest days of the year, but they are by no means confined to the winter months. The many beautiful forms of *Helleborus* × *hybridus*, the Lenten rose (see pages 180–81), continue their lavish display into early spring. Alongside them other outstanding hellebores begin to perform.

Helleborus argutifolius ♀ (formerly known as *Helleborus corsicus*) has handsome, stout, bushy stems clad in evergreen, leathery, dark green leaves. Each is divided into three segments gently edged with spines and exhibiting a faint network of pale green veins. In early spring of the second year, stems 1m (40in) tall are topped with slightly pendent, cup-shaped flowers in the palest green, lasting for a number of weeks. Rather shrub-like in habit, this Mediterranean beauty is very useful for a mixed border or it can be used as a specimen plant in gravel or alongside paving. (See also page 103.)

Helleborus foetidus ♀ is a native of southern Europe and Britain, and is also known as the stinking hellebore because of the odour given off by the foliage when bruised. Even so, its dark, glossy, deeply divided, evergreen leaves have long ensured its popular use in gardens. *Helleborus foetidus* grows to 80cm (32in). Flowers start arriving at the end of winter, borne at the top of mature stems: clusters of pendent, bell-shaped, pale green blooms usually delicately tipped with purple.

Helleborus lividus ♀ is another Mediterranean beauty, native to Majorca; it is slightly less hardy than *Helleborus argutifolius*, so in cold areas

GROWING SPRING-FLOWERING HELLEBORES

All early spring hellebores should be sited in full sun or light shade, avoiding icy cold winds, and in free-draining, neutral to alkaline soil. Cut out the flowered stems as they deteriorate to allow fresh foliage to come through.

will need protection from frost. Stems of purple-green are clothed in leathery silvery-green leaves, each with three oblong-elliptic leaflets, lightly toothed. All have fine creamy-white veins, and the leaf stalks have a pink-purple flush, which extends through the main veins beneath. In early spring of the plant's second year, purplish-green stalks, 45cm (18in) high, bear clusters of bowl-shaped creamy-green flowers, lightly flushed with pink or purple.

Helleborus × *sternii* is a popular hybrid between *Helleborus argutifolius* and *Helleborus lividus*, with many of its parents' attributes. A seed-raised plant, it may sometimes look more like one parent than the other, but it is always relatively dwarf, seldom exceeding 40cm (16in) tall. Two reliable strains are **Blackthorn Group** ♀, with purple

Omphalodes cappadocica 'Starry Eyes'

Pulmonaria 'Roy Davidson'

Pulmonaria saccharata 'Leopard'

stems, clearly veined grey-green leaves, and flowers suffused purple-pink; and **'Boughton Beauty'**, which has pink-red stems, mid-green leaves with cream veins, and flowers that are green inside and satin pink-red to purple outside. Both are in full flower in early spring.

Omphalodes (navelwort) are little-known, yet fantastic garden plants. Once established in rich, moist soil, these hardy evergreens will reward with a long period of bloom from early spring onwards. Hard frosts may damage the foliage, although their preference for a shady site affords enough protection in all but extreme conditions. Be prepared to fend off slugs and snails looking for an early meal.

The most favoured species is *Omphalodes cappadocica* ♀, a Turkish woodland native that forms a spreading clump just over 20cm (8in) high. The slender, dark red-brown stems carry numerous small, five-petalled, inky-blue forget-me-not flowers. **'Alba'** is pure white, while the popular **'Cherry Ingram'** ♀ has larger flowers in rich, deep blue. **'Starry Eyes'** is a similar shade, but each petal boasts a fine white margin.

Pulmonarias (lungwort) are hardy perennials originating from Europe and Asia, where they are found growing freely on mountains, in woodland and at streamsides. As garden plants, they have many attributes: attractive foliage, wonderful early spring flowers, and the ability to thrive in relatively poor soil in sun or shade. Of the many varieties and cultivars, virtually all are evergreen and some only shed their leaves just before flowering, after which they soon regrow. Many have ornately marked foliage, which may be flashed, spotted or variegated with silver-white. (See also page 106.) Seldom bothered by slugs or snails, they present a real alternative to dwarf hostas for foliage effect. None grows to more than about 30cm (12in) high, and all have numerous delicate,

OTHER GOOD PULMONARIAS

OTHER GOOD PULMONARIAS

Pulmonaria **'Lewis Palmer'** ♀ See page 63.

Pulmonaria longifolia **'Ankum'** Long-lasting mauve-blue flowers throughout spring.

Pulmonaria OPAL (**'Ocupol'**) Mid-green, silver-centred leaves that show off pearly-blue flowers.

Pulmonaria **'Roy Davidson'** (top right) Pale ice-blue flowers above strongly spotted foliage.

Pulmonaria **'Victorian Brooch'** Magenta-coral flowers set against white-spotted, mid-green foliage.

funnel-shaped flowers, which may be white, pink, red, violet or purple to deep blue, some displaying both pink and blue flowers in the same cluster.

Pulmonaria saccharata is the best known of those with dual-coloured blooms. The old cultivar **'Mrs Moon'** is a fine example: it has felty leaves heavily spotted with silver-white and a good mix of pink and blue flowers. **'Leopard'** is one of a number of pink varieties, with flowers of a crushed strawberry shade and well-spotted leaves.

Pulmonaria **'Sissinghurst White'** ♀ is the only widely grown variety derived from the common lungwort, *Pulmonaria officinalis*. Its pure white bells brighten a shady spot, and the fresh green, white-spotted leaves complement the pale blue of *Chionodoxa luciliae* (glory of the snow) and *Anemone blanda* ♀.

115

Pulsatilla vulgaris

Pulmonaria longifolia, widespread in western Europe, is a reliably tough plant with narrower, white-spotted leaves and usually blue flowers. It is more tolerant of drought than other pulmonarias. The cultivar *Pulmonaria longifolia* 'Bertram Anderson' is taller, with longer, narrower leaves and a profusion of rich blue flowers.

In most gardens the pasque flower, *Pulsatilla vulgaris* ♀, is grown as an alpine: a sunny, free-draining situation is the key to success. Like most plants from mountain regions, pulsatillas are hardy but hate the wet of winter. On heavy soil dig in plenty of shingle, grit or sand before planting; alternatively grow pulsatillas in a raised alpine scree bed or in a container.

The emerging foliage is covered in fine silvery-white hair and unfolds to mid-green, fern-like, feathery leaves. In spring short stems bear individual, gently nodding, bell-shaped flowers of silky texture, often purple-blue, but sometimes white or red, with vibrant golden yellow-orange stamens. These are followed by long-lasting, rounded, fluffy white seedheads. Several named cultivars exist, all growing to about 20cm (8in) high.

Pulsatilla alpina, the alpine pasque flower, forms a clump of finely divided mid-green foliage, above which short stems, 25cm (10in) high, bear showy, cup-shaped white flowers. The species grows on chalk while *Pulsatilla alpina* subsp. *apiifolia* ♀, with yellow flowers, grows on acid soil. Flowers and stems are covered in soft, silky hair. *Pulsatilla halleri* ♀ is slightly later to flower, with erect, silky bells of lilac to lavender-blue on 20cm (8in) stems.

Pulsatilla patens is the eastern pasque flower of Russian Siberia. In North America, the same species is celebrated as the prairie crocus, floral emblem of both Manitoba and South Dakota. Here it is found in mountains, although it makes its full impact in the vast plains, where its upright, cupped flowers, on stems only 15cm (6in) high, create a sea of blue-purple (occasionally white), followed by a carpet of fluffy white seedheads.

Symphytums, or comfreys, can be found in a range of habitats from Europe to North Africa and Asia. Fairly coarse plants growing from rhizomes, they have large crinkled, deciduous foliage and usually branched, leafy stems topped with clusters of pendent tubular flowers. They often start to flower in early spring and go on into summer; some may bloom again in autumn if cut back after the first flush. Symphytums grow well on any moist soil, and the thick carpet of foliage thrives in shady situations, keeping weeds to a minimum. They are excellent for ground cover under rhododendrons, and the rich reddish-brown foliage of *Lysimachia ciliata* 'Firecracker' ♀ (see page 91) is an attractive planting partner where soil is not too dry.

Symphytum caucasicum ♀ has oval to lance-shaped, deeply veined leaves, mid-green in colour. A tough, reliable ground-cover plant, 60cm (24in) high, it often goes unnoticed until spring, when it produces tight clusters of tubular

Symphytum caucasicum

flowers in an intensely bright ink-blue – a stunning shade, which rivals that of anchusas and delphiniums.

Symphytum ibericum, 40cm (16in) high, has pleasant creamy-yellow flowers, opening from red-tipped buds. The popular symphytums 'Hidcote Blue' and 'Hidcote Pink', originating from Hidcote Manor in Gloucestershire, are possible hybrids of this species. The hybrid *Symphytum* × *uplandicum* is distinctive in habit with upright, well-branched stems, up to 2m (6ft) high, clad in coarse, lance-shaped leaves. In late spring, clusters of pink-violet buds open to lilac-blue tubular flowers. (See also pages 63 and 101.)

Members of the lily family, **trilliums** are spectacular spring-flowering plants, originating from woodland and scrub in North America and, to a lesser extent, the western Himalayas and north-east Asia. The name *trillium*, from the Latin for 'three', refers to the fact that the leaves, petals and sepals are all borne in groups of three.

Trillium erectum ♀ (birth root) has stems up to 50cm (20in) high, each with three oval, glossy, mid-green leaves. Above the foliage, a short, arching stalk bears a single outward-facing, cupped, deep red-purple flower, occasionally white or yellow, with incurved petals.

Trillium grandiflorum

Trillium ovatum also grows to 50cm (20in), its stems topped with three oval to rounded mid-green leaves, above which appears a loosely cupped flower. The pure white, oval petals open fully to reveal mid-yellow stamens in the centre. *Trillium grandiflorum* ♀, also known as wake robin, is very similar, except that the large white petals have gently wavy edges and fade to pale pink with age. It is also slightly shorter, at 40cm (16in).

Trillium luteum ♀, too, has stems of up to 40cm (16in) tall, each proudly holding three mid-green leaves strongly marbled with pale green-white. The upward-facing flowers have narrow, pale yellow petals, sometimes bronze-green, and are sweetly scented *Trillium sessile* (toad-shade) is similar in habit and leaf markings, but generally shorter, at only 30cm (12in), with deep red-maroon, narrow-petalled flowers.

GROWING TRILLIUMS

Available from only a few specialist nurseries, trilliums are expensive to buy. If purchased as dormant plants, check the rhizomes are firm and healthy. Ideally buy in early spring, when the first flush of growth is visible. They require cool deep or partial shade, provided by large shrubs or small trees, and humus-rich, moist but well-drained soil, preferably neutral to acid. Once established, trilliums perform well, but try to avoid disturbing them.

GOOD COMPANIONS

The vivid greenish-yellow flowers of *Euphorbia cyparissias* 'Fens Ruby' (1) stand out sharply against the velvety foliage of the purple sage, *Salvia officinalis* 'Purpurascens' ♀ (2).

The large, glossy purple leaves of *Bergenia purpurascens* ♀ (3) contrast with the soft, woolly grey foliage of *Stachys byzantina* ♀ (4).

Late spring

As the days lengthen, colours intensify in the garden. Plants grow quickly in the warmer temperatures and leaves unfurl from the pale acid green of early spring towards the full emerald shades of summer. Spring-flowering trees and shrubs are laden with blossom, and tulips and wallflowers colour pots and borders. Herbaceous perennials fill out to cover the bare soil; suddenly all those empty spaces in the borders seem to be occupied.

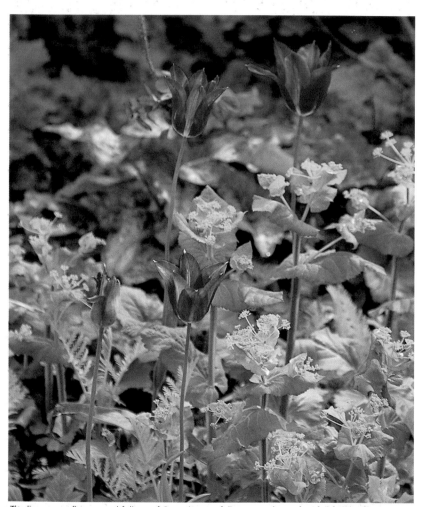

The lime-green flowers and foliage of *Smyrnium perfoliatum* are the perfect foil for the elegant glowing blooms of *Tulipa* 'Mariette'.

Ajuga genevensis (blue bugle) forms a spreading clump of strong mid-green, oblong-rounded foliage, with stems 30cm (12in) tall carrying whorls of dark blue flowers. Its flowering height lends it to naturalistic combinations with grasses, ferns and primulas.

Ajuga pyramidalis forms a rosette of spreading, dark green foliage and produces spires of tightly packed, violet-blue to deep blue flowers on 20cm (8in) stems. Pink- or white-flowered forms also occur naturally.

Ajuga reptans has spreading, spoon-shaped, dark green foliage, with 15cm (6in) spikes of sapphire flowers. The species itself is invasive, but the cultivars are less badly behaved. Some have fancy, winter-hardy foliage, the most common being the deep bronze *Ajuga reptans* 'Atropurpurea' (see also page 86), cream-splashed *Ajuga reptans* 'Variegata', and bronze, red

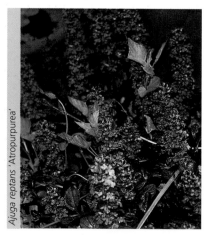

Ajuga reptans 'Atropurpurea'

Commonly known as bugle, **ajugas** are grown mainly for the metallic beauty of their often evergreen foliage, but the showy flowers are a delight in spring. Carried on spikes 5–15cm (2–6in) high, the tiers of tubular, two-lipped blooms may be mid- to dark blue, purple, pink or white. Ajugas' natural habitats are varied: hedgerows, woodland clearings, young coppice, scrub and meadows, all areas where moisture-retentive, slightly acid soil may be found.

Ajuga reptans 'Catlin's Giant'

Anchusa azurea 'Loddon Royalist'

Anthemis tinctoria 'E.C. Buxton'

Anthemis tinctoria 'Sauce Hollandaise'

and cream *Ajuga reptans* 'Multicolor'. The less ostentatious foliage of *Ajuga reptans* 'John Pierpoint' is glossy mid-green, which serves as a fine backdrop to the larger, pure white flowers. The same can be said of *Ajuga* 'Little Court Pink', a mid-pink form.

Ajuga reptans 'Catlin's Giant' ♈ is large enough to mix with the big boys of the border. In its preferred conditions of rich, moist soil and partial shade, the lush, rounded, glossy leaves of bronzed purple can be 15cm (6in) long. Tightly packed spikes of dark blue flowers bring its height to above 20cm (8in).

The flowers of **anchusas** provide one of the most stunning blues in the late spring border. Native to Europe, Africa and Asia, they grow well in moist but well-drained soil, with plenty of sun. The best species for gardens is *Anchusa azurea*, a herbaceous perennial of exceptional flower power, sadly often found to be short-lived; it can, however, be propagated from basal shoot or root cuttings. In favourable conditions, it will perform for a number of years, forming a rosette of narrow, lance-shaped, hairy mid-green leaves and branching stems, up to 1.5m (5ft) high, clad in numerous cup-like, vibrant ink-blue flowers, which mature to blue-purple. *Anchusa azurea* 'Loddon Royalist' ♈ is the most prized variety, with equally vibrant deep blue flowers borne on sturdy, self-supporting stems 90cm (3ft) tall. *Anchusa azurea* 'Opal' is of similar height, and just as floriferous, with powder-blue flowers.

The delightful, bright daisy flowers of *Anthemis* radiate their own sunshine, over a long period from late spring through to late summer. Mixing well with Mediterranean companions such as lavender, rosemary and thyme, they are sun-loving perennials similar in their requirements to salvias and many of the herbaceous geraniums. Anthemis fare best in free-draining, fertile soil; they dislike winter wetness. Many varieties are excellent for cutting.

Anthemis tinctoria has a number of cultivars, all with fern-like foliage that varies from mid- to dark green, some with downy grey on the underside, and all flowering at 60–80cm (24–32in). By late spring the sensational show of *Anthemis tinctoria* 'E.C. Buxton' is well under way, the flowerheads having soft yellow petals surrounding golden yellow, button-like centres. One of the most popular is *Anthemis tinctoria* 'Sauce Hollandaise', with pale cream-white flowers. Much bolder in colour are *Anthemis* 'Beauty of Grallagh', which is golden orange, and the pure gold *Anthemis* 'Grallagh Gold'.

Anthemis sancti-johannis, native to south-west Bulgaria, is a short-lived perennial, more often used as annual bedding. Borne on stems 60–90cm (24–36in) tall, the golden flowerheads of short petals make a strong impact. Its meeting with *Anthemis tinctoria* has resulted in a number of hybrids.

The diminutive **Anthemis punctata subsp. *cupaniana*** ♈, only 30cm (12in)

BLUE, WHITE AND SILVER COMBINATIONS

Blue and white flowers are always an appealing combination in the garden. Being among the bluest of them all, anchusas are natural planting partners. *Anchusa azurea* mixes well with the white willowherb, *Chamerion angustifolium* 'Album' (see page 133), and the pale lilac of perennial honesty, *Lunaria rediviva* (see page 126). It creates a cool, refreshing mix with the silver of *Artemisia ludoviciana* 'Valerie Finnis' ♈ (see page 51) or the multi-stems of hard-pruned *Eucalyptus gunnii* ♈.

Columbines (Aquilegia)

Commonly known as columbine or granny's bonnet, aquilegias are familiar favourites from the crowded borders of the cottage garden. The British native *Aquilegia vulgaris*, long cultivated in English gardens, was joined by species from Europe and North America as early as the 17th century, and many years of close association have produced a great variety of hybrids.

From a rosette of deciduous foliage come long-stalked, mid-green or blue-green leaves, each made up of three leaflets. In late spring and early summer, fine stems, up to 1m (40in) high and sometimes branched, carry clusters of teardrop buds opening into bell-shaped flowers, which in some forms have spurs. Single-coloured or bicoloured blooms of white, pink, red, blue to purple-mauve and even yellow and orange can be found in numerous shades and combinations.

In the wild, aquilegias are found in damp woodland, marshes and meadows; in the garden they thrive in rich, moist, free-draining soil in full sun or partial shade. On heavy, wet soils plants can be shorter-lived, often failing in winter. On light, well-drained soils

Aquilegia vulgaris is still widely cultivated in English gardens, and numerous selections and hybrids have arisen over the years.

aquilegias seed themselves rather too freely. Removing the flower stems once the blooms have faded prevents seeding and encourages a new flush of leaf growth.

Garden aquilegias can produce muddy-coloured offspring, and these are worth weeding out. Grow named hybrids in isolation, to prevent dilution of colours in the population.

Aquilegia vulgaris hybrids, growing up to 1m (40in) high, with a reliably robust constitution, are the most popular of aquilegias.
Aquilegia vulgaris **'Nivea'** ♀ (right) has erect stems of olive-green foliage carrying stunning, pure white flowers. *Aquilegia vulgaris* var. *stellata* **'Nora Barlow'** ♀ has large, spurless, pompon flowers in pale greenish white and red.
Aquilegia vulgaris **Vervaeneana Group** have yellow-variegated leaves and blue-mauve or pink flowers.

Aquilegia McKana Group, up to 70cm (28in) tall, have bright bicoloured flowers in shades of blue, yellow, red and white. These are short-lived perennials, but they will self-seed. Often used as early summer bedding.

Aquilegia alpina (alpine columbine) has compact foliage and stems 30cm (12in) tall carrying numerous ink-blue flowers, often tipped with white.

OTHER GOOD AQUILEGIAS

Aquilegia canadensis ♀ Lemon-yellow and scarlet flowers and dark fern-like foliage. Height 60cm (24in).

Aquilegia coerulea ♀ White and blue flowers on 60cm (24in) stems. Very hardy.

Aquilegia flabellata ♀ Compact habit, at 30cm (12in) high. Blue to purple petals tipped creamy white. Needs a moist, shady site.

Aquilegia longissima Dark and pale yellow flowers on 60cm (24in) stems. Short-lived but readily self-seeds.

tall, is worthy of special note. Its simple, long-lasting flowerheads of white petals and golden yellow centres work well with the fine silvery foliage. It is good for a dry, sunny wall or alongside paving. (See Good Companions, page 126.)

Cerinthe major '**Purpurascens**' is a captivatingly distinctive plant. Its fleshy growth is often a glaucous powdery blue. Branched stems are clad in spoon-shaped leaves, lightly spotted white, and bear unusual purple-mauve, tubular flowers, sometimes tipped in white or yellow, from spring all through summer. The clustered flowers are swathed in gentle folds of purple-flushed bracts that look almost iridescent. (See Good Companions, page 126.)

Found on clifftops, scrub and waste-land in the Mediterranean, cerinthes will grow in poor, free-draining garden soil. The bluish foliage of *Cerinthe major* 'Purpurascens' is more intense in plants that are carefully neglected. Grown as an annual, a biennial or a short-lived perennial, it is surprisingly hardy and reliably sets seed that germinates freely in the vicinity of the parent plant. It is an excellent mixer, combining superbly with purple foliage plants such as

Cerinthe major 'Purpurascens'

Dicentra spectabilis 'Alba'

heucheras and adding depth to silver planting. If buying seed choose a named variety: the offspring will more reliably produce those purple bracts.

Most gardeners know *Dicentra spectabilis* ♥, through its many years of cultivation as a cottage-garden plant. Usually called bleeding heart, it is also known by many other common names, including Dutchman's breeches and lady's locket. From late spring into early summer, gently arching, delicate stems, 90cm (3ft) high, present a succession of heart-shaped pink-red buds that, on opening, reveal inner petals of pure white. The foliage is distinctly beautiful: lush, mid-green, divided and almost fern-like, it makes a perfect setting for the flowers.

Most species of dicentra come from moist, wooded habitats in mountainous regions, often growing on stream banks. Cool, moist but well-drained, slightly alkaline soil brings the best results. The direct sun of midsummer often leads them to become dormant prematurely. Hybrid dicentras are good companions for hostas and ferns, and enjoy similar conditions. Their light, fern-like foliage is a useful contrast to heavier subjects and is every bit as important as the flowers. (See also pages 92–93.)

Dicentra spectabilis originates from Siberia, China and Korea, where the

Dicentra formosa

pure white form *Dicentra spectabilis* '**Alba**' ♥ is also found. Other species originate from North America, Japan and the Himalayas. Though less well known, many are excellent perennial plants for the garden.

Dicentra eximia comes from the eastern USA. The cool blue-green, finely divided leaves grow to 50cm (20in) long; pale to dark pink flowers hang daintily from arching stems, 30cm (12in) high, above the leaves, appearing in late spring and intermittently through to early autumn.

Dicentra formosa, from western North America, has deeply divided mid-green leaves, blue-green beneath, which form a tight, fern-like clump up to 60cm (24in) high. In late spring and early

Dicentra 'Bacchanal'

Euphorbia griffithii 'Fireglow'

summer, slender stems of up to 90cm (3ft) high bear rosy-pink buds, which open to pink flowers that fade to white. This species and the white form, *Dicentra formosa alba,* make excellent ground cover under shrubs and in semi-woodland situations.

Dicentra macrantha is much sought after: in late spring its short stems, 55cm (22in) high, bear creamy-yellow flowers, each up to 8cm (3in) long; the foliage is similar to that of *Dicentra spectabilis.* This Chinese beauty is not easy to grow, requiring shelter from wind and frost and protection from slugs. Moist but well-drained soil with plenty of organic matter is a must.

A SELECTION OF GOOD DICENTRA HYBRIDS

All of the following grow to about 30cm (12in) high.

Dicentra 'Bacchanal' ♥ (above)
Fine green foliage and deep red flowers.

Dicentra 'Langtrees' ♥ (see page 106) and *Dicentra* 'Pearl Drops' Both have silver-grey leaves and pink-flushed white flowers.

Dicentra 'Luxuriant' ♥ Fine foliage with showy red flowers.

Dicentra 'Stuart Boothman' ♥
Blue-grey foliage and dark pink flowers.

Euphorbia griffithii 'Fireglow' can be an invasive plant, with vigorous upright shoots growing from spreading underground rhizomes. In late spring its flame-coloured stems are topped with bright orange-red flowerheads framed by orange-flushed bright green leaves. The colour fades as the stems reach 1m (40in) high in midsummer. In autumn stems and leaves colour orange-red on plants in full sun, before dying down in winter. This is an excellent perennial for moist, fertile soil in sun or shade.

Euphorbia mellifera ♥ has stout shoots clad in lance-shaped leaves and forms a rounded bush growing 2m (6ft) high in a sheltered site. A native of Madeira, it is not regarded as being very hardy but it seems to tolerate low temperatures if soil is well drained. In late spring orange-brown flowerheads appear; these are honey-scented, hence the Latin name *mellifera.* The flowers are followed by waxy, rounded capsules. (For other euphorbias see page 113.)

Hesperis matronalis (sweet rocket) has been in cultivation since early times. It forms a loose rosette or clump of oval, pointed, dark green leaves, from which arise stems 90cm (3ft) tall carrying loose heads of fragrant, four-petalled, pale lilac to purple flowers. The scent is of

stocks, which are close relatives. The pure white *Hesperis matronalis* var. *albiflora* is a wonderful addition to a blue and white border; it also has a double form, 'Alba Plena'. *Hesperis matronalis* 'Lilacina Flore Pleno' has double lilac flowers.

Sweet rocket prefers full sun or light shade, in rich, moist but free-draining, slightly alkaline soil. Often a short-lived perennial or biennial, it should be cut back hard after flowering. The resulting flush of new growth will help with longevity, providing the plant is not crowded by neighbours or in wet soil. Ideally leave one plant to set seed: it will produce plentiful seedlings that can be transplanted. A member of the cabbage family, sweet rocket is prone to attacks by flea beetle, which can be controlled with an appropriate insecticide.

Hesperis matronalis

Irises are treasured for their extensive colour palette and the exquisite beauty of their complex flowers. Each of these is made up of three outer petals known as 'falls', which may be pendent, reflexed or spreading, and may have distinctive beards or crests; and three, usually smaller, inner petals known as 'standards'. These inner petals are often erect, but they may be horizontal or pendent. Many have evolved petal-like flaps to the flowers and some have ruffled or frilly petal edges. The foliage is often sword-like and upright, but

The architectural forms of *Euphorbia mellifera* and *Acanthus spinosus* combine well with stone and ceramic.

Iris lazica

many irises have distinctive fans of strap-shaped leaves. Most are deciduous, although a few are evergreen.

Irises originate from diverse natural habitats. In the garden they are grouped according to both physical make-up and the growing conditions they require. Some irises like dry, sunny situations. *Iris bucharica* ♥, for example, thrives in a hot, sunny site with free-draining soil and in these conditions it is hardy. Unlike other irises, it has short, broadly lance-shaped leaves in sheaths at intervals up rounded stems. In late spring, as the

stems reach 20–40cm (8–16in) high, the uppermost leaf axils bear pale to lemon-yellow, sometimes white, flowers.

A native of Turkey and the Caucasus, *Iris lazica* ♥ is similar to the winter-flowering *Iris unguicularis* ♥ (see page 179) in its fans of dark evergreen foliage, up to 30cm (12in) high. In late spring, it has stemless, lavender-blue flowers, with partly white falls spotted and veined lavender, each with a yellow stripe. Unlike other Unguicularis irises, it will thrive in light shade and moist soil.

The so-called crested irises prefer moist, humus-rich soil in full sun or part shade and many of these flower in spring. *Iris cristata* ♥, a native of the eastern USA, forms a fan of fresh, mid-green, lance-shaped leaves. Stemless blooms consist of blue-lilac petals, each with a blotch of white and a yellowish-orange crest on each fall. This is a striking iris, although it grows only 15cm (6in) tall; there is also a white form, *Iris cristata* 'Alba'. Broad, pale green leaves

make up the fan of *Iris milesii* ♥, and branching stems bear unusual, purple-splashed lavender-pink flowers, with yellow crests. It grows to 90cm (3ft) tall.

Lunaria annua (honesty), prized for its silver, papery, moon-like seedpods, is truly a biennial but is usually a perennial resident in the garden since it seeds so freely. In late spring and early summer, as the stems reach 80cm (32in) high, fine stalks carry clusters of four-petalled purple, sometimes white, flowers; these are followed by the translucent seed-pods, which are often dried for winter arrangements. An undemanding plant, it succeeds in many situations, although it is best in rich, moist, free-draining soil, in partial shade or full sun. Self-sown seedlings need thinning so that each one has enough space to develop. Purple honesty is an excellent mixer in the spring garden, superb with bluebells and lovely with the rich silky shades of hardy hybrid rhododendrons.

(continued on page 126)

123

Bearded irises

The largest selection of irises available comprises the modern cultivars of bearded irises, producing their distinctive flowers in an immense variety of colours from mid-spring into early summer. They are hybrids of often complex origin, although they are frequently incorrectly referred to as hybrids of *Iris germanica*. Growing from large, rounded surface rhizomes, they are classified by the height of the flowering stem. While the larger cultivars produce bold fans of sword-shaped, light green to green-blue foliage, the dwarf varieties often have a more random, dense arrangement of leaves; they also tend to flower earlier in the season than the medium to tall ones.

All need full sun to thrive and ripen the rhizomes. They like good drainage but benefit from moisture in the early part of the year and through the flowering period. They enjoy reasonably fertile soil, with plenty of organic matter added. Bearded irises can be planted as container-grown plants in spring or as bare, semi-dry rhizomes in autumn. If planting bare rhizomes, group them in threes, 30cm (12in) apart. They need to be set on or just below the soil surface; if they prove difficult to anchor in position, hold them in place with short canes or wire hoops.

Most varieties need lifting, dividing and replanting every three to four years, or when the rhizomes become overcrowded (see page 20). Many of the medium to tall bearded irises need support, as a windy, wet day can flatten the stems. Once the flowers fade, the foliage often becomes marked and can be quite unsightly. If leaves start to brown at the tips, they can be trimmed back to two-thirds or half their original height. Although this looks a little unnatural, it is tidier and less obtrusive than the fading foliage.

If bearded irises have one fault it is their relatively short flowering season. Because the rhizomes need to ripen in the sun, they are not suitable for planting among other perennials that will crowd and shade

In a softly harmonious planting, white *Geranium* clarkei 'Kashmir White' provides light cover at the feet of *Iris* 'Desert Song'.

them. Early tulips are useful to provide interest at the beginning of the season. *Nerine bowdenii*♥ and *Amaryllis belladonna*♥ are excellent to bring autumn colour to iris beds, particularly at the base of a wall. Low-growing sedums such as *Sedum acre* and *Sedum kamtschaticum* 'Variegatum'♥ can be planted to cover the soil between the plants.

GOOD DWARF BEARDED IRISES

'Brannigan' (above) Rich royal blue flowers with darker ink-blue fall petals.

'Green Spot' ♀ Greenish white with spotted green fall petals and yellow markings. Very early to flower.

'Mrs Nate Rudolph' Unusual, soft lavender-grey flowers flushed with gold.

'Southern Clipper' Free-flowering; fresh light blue flowers with darker spots.

GOOD MEDIUM BEARDED IRISES

'Aunt Martha' Frilly, pale yellow petals spotted white.

'Jasper Gem' Rich red-brown flowers flushed with gold.

'Rare Edition' (above) Eye-catching dark purple flowers with purple-edged white falls.

Dwarf bearded irises, height 20–40cm (8–16in), start to flower in mid-spring, just before the taller varieties. They are useful plants to prolong the interest in a bed devoted to bearded irises and combine well with low-growing plants such as helianthemums, *Helichrysum italicum* ♀ and *Artemisia schmidtiana* 'Nana' ♀. Their upright leaves and bold flowers provide a dramatic contrast to the fine foliage of most sun-loving plants. **'Laced Lemonade'** (above) is a softly pretty cultivar with frilly yellow petals and white beards.

Medium bearded irises reach 40–70cm (16–28in) tall. These have all of the dramatic flower quality of the tall varieties but without the possible problems of support; they are the ideal choice for more exposed sites and sit well at the front of a mixed border. They tend to flower earlier than the tall varieties, following on from the dwarf cultivars. In a border devoted to bearded irises they provide the essential link in the flowering season between tall and dwarf. **'Langport Wren'** ♀ (above) has magenta-brown flowers, strongly suffused black.

Tall bearded irises, growing to 70–90cm (28–36in), flower from late spring into early summer. These are the classic flag irises of the English garden, producing perhaps the most exotic and flamboyant blooms in the border. They benefit from some additional support when in full flower because of the weight of the blooms. They do not like to be crowded by their neighbours, but associate well with peonies, daylilies (hemerocallis) and geraniums. The flowers of **'Caliente'** (above) are deep velvety red-brown, suffused chocolate, with gold beards.

GOOD TALL BEARDED IRISES

'Dancer's Veil' Beautiful white ruffled flowers flushed violet.

'Frost and Flame' Frosty white petals and tangerine-flamed beards.

'Jane Phillips' ♀ Soft powder-blue, ruffled blooms. Vigorous.

'Stepping Out' ♀ Flowers of the palest lavender edged with purple.

'Top Flight' Deep apricot flowers with ruffled petals.

Lunaria annua var. albiflora

Lunaria annua var. albiflora 'Alba Variegata' has leaves margined creamy white and white flowers, while *Lunaria annua* **'Variegata'** has similar leaves but pinkish-purple flowers. Of those with green foliage, *Lunaria annua* var. *albiflora* ♀ has pure white flowers, and *Lunaria annua* **'Munstead Purple'** is dark red-purple.

Lunaria rediviva (perennial honesty) forms a strong clump that reaches 60–90cm (24–36in) in height, with more refined apple-green foliage, the margins gently toothed. The pale lilac flowers, carried loosely, are pleasantly fragrant and followed by the distinctive seed-pods, which are narrower than those of biennial honesty. Left to itself, perennial honesty will self-seed and become semi-naturalized. It is superb for providing tall ground cover in semi-shade and is most attractive in a woodland setting. (See Good Companions, below).

Mimulus (monkey flower or musk) are native to South Africa, Asia, Australia and the Americas, but three species have escaped from gardens in Britain and become naturalized in the countryside. *Mimulus luteus* is most commonly seen, its yellow, late spring flowers thriving alongside rivers and streams, which help to spread the seeds.

Mimulus **Highland hybrids** are garden cultivars with lush growth and many bright flowers, their bold, simple colours easily rivalling those of many annual bedding plants. From late spring into early summer, 20cm (8in) stems carry numerous trumpet-shaped flowers of orange (**'Highland Orange'**), pink (**'Highland Pink'**), rose-pink (**'Highland Pink Rose'**), red (**'Highland Red'** ♀) or yellow (**'Highland Yellow'**). Mimulus thrive in any moist, well-drained soil in full sun or light shade. By midsummer supplementary feeding may be required to maintain performance.

Other colourful cultivars are hybrids between the species *Mimulus guttatus* and *Mimulus luteus*. The early-flowering **Magic** and **Mystic** series offer a wide range of shades, including pastels.

Ranunculus aconitifolius

Ranunculus is a wonderful genus that includes many varied and garden-worthy plants; however, the notorious perennial weed *Ranunculus repens* (creeping buttercup) is the one that most gardeners know best. Native to temperate regions, ranunculus grow in a variety of conditions. Rich, moist soil is a basic requirement, although some dislike over-wet soil, especially in winter. Full to light shade is preferred, but some tolerate full sun.

Ranunculus aconitifolius, commonly known as bachelor's buttons, produces distinctive palmate, glossy, dark green leaves on branched stems of up to 60cm (24in). It is a favourite for its numerous white flowers, opening from red-tinged buds in late spring to early summer.

GOOD COMPANIONS

Perennial honesty, *Lunaria rediviva* (1), is good in combination with snowdrops such as *Galanthus nivalis* ♀ (2) as the emerging honesty covers the fading foliage of the snowdrop.

The fine silver foliage of *Anthemis punctata* subsp. *cupaniana* ♀ (3) complements the blue-green leaves of *Cerinthe major* 'Purpurascens' (4). Both enjoy poor, well-drained soil.

Solomon's seals (Polygonatum)

Commonly known as Solomon's seal, polygonatums are native to woodlands of North America, Europe, Asia, and Siberia. These are appealing garden plants, most with arching, leafy stems from which hang dainty, usually white, tubular flowers in late spring. Their natural elegance lends them both to structured contemporary plantings and to semi-naturalistic settings. The species native to Britain are found on chalk as well as acid soils, often in moist but well-drained places, although they may tolerate drier sites if shaded; they are ideal in a light woodland planting. Their potential to thrive in most gardens is evident: they will share a shady corner with pulmonarias, primulas, *Arum italicum*, hellebores, ferns and evergreen grasses such as *Carex pendula*. Late summer brings an early turn towards winter dormancy for Solomon's seal; by autumn, leaves and stems will become a pleasant shade of creamy yellow.

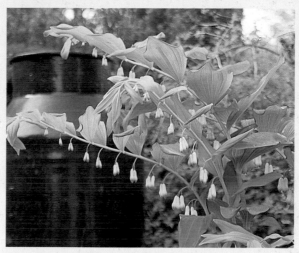

Polygonatum × *hybridum* enjoying a shady corner.

Several species are commonly cultivated, including *Polygonatum multiflorum*, *Polygonatum odoratum*♀ and *Polygonatum* × *hybridum*♀ – these are so alike that few gardeners are aware of which one they grow.

Polygonatum odoratum♀ (also known as David's harp as well as Solomon's seal) has arching stems, 85cm (34in) high, of oval olive-green leaves, with a charming cascade of white teardrop buds from the upper leaf axils. The white tubular flowers are lightly tipped green, and are followed by rounded black fruit. **'Flore Pleno'**♀ has double flowers strongly marked in green. *Polygonatum odoratum* var. *pluriflorum* **'Variegatum'**♀ (above) has attractive cream-edged foliage.

Polygonatum biflorum is an impressive architectural plant, commonly growing to about 1m (40in) tall, although many specimens reach double that height. It is similar to other Solomon's seals but the leaf undersides are finely hairy and veined. The flowers are greenish white, and are borne singly or in clusters of two to four.

Polygonatum stewartianum is distinctly different from other Solomon's seals: upright, rounded, boxy stems of mid-green flecked with reddish purple are clad in tiers of lance-shaped foliage. Above each tier appear clusters of up to four bell-shaped, pale creamy-pink flowers with faint red flecks. Height 20–90cm (8–36in).

Polygonatum × *hybridum* **'Striatum'** Has mid-green leaves with creamy-white stripes and green-tipped white flowers. Height 90cm (3ft). Grows much more slowly than most.

Ranunculus aconitifolius 'Flore Pleno'♀ is the double form, made up of layered, pure white petals.

The meadow buttercup, *Ranunculus acris*, is often considered a weed by gardeners in Europe but it is certainly worthy of a place in a wildflower meadow. *Ranunculus acris* 'Flore Pleno'♀, 40–80cm (16–32in) high, is the usual form cultivated, producing double, dark yellow flowers between late spring and early summer. Both will do well in full sun, but dislike wet soil.

Ranunculus constantinopolitanus forms a tidy clump of handsome foliage. Stems 20cm (8in) high are clad with attractive mid-green, deeply divided leaves; bright yellow, cup-like flowers appear from mid-spring through to mid-summer. The double form *Ranunculus constantinopolitanus* 'Plenus' bears blooms with layers of bright yellow petals; the central ones are lime green.

Ranunculus ficaria grows only 5cm (2in) tall, with heart-shaped, glossy leaves and bright yellow, saucer-shaped flowers in mid-spring. This species becomes dormant soon after flowering, especially when in full sun and dry soil. To control its spread, dig it out immediately after flowering, before the bulbs multiply. 'Brazen Hussy' has glossy, chocolate-brown foliage that sets off the flowers (see Good Companions, below right).

Tiarella 'Spring Symphony'

Smilacina racemosa♀ flowers from mid- to late spring and is an impressive sight when in full bloom. The plant forms a mass of unbranched stems, 80cm (32in) tall, carrying attractive oval, pointed leaves, their veins prominent on the fresh mid-green of the new growth. At the top of each stem, a conical head of short, branched stalks is crowded with small, star-shaped, white to cream, scented flowers. Often the flowers are succeeded by bright red berries, which stand out against the creamy-yellow autumn foliage.

In the wild, smilacinas can be found growing in rich, moist, well-drained soil, enjoying the partial or full shade of light woodland, in parts of Asia and in North and Central America. In cooler climates full sun will be tolerated. They are not suited to alkaline soils, which always result in poor growth. Any number of plants enjoying the same conditions work well in partnership with smilacinas, especially neighbours of striking form such as rodgersias, ligularias, rheums or evergreen ferns.

Smyrnium perfoliatum (commonly called perfoliate Alexanders) is actually a slow-growing biennial, but seeds itself readily, especially on light soils, and combines perfectly with perennials. Its lime-green spring flowers and foliage offer a lighter alternative to euphorbias and a taller, more definite form than that of alchemilla. It grows to a height of 60cm (24in). (See page 118.)

Tiarellas are commonly known as foam flower, because of the frothy flowers that rise above the low green foliage. Happy in a range of soils as long as they are moist and free-draining, they grow best in shade, although they do perform adequately, if slowly, in full sun. They combine well with hostas, bergenias and pulmonarias and with evergreen grasses and ferns.

Tiarella 'Spring Symphony' forms a tight semi-evergreen clump about 40cm (16in) high. The deeply divided, maple-like leaves are mid-green with an attractive red-brown stripe, bronzing in winter. Dark red flower spikes push through the foliage one after another, forming candle-like heads of numerous starry white flowers, which open from pink buds in early spring right through to autumn.

Smilacina racemosa

Tiarella cordifolia

Tiarella cordifolia ♀ produces more rounded, heart-shaped leaves of a lighter green, each with three to five distinct points and a jagged margin (see Good Companions, below right), while those of *Tiarella trifoliata* are palmate and mid-green, each with three distinct points. *Tiarella wherryi* ♀ is a parent of many of the new hybrids: its rounded leaves have three sharp points and are light green flushed to varying degrees with reddish maroon. The airy heads of white flowers often show a hint of pink. All three species range in height from 20 to 50cm (8–20in).

Tiarella 'Iron Butterfly' is one of many new selections; it has large, deeply divided mid-green leaves, with a striking dark red-black stripe on each segment, and flowers similar to those of *Tiarella* 'Spring Symphony'. *Tiarella* 'Jeepers Creepers' differs in its spreading habit, forming a dense carpet of green with red-black veining: an attractive ground-cover plant, useful in dappled shade. Both grow 30cm (12in) high.

Species of *Veronica* (speedwell) are widespread throughout Europe. Some colonize the margins of rivers and streams, others are found in moist meadows, light woodland and sunny grassland and on rocky hillsides. In the garden they are easy to grow in sun or in partial shade. Some are prone to mildew, but this is easily controlled with a proprietary fungicide.

Growing as thick ground cover, the stems of *Veronica peduncularis* 'Georgia Blue' are clad in rounded, toothed, glossy, mid-green leaves, tinged purple with maturity. From early spring through to early summer, a mass of small, saucer-shaped sapphire flowers covers the 10cm (4in) high stems.

The variety *Veronica austriaca* subsp. *teucrium* 'Knallblau' produces a multitude of blue spikes above lush grey-green foliage, from late spring onwards. Growing no more than 25cm (10in) high, it is perfect for a patio container or for the edge of a border. The lovely *Veronica austriaca* subsp. *teucrium* 'Crater Lake Blue' ♀ is taller, reaching 45cm (18in), with equally arresting flowers.

Veronica gentianoides ♀ is an old garden favourite. From tight winter rosettes develop thick, rounded, dark green leaves, slowly forming a mat. In late spring through into early summer, these produce stems 40cm (16in) tall, bearing a succession of pale to mid-blue flowers. *Veronica gentianoides* 'Alba' is white but rarely purely so: it usually exhibits a pleasing hint of blue.

Veronica spicata is tidy and compact in habit. Stems up to 60cm (24in) tall

Veronica gentianoides

bear lance-shaped, softly hairy leaves and generous spikes of small, bright blue flowers right through to the end of summer. The cultivars tend to be smaller plants, only about 30cm (12in) high: 'Heidekind' has green-grey foliage and raspberry-pink flowers; 'Rotfuchs' (RED FOX) is deep pink. *Veronica spicata* subsp. *incana* is outstanding, with silver-grey foliage and silver-white stems carrying deep blue flowers.

Late spring is a time when the pool side and bog garden are at their best: irises and primulas are joined by a host of perennials with bright flowers and lush foliage (see pages 74–79).

GOOD COMPANIONS

Tiarella cordifolia ♀ (1) and *Vinca minor* 'Argenteovariegata' ♀ (2) make a successful partnership for ground cover in shade.

Ranunculus ficaria 'Brazen Hussy' (3) and the winter aconite, *Eranthis hyemalis* ♀ (4): the ranunculus flowers after the aconite, extending the season of interest.

Early summer

As the borders start to billow in early summer, herbaceous perennials come to the fore. This is the season for their variety show; there is no holding back, just sheer floribundance. Stately spikes of delphiniums and lupins rise above mounds of geraniums and lady's mantle. The exotic blooms of poppies, peonies and daylilies punctuate the planting. Foliage plays second fiddle now, a supporting role to the mass of flowers and riot of colour.

Cultivars of *Alcea rosea* (hollyhock) are at their best growing from the dry soil at the base of a sunny wall.

Acanthus (bear's breeches) are truly architectural perennials with striking foliage and statuesque flower spikes, borne from late spring into midsummer. A number of species are found in dry, rocky areas in the Mediterranean region and so enjoy free-draining, fertile soil; winter wet is not appreciated. Although acanthus will grow in partial shade, full sun results in better flowering. Watering during periods of drought in summer will help maintain the quality of the foliage. *Acanthus spinosus* ♥ is the most impressive species. The dark green, thistle-like leaves can be up to 1m (40in) long on a mature plant. Its spires of hooded flowers reach skywards, often attaining 1.5m (5ft). The blooms are produced in succession: pure white, tubular, two-lipped flowers, each with a pink-purple hood-like bract. It is best planted as an individual specimen, against a south-facing wall, alongside a path, or on the edge of a terrace; give it space to be admired.

Acanthus mollis equals the height of *Acanthus spinosus*, but has much broader, less thistle-like leaves and its white flowers with purple-shaded bracts appear much later in summer. *Acanthus* 'Summer Beauty', a garden hybrid producing 1.2m (4ft) spires of white flowers with purple bracts, has

Acanthus spinosus

Achillea filipendulina 'Gold Plate'

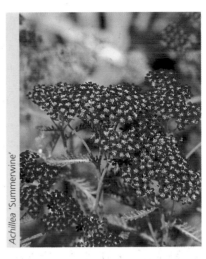

Achillea 'Summerwine'

proved most popular in recent years. Its impressive, dark glossy leaves, 1m (40in) long, are similar to those of *Acanthus mollis* but more deeply cut. *Acanthus dioscoridis* is less common but equally garden-worthy. Reaching no more than 40cm (16in) high, its spikes of mid-pink flowers and green bracts appear above variable foliage. *Acanthus hungaricus* produces dark green, spineless leaves 60–90cm (24–36in) long, and towering spires up to 1m (40in) high clad in white or pale pink flowers with purple-shaded green bracts.

Achilleas (yarrow) add welcome colour and different flower form to any sunny border. Each plate-like head is made up of many tiny, daisy-like flowers in numerous shades: creamy white through pinks, spicy oranges and reds, pure whites and golden yellows. The flowers are carried on stiff stems above fine fern-like, often aromatic foliage in grey, silver or green.

Achilleas are hardy plants that thrive in a variety of situations. Some are found wild in rough grassland and meadows, and on roadside verges and wasteland. Shorter species, forming mat-like growth, grow in mountainous regions, the harsh conditions resulting in silver-grey foliage. In the garden, achilleas grow on most well-drained soils; full sun is preferred, but partial shade is acceptable. Usually reaching a height of 70–90cm (28–36in), many of the showiest achilleas need support. All have a long flowering period, from early summer right through to early autumn. When the blooms are past their best, cut the stems back to the base, water thoroughly and apply a light dressing of fertilizer; the plants should flower again within a few weeks.

OTHER GOOD ACHILLEAS WITH COLOUR

Achillea clypeolata Exquisite feathery silver foliage, and small heads of golden yellow flowers, less showy than most, on stems 50cm (20in) high.

Achillea 'Fanal' Grey-green foliage and vibrant heads of bright red, yellow-eyed flowers.

Achillea millefolium cultivars are all around 60cm (24in) high, with fine, feathery, dark green leaves. 'Cerise Queen' has bright magenta-pink flowers with white centres. 'Lilac Beauty' has divine pale lilac flowers. 'Paprika' has pretty pink and cherry-red flowers with yellow centres.

Achillea sibirica var. *camschatica* 'Love Parade' Shiny, dark green, finely toothed foliage and tightly packed heads of soft pink flowers.

Achillea 'Walther Funcke' Captivating orange-red flowers in broad, flat heads.

PLANTING PARTNERS

Achilleas look wonderful planted randomly among ornamental grasses such as *Stipa calamagrostis*. The simple upright foliage of the grass contrasts with the solid, plate-like achillea flowers, which appear to float among the stipa's moving leaves.

Achillea filipendulina is the tallest of the species, reaching over 1m (40in) high. The most popular cultivar is 'Gold Plate' ♥, with large golden flowerheads 15cm (6in) across. 'Cloth of Gold' ♥ is similar, and *Achillea* 'Moonshine' ♥ offers a soft pale yellow alternative. All are excellent companions for *Salvia nemorosa* (see page 166). *Achillea* 'Coronation Gold' ♥, often reliably evergreen, has silver-grey foliage and flowers of rich golden yellow. *Achillea* 'Lachsschönheit' (SALMON BEAUTY) ♥ has fine, feathered, dark green foliage and salmon-pink flowerheads, while *Achillea* 'Summerwine' ♥ is a lovely deep cherry-red that goes on flowering well into autumn. *Achillea* 'Terracotta' is a well-named favourite, producing delightful dusky orange flowers that turn yellow with age.

Achillea ptarmica (sneezewort) is very different, with narrow, dark green leaves and branched stems bearing

131

button-like, grey-white flowers; **'Boule de Neige'** is pure white, flowering at 50cm (20in).

Aconitums, commonly known as aconite, monkshood and wolfsbane, are popular garden plants: their distinctive foliage, bold, upright form and striking flowers over a long period all guarantee them a place in any border. Most do especially well in moist soil in partial shade. (See page 46.)

Like all plants in the mallow family, **alceas** (hollyhock) thrive in full sun. For well over 300 years the patient gardener has propped and tied up these ungainly beauties, choosing to overlook the rust-spotted, insect-nibbled foliage for the sake of a glorious show of summer flowers. Hollyhocks are at their best in rather dry, well-drained conditions, thriving near the coast and alongside sunny walls.

The most garden-worthy hollyhocks are selections of *Alcea rosea*. Usually ranging in height from 1.5 to 2.5m (5–8ft), their towering stems are clothed in rounded, light green leaves, each with three to seven shallow lobes. Lightly cupped, funnel-shaped flowers in shades of yellow, white, pink or purple open in succession from halfway up the stem. The double-flowered forms, such as the mixed *Alcea* 'Chater's Double', have layer upon layer of ruffled petals,

Alcea rosea 'Nigra'

Alcea rugosa

resembling the blooms of a peony. *Alcea rosea* 'Majorette' has a bushy habit with stems about 1m (40in) tall, useful for smaller gardens; the flowers are semi-double in pastel colours. Few flowers are as dark as those of *Alcea rosea* 'Nigra': black at first glance, they have a dark red, velvet sheen. *Alcea rugosa* is a lovely species, with spikes over 2m (6ft) tall. The flowers are clear pale yellow, the leaves lobed and less heavy than those of *Alcea rosea*. Where it is happy, it is a good self-seeder.

Often confused with *Alcea*, the various forms of **Althaea** come very close in height, although their stems are usually numerous and much finer. The

flowers, borne throughout summer, are smaller and carried on short stalks on almost the entire length of the stems. Given some support, althaeas will prove their worth in any herbaceous border. *Althaea armeniaca* has deep rose-pink flowers, a colour also found in *Althaea cannabina*, along with pleasant shades of lilac-pink.

Baptisias (false indigo) are natives of the eastern and southern USA, where they grow in woodland and grassy scrub on dry, sandy, acid soils. In the garden they are drought-tolerant, hardy plants enjoying free-draining soil and a sunny aspect. Grey-green stems, up to 1.5m (5ft) high, are clad in leaves made up of three oval leaflets, blue-green maturing to soft green. Airy spikes of pea-like flowers in early summer are followed by large, often inflated seedpods. Early frosts blacken the stems and foliage which, along with the dark pods, are useful for floral decoration. *Baptisia australis* ♥ is the most widely grown, with upright stems terminating in a 50cm (20in) spike of rich blue flowers (see Good Companions, right). *Baptisia alba* is often half the height and has narrower leaflets; its stunning white flowers sometimes have delicate purple

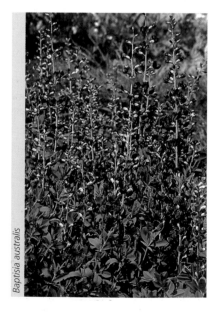

Baptisia australis

HOLLYHOCK RUST

Hollyhocks are notorious for their susceptibility to rust, a fungal disease that appears as reddish-brown spots all over the foliage. A severe infestation can drastically affect performance. To avoid this problem, hollyhocks are often treated as annuals or biennials: plants are destroyed after flowering to prevent the fungus overwintering. New stock is planted out in spring to flower the same summer. Rust is less of a problem in coastal areas.

markings on the upper petals. *Baptisia alba* var. *macrophylla* has broader foliage and white flower spikes up to 60cm (24in) high. *Baptisia* 'Purple Smoke' is a recent selection from hybrid seedlings found in the North Carolina Botanical Gardens, USA. Dark stems carry dusky purple flowers in spikes up to 60cm (24in) high.

Campanulas (bellflower) perform throughout the garden, providing tight, low-growing clumps, spreading, trailing mats and some of our favourite border perennials. Some species and varieties are in flower from late spring through to late summer, and early summer sees some of the best border campanulas at their peak. (See page 40.)

Our lovely native annual cornflower, *Centaurea cyanus*, once commonly grew in cornfields, where it became a persistent weed. Its slender growth topped in dark blue flowers was a real spectacle in early summer, a treat for all but the farmers! The cornflower is a popular garden flower today and there are a number of equally lovely perennial species. *Centaurea hypoleuca* forms a spreading clump of broad, deeply divided, pale green leaves, grey-white beneath. Borne on 60cm (24in) stems, the early summer flowers are light to deep pink, each pincushion-like centre surrounded by a showy, feathery ruff. Needing full sun and moderately fertile, free-draining soil, it enjoys the company of lavender and rosemary. *Centaurea hypoleuca* 'John Coutts' is a rich, deep rose-pink, and flowers intermittently until early autumn; it was a favourite of Graham Stuart Thomas, who likened the seedheads to 'silvery daisies'.

Long cultivated in cottage gardens, *Centaurea montana* is a very easy perennial to grow. It forms a mass of mid-green foliage and rather ungainly stems up to 45cm (18in) high. These bear one or more large, inky-blue cornflower heads, more spidery than most,

Centaurea hypoleuca 'John Coutts'

with centres of pinkish purple. (See Good Companions, below.) The flowers reach their peak in early summer; if plants are then cut back hard, new foliage appears, along with occasional later flowers. The white form, *Centaurea montana* 'Alba', looks wonderful with the vibrant deep blue flowers of *Anchusa azurea*. *Centaurea montana* 'Carnea' is a pink-flowered form, while 'Parham' boasts large heads of deep lavender-blue, and those of 'Violetta' are a striking violet-blue.

Cephalaria gigantea is a surprising perennial, a truly statuesque plant, which can reach heights of up to 2.5m (8ft). It is often mistaken for a scabious, to which it is closely related. From early

Centaurea montana

Cephalaria gigantea

to midsummer, its branched stems hold numerous primrose-yellow flowerheads, which make marvellous partners for blue delphiniums. It likes rich soil with adequate moisture and will grow either in sun or in partial shade.

GOOD COMPANIONS

Centaurea montana (1) and *Papaver orientale* 'Allegro' (2) create the classic combination of cornflowers and poppies in the perennial border.

The indigo spires of *Baptisia australis* ♀ (3) are wonderful with the graceful, pure white spikes of *Chamerion angustifolium* 'Album' (4). Both enjoy well-drained soil in full sun.

133

Delphiniums

The garden scene has its leading players but few hold centre stage with such splendour as the delphiniums. Their impressive flowers and stunning colours make them the most popular perennials: the very essence of the summer garden.

Few genera claim such world-wide distribution; only the polar regions and Australia lack native species. Many have enchanting, simple flowers resembling a pointed hat or bonnet, occasionally hooded and often spurred. From these, numerous hybrids have evolved to exuberant beauty and proportions.

There are annual and biennial types, but it is the perennials that dominate the summer border. They produce deciduous clumps of divided, pale to dark green leaves, from which emerge tall spikes or spires in early summer and often again in early autumn. These carry blooms of numerous shades, both subtle and vibrant, not only much-loved blues but lilacs, purples, pinks and whites. Most species and hybrids are usually considered short-lived; however, attention to their needs will bring years of loyal service, especially from *Delphinium elatum* hybrids.

Delphiniums need some space: if they are crowded or shaded by vigorous neighbours, the resulting damp-ness and poor light can have disastrous effects. They also need shelter from strong winds. Plant them in a fertile, well-drained soil in full sun.

Twiggy or metal grow-through supports should be put into position before new growth exceeds 30cm (12in), with the large-flowered hybrids needing a stout cane to match their ultimate height. For the most impressive blooms thin out the young shoots in spring, to two or three shoots on young plants and five to seven shoots on mature clumps. The unwanted shoots should be removed at the base with a sharp knife and can be used as cuttings. Routine feeding throughout the growing season with a high-potash liquid fertilizer reaps dividends. Once the blooms have faded, the

Statuesque spires of blue delphiniums are set against a yew hedge, with the dramatic silver foliage of the cardoon, *Cynara cardunculus*, in front.

spikes should be cut back hard to encourage plants to produce a second flush of flowers.

The breeding of delphinium hybrids was started in earnest by Kelway of Langport in 1875, and the Somerset nursery Blackmore and Langdon in 1901. Blackmore and Langdon gained their first RHS Gold Medal in 1903 and are still producing, exhibiting and selling prize-winning delphinium hybrids today.

Most commonly available delphiniums fall into one of three groups: the Elatum group, with stately upright spikes; the similar but shorter Pacific hybrids; and the Belladonna hybrids, whose looser, branched spikes give them a less formal habit. (See also page 41.)

Delphinium hybrids of the Elatum group produce some of the showiest flowering spikes, usually 1.5–2m (5–6ft) tall, tightly packed with large blooms. In the best varieties these are semi-double and consist of large outer petals and an inner smaller cluster, often in a contrasting colour. *Delphinium* 'Lord Butler' ♀ (above) is shorter than most, at 1m (40in), and has white-centred sky-blue flowers.

OTHER GOOD ELATUM GROUP DELPHINIUMS

Delphinium 'Cassius' ♀ Rich blue flowers overlaid with pinkish purple, with golden brown centres.

Delphinium 'Faust' ♀ Statuesque spikes of aquamarine-purple.

Delphinium 'Fenella' ♀ An old variety, still held in high esteem; the flowers are true deep blue with black centres.

Delphinium 'Gillian Dallas' ♀ Lavender-blue flowers with gently frilled edges and white eyes.

Delphinium 'Langdon's Royal Flush' ♀ A shorter hybrid, at 1m (40in) tall. Rich mid-pink flowers with creamy-white centres.

Delphinium 'Moonbeam' One of the finest pure whites.

Delphinium nudicaule, a short-lived perennial usually grown as an annual, has flowers in vibrant scarlet-red, orange-red or yellow. Grows only 60cm (24in) high, with finely divided foliage.

Delphinium 'Völkerfrieden' ♀, one of the Belladonna Group of hybrids, has graceful flowers of brilliant gentian-blue. Mixing well with fellow perennials, Belladonna delphiniums rarely exceed 1.2m (4ft) tall, with finely cut foliage and slender, branched spikes bearing loosely arranged, small, long-spurred, bonnet-like flowers.

OTHER GOOD BELLADONNA GROUP DELPHINIUMS

'Atlantis' ♀ Vivid gentian-blue with dark eyes; a good cut flower.

'Casa Blanca' Pure white flowers.

'Cliveden Beauty' Flowers in a lovely, refreshing sky blue.

Delphinium grandiflorum 'Blue Butterfly' is a short-lived perennial often grown as an annual. It has bright turquoise-sapphire flowers with black eyes, borne on slender, branched stems only 60cm (24in) high, with finely divided foliage. In well-drained soil in full sun, it can survive for a few years.

Delphinium Pacific hybrids are the ones often available from garden centres. They have semi-double flowers and are similar to those of the Elatum group but shorter, at only 1.2m (4ft), and not as long-lived. However, they are easily replaced on a regular basis; they grow quickly and, being raised from seed, are less expensive.

OTHER GOOD SEED-RAISED DELPHINIUMS

Black Knight Group

Blue Bird Group

Cameliard Group

Guinevere Group

King Arthur Group

Summer Skies Group

Cirsium rivulare 'Atropurpureum'

Dianthus 'Gran's Favourite'

Dianthus 'Widecombe Fair'

Cirsiums have become firm favourites in recent years for their tall stems of thistle-like flowers. They like a sunny position on moist, well-drained soil, where they will flower intermittently from early summer to early autumn. *Cirsium rivulare* 'Atropurpureum' is the most desirable, with rosettes of dark green thistle foliage and 1m (40in) stems carrying very dark red pincushion flowers. It combines well with pinks, purples and blues and its light see-through habit makes it valuable for use at the front of the border.

A long history of travel and trade between Europe, Asia and South Africa has seen the evolution of *Dianthus* as some of the best-loved flowers for the garden and for cutting. From mountain slopes and meadows, numerous species have been collected and hybridized to deliver the dazzling beauties we know as carnations and pinks. From the tight, mounded, needle-like growth of alpine varieties to the looser, longer, lance-shaped leaves of border perennials, they all thrive in well-drained, alkaline soil with plenty of sun.

Carnations are not popular border plants but they are good in the cutting garden. They are taller than pinks, with stems 60–90cm (24–36in) high, each carrying up to six large double flowers. By midsummer, an established plant produces ample blooms for cutting. The creamy-yellow petals of **Dianthus**

'Bookham Fancy' are solidly margined in royal red. 'Bookham Perfume' is crimson and very fragrant. 'Eva Humphries' has bright white flowers edged purple.

Pinks offer a neater, more compact alternative, flowering at heights of 25–45cm (10–18in). Early summer sees the first blooms arrive, ideal along a path where their scent can easily be enjoyed. Most modern cultivars flower repeatedly. Lovely *Dianthus* 'Doris'♥ is pale salmon-pink. 'Bovey Belle'♥ has deep pink flowers against silver-blue foliage. 'Joy'♥ is a vivid salmon red. 'Gran's Favourite'♥ is fragrant, with pale pink flowers laced and centred with red. All these have double flowers; 'Widecombe Fair'♥ is semi-double, a delightful blush pink and very fragrant. (See also pages 71 and 81.)

Dianthus barbatus (sweet William) is a hardy, short-lived perennial that is

---

PINKS FOR FOLIAGE

Although grown mainly for their fragrant, long-lasting flowers, garden pinks are extremely valuable for their blue-grey foliage. Evergreen and healthy, the fine, pointed leaves look particularly attractive in winter and make textural mounds or mats at the border's edge. The dwarf alpine varieties such as *Dianthus* 'Pike's Pink'♥ are also useful in winter patio containers.

---

traditionally grown as a biennial for bedding. Stems 70cm (28in) high bear clusters of small single, sweetly aromatic flowers. A true cottage-garden plant, it has richly coloured blooms that impart a period character to any planting scheme. They are usually a mix of shades of pink and red to purple, sometimes bicoloured, with contrasting banding or paler, suffused eyes; the darker shades are increasingly in demand. *Dianthus barbatus* Nigrescens Group♥ and the almost black *Dianthus barbatus* 'Sooty' are wonderful plants for rich, dark colour schemes.

Dianthus carthusianorum is not well known but deserves to be more widely used. Growing to 30cm (12in) high, with well-branched stems and fine grey-green leaves, it produces small double, strong pink flowers throughout summer (see Good Companions, page 142). The flowers are borne in clusters, like those of sweet William but looser, and the individual blooms are like those of a miniature border pink. It is a good choice in a sunny border with roses.

Digitalis, the foxgloves, are not only much-loved wildflowers but also some of our most popular and useful garden plants. Their versatility enables them to fit into both traditional borders and more naturalistic plantings. They provide both subtle colour and elegant spikes in the early summer garden. (See pages 47 and 56–57.)

The herbaceous **geraniums** are adept at stitching together the patchwork of the summer border. These are accommodating plants, various types performing well over a long period, and most are robust and hardy. The divided leaves vary in size, and some are highly aromatic. Most are deciduous; some such as *Geranium cinereum* are evergreen. (See also pages 47–48 and 67.)

Geranium × *cantabrigiense* has inherited the dwarf habit and evergreen foliage of *Geranium dalmaticum* ♥ and

Geranium cinereum 'Ballerina'

the strongly aromatic foliage of *Geranium macrorrhizum* (see page 62). From early into midsummer, lovely pale pink or white flowers appear on slowly spreading stems, only 30cm (12in) high.

Geranium cinereum is a star among geraniums, forming an evergreen rosette of fine grey-green foliage topped with upward-facing, white to pink flowers in early to midsummer. Its slowly spreading growth, 15cm (6in) high, makes it ideal for the edge of a raised border or a container. The cultivar 'Ballerina' produces mid-pink flowers delicately patterned with thread-like, pinkish-red veins, leading to dark eyes. 'Purple Pillow' has gorgeous vibrant purple blooms.

Geranium subcaulescens ♥ is of similar height, but more vigorous, and from late spring into early summer boasts the most dazzling magenta-pink flowers, enhanced by dark eyes.

Geranium cinereum 'Purple Pillow'

All these are neat, compact plants, ideal on scree or in rock gardens or for the edges of paths. The more vigorous and sprawling geraniums are superb border perennials, mixing readily with other plants. *Geranium clarkei* reaches 50cm (20in) high and spreads freely through the border, producing large blooms in succession from early to late summer. Its native origin is recognized in the named selections 'Kashmir Pink', 'Kashmir Purple' and 'Kashmir White' ♥.

The upward-facing, funnel-shaped flowers of *Geranium endressii* ♥ are pale pink, darkening with age as the petals gently recurve. They appear from early summer into autumn, among evergreen foliage on 45cm (18in) stems.

One of only a few herbaceous perennials that provide autumn leaf colour, *Geranium himalayense* forms a spreading mat of foliage, 45cm (18in) high, which gives way to loose clusters

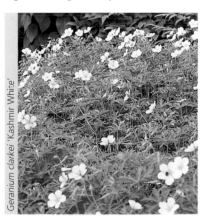
Geranium clarkei 'Kashmir White'

of lilac-blue to deep blue, saucer-shaped flowers in early summer. 'Gravetye' ♥ boasts larger blue flowers; it is a parent of *Geranium* 'Johnson's Blue' ♥, the most popular blue geranium (see page 48 and Good Companions, page 149). 'Plenum' (often available as 'Birch Double') has double purple-pink flowers flushed with blue, which gives a pearly finish. It forms a compact, spreading clump, 50cm (20in) high.

Geums, like the closely related potentillas (see page 82), are not noted for the size of their blooms; however, they compensate with strength and vibrancy of colour. In shades of yellow, orange and red, the charming, usually saucer-shaped flowers appear from late spring into summer. They are borne on slender stems rising above either a prostrate rosette or a more upright clump of softly hairy mid-green leaves, with rounded, toothed leaflets. Geums are easy to grow in full sun in fertile, well-drained soil, although *Geum rivale* prefers richer, moister conditions.

Geum 'Mrs J. Bradshaw' ♥, 45cm (18in) tall, is perhaps the most striking, with scarlet orange flowers of glowing intensity, brilliant with early summer blues and purples such as *Iris sibirica* 'Tropic Night'. *Geum coccineum* grows taller, to 60cm (24in), with flowers of rich orange-red; 'Cooky' is apricot-orange. *Geum* 'Lady Stratheden' ♥ is

(continued on page 140)

Geum coccineum 'Cooky'

Daylilies (Hemerocallis)

One of the major attractions in the herbaceous or mixed border, hemerocallis are known as daylilies because each flower supposedly lasts one day (around ten hours). Established plants produce a succession of blooms over a few weeks, with many performing repeatedly from late spring to late summer.

Native to China, Korea and Japan, daylilies are found growing on the forest edge, on hillsides, in rich river valleys and in meadows. They are very hardy perennials that may be deciduous, semi-evergreen or evergreen. The grass-like, mid- to dark green foliage is tough and resilient, forming dense clumps that make effective ground cover. In gardens, daylilies prefer moist, free-draining conditions, but many will succeed on wet sites and by water. All will grow in partial shade, but they perform best in sun. In cooler areas, they are best planted where the sun can bake them, perhaps against a sheltered wall. The smaller-flowered varieties, such as *Hemerocallis lilioasphodelus* ♡, can be naturalized in unmown grass.

From the 13 species in cultivation, breeders and gardeners have produced countless cultivars, certainly in excess of 40,000. Every attribute of the original species – flower size, shape, colour, scent, quantity, and period of bloom, along with foliage characteristics and height – has added to the wonderful mixing pot.

Daylily flowers come in a number of different forms, including triangular, circular, double, spidery and star-shaped. Colours include whites and creams through yellows, oranges and reds to deep purples, often with contrasting details in the throat. Some are nocturnal, opening in the middle of the afternoon and lasting into the night; in some cultivars, the life of individual flowers has been extended by breeders.

Hemerocallis 'Hyperion' produces large, lily-like pale yellow flowers with sweeping petals, borne on slender stems above the clump of narrow foliage; the blooms are nocturnal and have a sweet fragrance. Midsummer flowering. Height 70cm (28in).

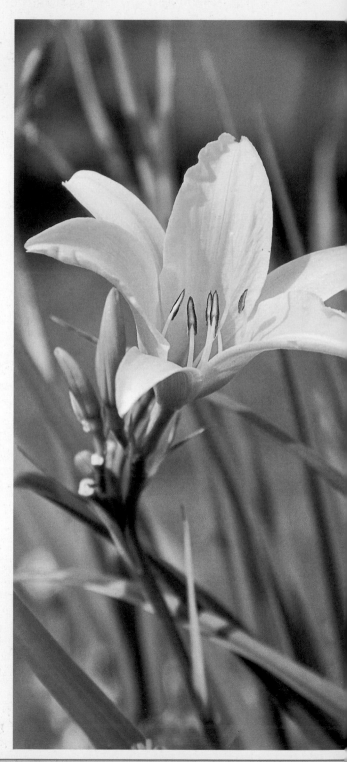

Hemerocallis fulva 'Flore Pleno', introduced in 1860, is a beautiful double cultivar with elegant orange-brown flowers in mid- to late summer. These are longer-lasting than most daylilies and surprisingly graceful for a double variety. A gorgeous combination with blue nepeta. Height 65cm (26in).

Hemerocallis 'Gentle Shepherd' has ivory blooms reminiscent of *Lilium regale* but with a hint of green in the throat. This is a cool and stylish daylily, perfect with white-variegated hostas, and follows on from white peonies and poppies in the summer border. Height 65cm (26in).

Hemerocallis lilioasphodelus ♀ has pale yellow, elegantly pointed flowers on graceful stems above fine foliage. The nocturnal blooms are lightly and sweetly scented. Flowering in early summer, it combines particularly well with blue *Iris sibirica* cultivars such as 'Flight of Butterflies'. Height 1m (40in).

Hemerocallis 'Stafford' is an ever-popular variety with strong red-brown flowers that have pointed petals and golden yellow throats. Free-flowering over a long period from mid- to late summer, it is reliable and an excellent choice for hot colour schemes, combining well with achilleas and early crocosmias. Height 70cm (28in).

Hemerocallis 'Little Grapette' is a compact variety with lovely small purple flowers with a silver bloom produced over a long period from midsummer onwards. Delightful planted with purple heucheras. Height 30cm (12in).

Hemerocallis 'Summer Wine' is one of the loveliest cultivars, with warm burgundy-pink flowers borne on stout stems in early summer. The blooms have lightly waved and ruffled petals and yellow throats. Rich and sophisticated when planted with purple foliage shrubs such as *Cotinus coggygria* 'Royal Purple' ♀ and *Physocarpus opulifolius* 'Diabolo' ♀. Height 70cm (28in).

OTHER GOOD DAYLILIES

Hemerocallis 'Anzac' Velvet-red flowers, with yellow throats and a faint yellow stripe on each petal. Midsummer flowering. Height 70cm (28in).

Hemerocallis 'Cherry Cheeks' Evergreen foliage and bright pink flowers with reflexed, white-striped petals and yellow throats. Blooms in midsummer. Height 70cm (28in).

Hemerocallis citrina Nocturnal, star-shaped, fragrant flowers in midsummer; green to pale yellow with brown tips. Height 1.2m (4ft).

Hemerocallis 'Edge of Darkness' Lavender flowers with dark purple petal edges and eyes, in midsummer. Height 60cm (24in).

Hemerocallis 'Eenie Weenie' A good dwarf cultivar with neat, compact foliage and yellow flowers from early into midsummer. Height 30cm (12in).

Hemerocallis 'Pandora's Box' Compact, with maroon-eyed cream flowers in midsummer. Height 30cm (12in).

of similar size and produces bright yellow, semi-double flowers. *Geum* 'Borisii' is compact with mid-orange flowers on 30cm (12in) stems. *Geum rivale* has pendent, bell-shaped flowers in dusky pink or darker orange-red. With slender, arching stems, 20–60cm (8–24in) tall, this species has a much softer, gentle habit.

Heucheras originate from the North American Rocky Mountains. Enjoying massive popularity in gardens today, modern varieties offer a wonderful choice of foliage (see pages 88–89 and 93). However, some cultivars also have fantastic flowers, borne over a long period in summer. Heucheras have been hybridized with their near relatives *Tiarella* to produce × *Heucherella*, also responsible for some valuable flowering cultivars. Growing on moist, well-drained, neutral soils, both form dense clumps of rounded to heart-shaped, semi-evergreen to evergreen leaves. They prefer light shade, tolerating full sun only in moist conditions. Their fine

Heuchera 'Raspberry Regal'

A FEW GOOD HEUCHERAS AND HEUCHERELLAS FOR FLOWERS

Heuchera 'Cherries Jubilee' Stems of showy, cherry-red flowers above rich chocolate-brown foliage.

Heuchera cylindrica 'Greenfinch' Popular with garden designers for its unusual green-cream flowers on 90cm (3ft) stems. Handsome, rounded, dark green leaves, overlaid or mottled with metallic silver.

Heuchera EBONY AND IVORY ('E and I') Ruffled, dark ebony-purple foliage and large, bell-shaped ivory-white flowers.

Heuchera 'Fireworks' ♀ An explosive display of coral pink-orange flowers above bronzed ruffled foliage.

Heuchera 'Leuchtkäfer' (FIREFLY) Dark green foliage and dark red stems of bright red, fragrant flowers; an established favourite.

Heuchera 'Magic Wand' ♀ Almost luminous pink-red flowers, double the size of most. Dark green leaves are flushed silver-bronze and finely margined in red.

Heuchera 'Raspberry Regal' ♀ (left) A profusion of fresh pink flowers on straight stems above copper and burgundy foliage.

× *Heucherella alba* 'Rosalie' A profusion of pretty pink, tubular bell-shaped flowers against rounded, maple-like red-flushed leaves.

× *Heucherella* 'Dayglow Pink' Distinctive foliage with chocolate-brown veining and stems of profuse fluorescent pink, tubular bell-shaped flowers. Looks glorious against the bold blue-grey leaves of *Hosta sieboldiana* var. *elegans* ♀ (see page 107).

green or red-brown stems usually reach 40–65cm (16–26in) high, at which point they lightly branch to bear numerous tubular flowers.

Incarvilleas (hardy gloxinia) are found in mountainous regions from Afghanistan to north-western China. The plants form thick tap roots and are perfectly hardy, although they detest

---

over-wet conditions, especially in winter. An ideal situation is a sunny raised bed of rich, gritty soil. Foliage varies from species to species: most form a rosette of dark, glossy green leaves each made up of a number of leaflets. The flowers, which are borne in early to midsummer, are all trumpet-shaped, opening to five well-defined petals.

Incarvillea delavayi

The most common garden species is *Incarvillea delavayi*. Growing to 45cm (18in), its height makes it suitable for the herbaceous or mixed border. Thick stems each carry around ten gloxinia-like flowers, which are rose-pink with clear yellow throats, followed by long, angular seed capsules. 'Bees' Pink' is a more subtle pale pink. 'Snowtop' is pure white. *Incarvillea mairei* is a Himalayan beauty of distinction, its bright pink flowers with white markings and yellow throats sitting proudly above the glossy, dark foliage on stems 15–40cm (6–16in) high.

Iris sibirica ♀ (Siberian iris) is one of the highlights of early summer. Its upright, grass-like clumps of foliage grow to 80cm (32in) high and produce much taller stems each with about five flowers. Parent of an ever-increasing list of cultivars, *Iris sibirica* prefers slightly acid soil, which must be reliably moist, and a site in full sun or partial shade. The elegant flowers occur in shades of blue through to purple-mauve, as well

Iris ensata thrives in the spring water of the rill at Hestercombe Gardens, Somerset.

as the white of **Iris 'Sibirica Alba'**. Intricate markings at the base of each lower petal (fall) often include a golden yellow flush and dark stripes or veins. (See also pages 75–76.)

Iris laevigata and its cultivars thrive in acid soil, rich in humus. They grow in the moist to wet conditions at the edges of a pond or stream and are ideally suited to a bog garden. The flamboyant flowers of **Iris ensata** can also be grown successfully in the border providing the soil is rich, deep and moist. Additional watering in summer may be necessary to keep the foliage in good condition and build the plants for the following season. Many beautiful named varieties are available, in colours from white through pinks to the deepest blues and purples. (See also page 76.)

Knautias are close relatives of *Scabiosa* (scabious) and were previously known by this name. Their dainty pin-cushion flowers are carried on fine stems above felty rosettes of foliage, and appear throughout summer, often repeating in autumn. These are easy plants to grow on any soil, including chalk, but they do need a position in full sun. *Knautia macedonica* has pleasing grey-felted leaves and glorious deep crimson-red flowers. It is invaluable in the mixed border, particularly combined with other grey foliage perennials and shrubs. The selection known as *Knautia macedonica* Melton pastels is widely available; it lacks the depth of colour of the species, but it is a pretty plant nonetheless. There are three colours: pink-lilac, lavender-pink and crimson-

---

A SELECTION OF IRIS SIBIRICA HYBRIDS

'Butter and Sugar' ♀ Gorgeous flowers with creamy-white standards and butter-yellow falls.

'Dance Ballerina Dance' Ruffled white-lilac standards above falls of darker lilac edged white.

'Flight of Butterflies' Masses of smaller flowers of sapphire-blue with darker veining. (See page 75.)

'Papillon' Soft mid-blue flowers.

'Tropic Night' Dark velvety-purple blooms with distinct veining on the petals. Looks lovely planted with *Carex elata* 'Aurea' ♀.

'White Swirl' ♀ Produces outstanding white flowers.

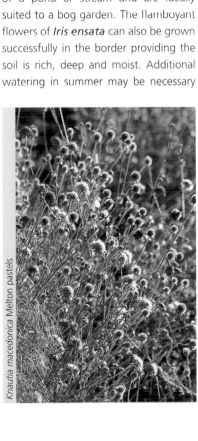

Knautia macedonica Melton pastels

141

Leucanthemum × superbum

Leucanthemum × superbum 'Aglaia'

red, usually available as mixed. All these reach heights of around 75cm (30in); *Knautia macedonica* 'Mars Midget' is dwarf at only 40cm (16in) high, with numerous small ruby-red flowers.

Leucanthemum × superbum, once named *Chrysanthemum maximum*, has long been enjoyed for its show of flowers from early to late summer. It is fondly known as the shasta daisy, and we could not wish for a more hardy, robust garden plant. A native of grass-

land, it thrives in moist, well-drained soils, and its simple to elaborate white flowers stand out in a sunny herbaceous border or brighten the partial shade of a mixed planting. It forms a clump of toothed, glossy, dark green leaves and carries its flowers on stems 25–90cm (10–36in) high. The taller cultivars often need some support.

Each usually pure white flowerhead can be up to 12cm (5in) across. Single forms have bold yellow centres, while the double cultivars are often paler and sometimes fringed around the centres.

Lychnis (campion or catchfly) include low-growing alpine perennials as well as larger, more familiar border plants. Most

have upright, usually branched stems with often hairy leaves and loose heads of five-petalled flowers in shades of red and pink in addition to white. They are undemanding plants, most requiring only moderately fertile, free-draining soil. Ideally grown in full sun, they will tolerate partial shade. Some species self-seed successfully, and this is certainly part of their appeal.

The alpine campion, *Lychnis alpina*, forms a compact tuft of growth, with dark green leaves. In summer, stems 15cm (6in) high each bear a cluster of saucer-shaped purple-pink flowers with notched petals. *Lychnis flos-jovis* ♀ (flower of Jove or Jupiter) is another alpine species, with a mat of white-hairy leaves and 30cm (12in) stems topped with loose clusters of white, pink or scarlet flowers in early summer.

Lychnis coronaria ♀ (dusty miller or rose campion) is an upright plant, with woolly, grey-silver leaves and silvery-white stems, 80cm (32in) high, of rounded, vivid magenta flowers, often with pale eyes. Borne in loose clusters, these open one at a time over a long period in summer and seed themselves freely. (See Good Companions, below.)

(continued on page 144)

SOME FINE CULTIVARS OF LEUCANTHEMUM X SUPERBUM

'Aglaia' ♀ (above right) A popular choice with delicate, fringed, semi-double flowers on 60cm (24in) stems.

'Cobham Gold' Double flowers with yellow centres fading through pale lemon to white. Height 60cm (24in).

'Esther Read' The familiar pure white double, stunning among the blue flowers of *Agapanthus campanulatus* later in the season. Height 70cm (28in).

'Snowcap' Dwarf and compact, at 45cm (18in) high, with single flowers, freely borne. Ideal for the front of the border.

'Sonnenschein' (SUNSHINE) Single, creamy-yellow flowers with dark yellow centres. Height 70cm (28in).

'Sunny Side Up' Bold and refreshing with large double, pure white flowers with deep yellow centres. Height 60cm (24in).

GOOD COMPANIONS

The raspberry-pink flowers of *Dianthus carthusianorum* (1) make a vivid combination with the wine-coloured leaves of *Heuchera* 'Plum Pudding' (2).

The bright magenta blooms of *Lychnis coronaria* ♀ (3) are striking with the lavender-blue flowers and sage-green foliage of *Lavandula stoechas* subsp. *pedunculata* ♀ (4).

Lupins (Lupinus)

Mixed hybrid lupins fill a box parterre at Anne's Grove Gardens, County Cork, Ireland.

Lupins are a welcome addition to any garden: their stems of up to 90cm (3ft) tall are an imposing sight as the dense spikes of pea-like flowers open from the bottom up. Cultivars come in shades of yellow, pink, red, and blue to mauve, as well as white and some striking bicolours. The clumps of large, softly hairy, palmate leaves are especially attractive when droplets of water are trapped in the centre of the leaflets.

A long history of cultivation is recorded; some were used by the Romans for animal fodder. *Lupinus luteus*, with fragrant yellow flowers, was the only lupin grown as a garden plant until the 17th century, when the first American perennial lupins arrived. The wonderful garden lupin was born of these original species, helped along by devotees such as George Russell, who set about a programme of hybridization to improve colour range, and size and shape of flower.

Reliably blooming in early summer, lupins are best planted among other perennials that can take over the show later in the season. Slightly acid, fertile, well-drained soil is ideal; heavy, wet clay is not appreciated. Full sun brings the best results, although light shade is tolerated. To encourage further blooms, remove spikes right to the base immediately after flowering.

Cultivars are often propagated from cuttings. These are taken from the young shoots in spring, cut right at the base, just above the roots. Today, many modern varieties come true from seed.

Lupinus 'The Governor' (Band of Nobles Series) is perhaps the most popular lupin of them all, with strong spikes of bold, deep blue and white bicoloured flowers. They look striking against the silver leaves of *Elaeagnus* 'Quicksilver' ♀ or rising through a cloud of white valerian, *Centranthus ruber* 'Albus' (see page 43).

OTHER GOOD LUPINS

'Chandelier' A subtle combination of mid- and pale yellow.

'My Castle' Lovely flowers of deep lipstick-pink.

'Noble Maiden' (Band of Nobles Series) White maturing to creamy white.

'The Chatelaine' (Band of Nobles Series) Bicoloured flowers in boldly contrasting white and rose-pink.

'The Page' (Band of Nobles Series) Subtle bicoloured flowers of red and mid-pink (left) .

A number of colour forms are available such as **Atrosanguinea Group**, deep blood red; **'Alba'** ♀, which is white; and **'Oculata'**, which is white with a pink flush. *Lychnis × walkeri* **'Abbotswood Rose'** is similar to *Lychnis coronaria* but shorter, at about 60cm (24in) high, with numerous bright pink flowers. *Lychnis × arkwrightii* **'Vesuvius'**, 45cm (18in) high, has chocolate stems and foliage, a perfect setting for the clusters of star-shaped, bright orange-red flowers in early summer.

Although most lychnis thrive in well-drained conditions, some prefer a richer, moister soil. *Lychnis flos-cuculi* (ragged robin), popular for wildflower meadows, has loose heads of purple-pink flowers with raggedly divided petals, on stems up to 70cm (28in) tall, in late spring and early summer. *Lychnis chalcedonica* ♀ (Jerusalem or Maltese cross) produces domed heads of star-shaped, bright

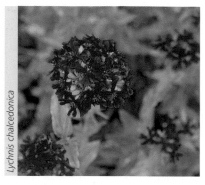

Lychnis chalcedonica

orange-red flowers in early and mid-summer and freely self-seeds. This is a more upright plant with bristly stems 1m (40in) high. *Lychnis viscaria*, the German catchfly, produces slender spikes of saucer-shaped, bright purple-pink flowers, borne on dark red-brown stems, 45cm (18in) high, in early and midsummer. **'Splendens Plena'** ♀ has double, bright pink flowers.

Lysimachias (loosestrife) are seldom praised despite their appearance in so

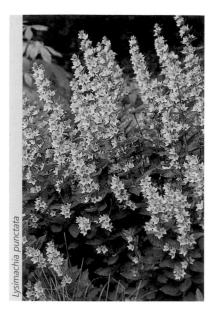

Lysimachia punctata

many gardens, where they perform year after year. Growing naturally in damp meadows and woodland, they thrive on rich, moist, free-draining soil in full sun or partial shade. They are superb border plants, and quickly become established. (See also pages 91 and 101.)

Lysimachia punctata, the best-known species, has whorls of golden yellow flowers borne from early summer onwards on pale green, upright stems 1m (40in) high. It is a useful plant since it requires no support and has enough foliage to dilute the brightness of the flowers. Roughly the same height, and in bloom at the same time, *Lysimachia ephemerum* has erect stems of narrow grey-green leaves topped by candle-like spires of numerous starry white flowers.

Lysimachia clethroides ♀ is glorious in bloom, especially when planted in drifts. Reaching 60cm (24in) tall, it has tightly packed spikes of pure white flowers, which open from the bottom up; the top of each spike dramatically arches or curls with age. Flowers start appearing early in summer and carry on throughout the season. *Lysimachia clethroides* **'Geisha'** is a more recent Japanese introduction that has a jagged creamy margin to the leaf.

The bright magenta blooms and silver foliage of *Lychnis coronaria* contrast with the lush green foliage and deep blue flowers of *Iris ensata*.

Lysimachia nummularia (creeping Jenny) is a valuable ground-cover plant for shady banks and under shrubs; its creeping stems carry fresh green leaves and flushes of yellow flowers from early summer onwards. **'Aurea'** ♥ is a lovely yellow-leaved form (see page 95).

Lythrum salicaria (commonly called purple loosestrife) thrives in a moist site, producing tightly packed spires of starry, purple-red or purple-pink flowers over long periods from early summer. (See page 77.)

Malvas (mallow) are closely related to lavateras and hollyhocks but are of more modest stature, at around 1m (40in) tall. The funnel-shaped blooms are white, pink or purple as well as striking shades of blue, and are borne from early summer to autumn. Liking good drainage and lots of sun, malvas suit planting in gravel and are excellent with roses and sun-loving shrubs.

Malva alcea (hollyhock mallow) has delightful purple-pink flowers. *Malva moschata* (musk mallow) is pale pink, and has finely divided leaves with a gentle musk scent. *Malva moschata* f. *alba* ♥ is a pure white form.

Malva sylvestris has open funnel-shaped flowers, in colours ranging from pink through purple to blue. Those of **'Brave Heart'** are large and purple, but **'Primley Blue'** steals the show: its pale blue flowers have dark purple-blue

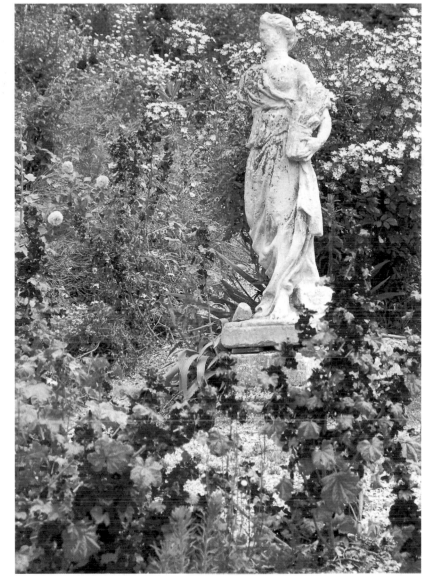

A purple form of *Malva sylvestris* associates well with old roses and with other sun-loving perennials.

SHRUBBY MALLOWS

Lavateras are woody-based plants that grow quickly to produce a spectacular show of funnel-shaped blooms throughout summer into autumn. They are related to malvas and are often sold alongside them as perennials. They enjoy the same conditions and suit coastal gardens. Although shrubby, they are short-lived, and on wet soils may need replacing every two or three years.

Malva alcea

veins and, at 20cm (8in) tall, it sits nicely at the front of a border with shorter campanulas and dwarf agapanthus.

Nepetas are unquestionably good companion plants, presenting their airy flower spikes over a long season from early summer through to autumn. Most are in blue and purple shades, but some are white or yellow. A number of hardy species and garden cultivars are universally known as catmint, although not all types stir cats to the same degree. (See pages 42, 67 and 69.)

Peonies (Paeonia)

Throughout gardening history peonies have been much treasured plants, a prominent statement of good taste and prosperity. Rich red young growth soon matures into bold, leathery, deeply cut blue-green foliage, with beautiful saucer- or bowl-shaped flowers carried above the leaves at heights of up to 1m (40in). Most flower in early to midsummer. The blooms may be single, semi-double or fully double; those described as 'anemone-formed' have a single or semi-double layer of smaller petals at the centre. Colours include white and cream to yellow, through pinks and reds, often blushed, tinted or streaked, with the occasional distinct bicolour; most have a central eye of yellow stamens, often hidden in fully double forms.

The majority of herbaceous peonies are hardy, easily grown perennials with winter-dormant tuberous roots. They are often sold in autumn as bare-root tubers. Careful inspection should reveal at least three firm reddish buds or eyes. Plant immediately in moist, free-draining soil enriched with well-rotted manure. Whether using bare tubers or container-grown plants, never plant too deeply: the top of the tuber should be no more than 2cm (1in or so) below the surface. Plant any deeper and your peonies will not flower.

Long, cold winters bring the best results with peonies. Where temperatures rarely drop below 10°C (50°F), plant in a cool, shady site; otherwise full sun to partial shade is preferred. In full sun individual blooms fade more quickly; those planted in shade will have fewer, longer-lasting flowers.

The greatest threats to new growth are frost and botrytis (a fungus that causes buds and stems to wilt). If shoots develop early, protect with fleece. If botrytis develops, apply a fungicide. Still, damp air tends to accentuate this condition, so always allow plenty of space around the plants.

Taller varieties will need some support (see pages 24–25). Peonies appreciate an annual mulch of well-

Paeonia officinalis 'Rubra Plena' ♀ is the old-fashioned double red peony of cottage gardens. Round, green, red-veined buds open into balls of silky ruby-red petals, which are delightfully scented. The mid-green foliage with broad leaflets is the perfect setting for the attractive horned seedheads that follow the flowers. Height 75cm (30in).

rotted manure or compost. This increases the organic content of the soil and aids water conservation, helping to keep the foliage in good condition. Healthy leaves through the summer build the plants up ready to flower freely the following year. Late winter or early spring is the best time to divide peonies (see page 21).

Most garden peonies are cultivars of the Chinese species *Paeonia lactiflora*. They were well developed as a garden flower in China as early as the 18th century and became popular in Edwardian England. The peonies of the English cottage garden are double forms of the European species *Paeonia officinalis*. All have large, rounded buds, are lightly fragrant and make wonderful cut flowers.

OTHER GOOD PEONIES

Paeonia anomala
Wavy red-purple petals surrounding a golden yellow centre. Height 50–60cm (20–24in).

Paeonia lactiflora 'Charm'
Large, ruffled, ruby-red flowers, red and yellow at the centre. Height 90–100cm (36–40in).

Paeonia lactiflora 'Dinner Plate' Large, double, soft lilac-pink blooms, gently fragrant. Height 75–100cm (30–40in).

Paeonia lactiflora 'Karl Rosenfield' A lovely deep red double. Height 70–80cm (28–32in).

Paeonia lactiflora 'Raspberry Sundae' Large, double, pink-red flowers streaked with white. Height 75–90cm (30–36in).

Paeonia lactiflora 'Sarah Bernhardt' ♀ Double, fragrant, rose-pink flowers. Height 90–100cm (36–40in).

Paeonia officinalis 'Alba Plena' Large, double flowers with white ruffled petals. Height 60–75cm (24–30in).

Paeonia officinalis 'Rosea Plena' ♀ Pale pink and very double. Height 65–75cm (26–30in).

Paeonia tenuifolia Deep velvety-red, single flowers with golden centres. Height 50–70cm (20–28in).

Paeonia mlokosewitschii ♀ (Molly the witch) One of the loveliest species peonies Emerging early with coppery young foliage, it may need frost protection. The pale yellow, kingcup-like flowers are not long-lived but are very beautiful, especially against the backdrop of purplish leaves. Height 60–90cm (24–36in).

Paeonia lactiflora 'Bowl of Beauty' ♀ is a glorious peony with bowl-shaped flowers. The shining pink outer petals hold a rich creamy centre of numerous smaller petals. Occasionally fully double, plain pink flowers appear early in the season. The plant is upright in habit with reddish stems and shining, dark green leaves that remain attractive throughout the year. Height 90cm (3ft).

Paeonia lactiflora 'Duchesse de Nemours' ♀ has very double flowers of creamy white, flushed yellow at the base of the petals, with a light and lovely fragrance. The blooms are sumptuous and extravagant against the handsome dark green foliage. Height 90cm (3ft).

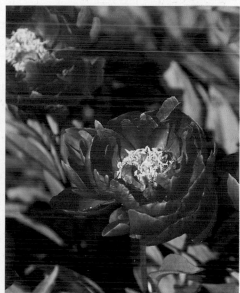

Paeonia lactiflora 'Lord Kitchener' is an old cultivar dating from the Edwardian era. It is upright in habit, with dark foliage, reddish stems and semi-double, bright scarlet blooms with yellow centres. Height 90cm (3ft).

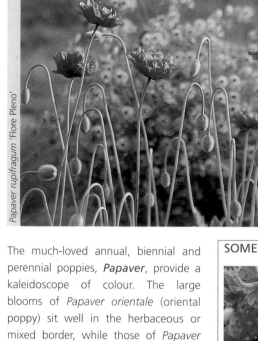

Papaver rupifragum 'Flore Pleno'

green leaves starts to die down soon after flowering; by late summer any remaining foliage is unsightly. The cup-shaped flowers are up to 15cm (6in) across, borne individually on stout, unbranched stems, usually 60–90cm (24–36in) high. Some varieties collapse all too easily under the weight of the flowers so some support is needed, either from well-chosen neighbouring plants or from artificial supports.

Persicaria (formerly *Polygonum*) species are widespread in the northern hemisphere. The hardy perennial types are popular garden plants, growing in

The much-loved annual, biennial and perennial poppies, *Papaver*, provide a kaleidoscope of colour. The large blooms of *Papaver orientale* (oriental poppy) sit well in the herbaceous or mixed border, while those of *Papaver nudicaule* and annual *Papaver rhoeas* are simply stunning en masse or drifting through cottage or wild gardens. Native to many countries, all need moderately fertile, free-draining soil and full sun.

Papaver nudicaule, the Icelandic or Arctic poppy, is a short-lived perennial forming tufts of blue-green, divided leaves. Numerous solitary, bowl-shaped, fragrant flowers in white, yellow, orange or pale red are borne on wiry stems 30cm (12in) tall, appearing from early summer onwards. There are a number of good garden selections.

Papaver rupifragum 'Flore Pleno' is wonderful along the edge of a gravel path or on scree. Compact tufts of grey-green foliage give rise to fine stems, 40cm (16in) high, carrying solitary, double tangerine-orange flowers from early summer. This is a hardy, short-lived perennial, which prolifically self-seeds.

Papaver orientale (oriental poppy) contributes a breathtaking display of glorious, oversized blooms that steal the show for a few weeks in early summer. Its clump of long, divided, bristly mid-

SOME RECOMMENDED PAPAVER ORIENTALE CULTIVARS

'Allegro' (above) Scarlet-orange petals with black blotches at the base. A shorter variety, 45cm (18in) high; popular but rather inelegant.

'Beauty of Livermere' (see page 55) Glorious dark red blooms on strong upright stems 90cm (3ft) high.

'Black and White' ♥ (below) Pure white petals with black basal blotches, which often bleed crimson into the petals.

'Cedric Morris' ♥ Large flowers made up of frilly, pale pink petals with dark basal blotches.

'Curlilocks' (below) Glowing orange-red flowers with cut edges to the petals; pretty and unusual.

'Karine' ♥ A lovely shade of apricot-pink with crimson-marked petals.

'Manhattan' Unusual lavender-rose, ruffled petals.

'Orange Glow' Large amber-orange flowers.

'Patty's Plum' (see page 45) Large, ruffled flowers of soft grey-purple.

'Picotee' (below) Pure white petals with a contrasting edge of clear orange.

sun or partial shade on almost any moist soil, including heavy clay. Varied in both habit and form, they range from low-growing, ground-cover subjects to stately border plants (see also page 48). Some are valuable for their attractive stem and foliage colour. *Persicaria virginiana* 'Painter's Palette' produces intricately patterned leaves in cream, brown and salmon pink (see page 101); while *Persicaria microcephala* 'Red Dragon' has purple-green foliage with striking brown and silver markings (see page 87).

Persicaria affinis 'Superba' ♥, with rich dark green, evergreen foliage, makes an excellent ground-cover plant, 25cm (10in) high. From early summer onwards, it has short spikes, 10cm (4in) high, of tightly packed flowers that open blush pink and turn deep crimson with age. With the onset of autumn the foliage turns bronze, then red-brown, looking wonderful with the remaining flowers. *Persicaria affinis* 'Darjeeling Red' ♥ is a slightly taller plant, with flowers that mature to rich red; 'Donald Lowndes' ♥ ages to deep pink.

Persicaria bistorta 'Superba' ♥ is a larger creature, very useful in the border, particularly in damp conditions. Its large evergreen leaves are conspicuously veined. Stems of up to 75cm (30in) in height are topped with dense cylindrical spikes of pale pink flowers from early summer onwards.

Persicaria vacciniifolia ♥, growing only 20cm (8in) high, has red, spreading stems with small, dark green leaves that turn rich red in autumn. Candle-like heads of numerous large, dark pink, bell-shaped flowers are borne in mid- to late summer.

Polemoniums (Jacob's ladder) are easily pleased border plants, happy in most conditions. From a winter-dormant clump develop ladder-like leaves of mid- to dark green. In early summer, erect or arching stems bear loose or clustered,

Persicaria bistorta 'Superba' is an excellent long-flowering perennial that thrives in moist soil.

tubular to funnel-shaped flowers in white, blue, lilac-mauve, pink or yellow. Most seed themselves freely.

Polemonium caeruleum is the best known, its upright stems, 60–90cm (24–36in) high, carrying funnel-shaped, lavender-blue flowers with pretty golden stamens. *Polemonium caeruleum* subsp. *caeruleum* f. *album* is the white form. *Polemonium caeruleum* BRISE D'ANJOU ('Blanjou') has leaves boldly variegated with creamy yellow. *Polemonium* 'Lambrook Mauve' ♥ is of similar stature; its pale lilac-mauve flowers blend effortlessly with both pale

Polemonium 'Lambrook Mauve'

and dark pink geraniums and with roses. *Polemonium carneum* produces flowers of pale pink, purple, lavender-blue or yellow, carried on stems 40cm

GOOD COMPANIONS

Scabiosa caucasica 'Clive Greaves' ♥ (1) looks delightful among clouds of *Gypsophila paniculata* 'Bristol Fairy' ♥ (2). Both plants enjoy a chalk soil in full sun.

The upright spikes of *Verbascum chaixii* 'Album' ♥ (3) look perfect above the soft mounds of *Geranium* 'Johnson's Blue' ♥ (4).

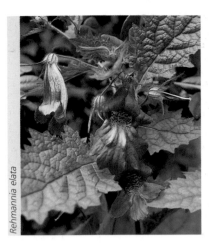

Rehmannia elata

(16in) in height. **'Apricot Delight'** is a pleasing apricot-pink form.

Polemonium pauciflorum is quite distinct among its fellows, having large, pendent, narrowly tubular flowers of pale yellow-green, on stems 50cm (20in) high. *Polemonium yezoense* **'Purple Rain'**, 60cm (24in) tall, has nodding, bell-shaped, pale blue flowers and green-purple leaves, lovely when mixed with fine silver foliage such as that of *Artemisia* 'Powis Castle' ♀.

Rehmannia elata ♀, the Chinese foxglove, is seldom seen in gardens, perhaps because it is thought to be tender, although in its native China, where it lives on cliff tops and in rock crevices, it is regularly exposed to low temperatures. The key to success in the garden is to give it well-drained soil; wet conditions, especially in winter, spell disaster. A sunny situation is preferred. The plant has softly hairy, mid-green foliage and lightly branched stems reaching 1.5m (5ft); from early summer until the first frosts, these carry large mid-pink, foxglove-like flowers with prominent divided lower lips and throats of pale yellow spotted red. If pinched at the tips, the lush growth will branch and maintain a modest height.

Rehmannias are fairly coarse-looking, but have beautiful flowers produced over a long period. Partner them with silver foliage subjects such as artemisias

Sidalcea 'Party Girl'

or herbaceous geraniums to conceal the lower part of the plants.

Scabiosa (also known as scabious or pincushion flower) are often found in grassland and meadows across many regions of Europe, Africa and Asia. They all like open, sunny situations and good drainage and generally thrive on chalk. Scabious flowers are popular with bees and butterflies, so are widely used in semi-natural or wild gardens. Some are annual or biennial. The perennial species are popular garden plants that produce a long succession of flowers from early summer sometimes into autumn. (See page 82.)

Sidalceas (prairie mallow) are natives of North America. The species *Sidalcea candida* and *Sidalcea malviflora* make an arresting sight, creating drifts of creamy-white or pink flowers in the moist, free-draining soils of meadows and river plains. Sidalceas are wonderful perennials for the herbaceous border. They form dense clumps of kidney-

shaped leaves from which arise erect, lightly branched stems, 30–90cm (12–36in) tall, carrying a succession of shallow, funnel-shaped flowers over a long period from early summer on.

Sidalcea candida is an old garden favourite, loved for its spikes of cream or white flowers. *Sidalcea malviflora* has pink to pink-lilac blooms and **'Alba'** is a silky white form. There are numerous garden varieties, which have larger flowers, 5cm (2in) across, on spikes reaching 70–90cm (28–36in) in height. *Sidalcea* **'Croftway Red'** is a rich, deep pink. **'Elsie Heugh'** ♀ produces showy purple-pink, fringed flowers. **'Party Girl'** lives up to its name with bright pink flowers, and is over 1m (40in) in height. **'Rosanna'** is a lovely satin, rosy pink, and **'Wine Red'** is pinkish red.

Stachys are usually associated with the wonderful silver mat of foliage belonging to *Stachys byzantina* and its cultivar **'Silver Carpet'** (see pages 103 and 105), but there are other species and cultivars with exceptional flowers. *Stachys macrantha* forms a clump of wrinkled, deeply veined, dark green leaves from which arise erect stems,

Stachys macrantha

60cm (24in) high, bearing many short, densely packed spikes of tubular, hooded, pinkish-purple flowers from early to late summer. **'Nivea'** is a less common white form; **'Robusta'**♀ is very floriferous in a lovely shade of purple. Of similar height and habit is *Stachys officinalis*, with more rounded heads of small pink, white, or reddish-purple flowers. **'Alba'** is the white form, **'Hummelo'** has purple flowers, and **'Saharan Pink'** is a bright mid-pink.

Verbascums (mullein) have enjoyed increasing popularity as easy-to-grow garden plants in recent years. Tall, upright flower spikes and felty leaves are their main features, useful to add a different shape and texture to the border. As a rule the tall species are biennial, the flower stems arriving in the second year, after which the plant often dies. The shorter species are regarded as perennials, albeit often short lived; the same is true of the garden hybrids.

Verbascum chaixii 'Album'

SOME VERBASCUM HYBRIDS

Verbascum **'Buttercup'** Good green, disease-resistant foliage and pretty yellow flowers. Height 1m (40in).

Verbascum **'Cotswold Beauty'**♀ A lovely shade of apricot-buff with dark eyes. Height 1m (40in).

Verbascum **'Helen Johnson'**♀ Pinkish orange-brown flowers above grey-green foliage. Height 90cm (3ft).

Verbascum **'Jackie'** A popular choice, with lovely pale apricot flowers on well-branched stems. Height 40cm (16in).

Verbascum **'Jackie in Pink'** (right) Delicious mid-pink flowers that age attractively to pale pink in light shade. Height 40cm (16in).

Verbascum **'Pink Domino'**♀ Purple-eyed, deep pink flowers. Height 1.2m (4ft).

Verbascum **'Raspberry Ripple'** Creamy-pink flowers flushed raspberry red in the centres. Height 60cm (24in).

The yellows of the tall species have been crossed with the white, pink, violet or dark purple of shorter species such as *Verbascum phoeniceum* to produce a

Verbascum 'Jackie in Pink'

wonderful palette of bold and pastel shades. Deciduous or semi-evergreen leaf rosettes give rise to a number of stems, each clad in numerous tightly packed, saucer-shaped flowers, often with darker eyes, from early to late summer. (See also page 104.)

Verbascum chaixii is a particularly useful plant that flowers for a long period and needs no additional support. It has grey leaves and yellow flowers with purple stamens, carried on spikes up to 1.5m (5ft) tall in early summer. **'Album'**♀ is a white form (see Good Companions, page 149). Both mix easily with most perennials and provide graceful vertical interest in the border.

Verbascums are happiest in full sun on poor, free-draining, alkaline soil. Fertile, wet soil produces tall, floppy growth and may result in mildew. The species are easily raised from seed, and some self-seed freely; garden hybrids can be propagated by root cuttings.

Late summer

Agapanthus africanus

Late summer is one of the richest seasons for perennials: warm pinks, blues and purples sit alongside the hot hues of crocosmias and alstroemerias. Deciduous shrubs, their flowers largely over, present no competition to this colourful display. Without late perennials the garden would be quiet and sombre; with their help the borders are alive and singing.

Agapanthus africanus 'Albus'

The grey-green and white striped foliage of *Iris pallida* 'Variegata' stays looking good into late summer. It contrasts beautifully with the vibrant purple blooms of *Verbena rigida.*

Agapanthus (African blue lily) are long-cultivated and widely naturalized plants, popular for their large, rounded heads of tubular, bell- or trumpet-shaped flowers in shades of blue or white, borne throughout summer. All form strong clumps of broad or narrow, fleshy, grass-like leaves, which may be evergreen or deciduous. They are at their most dramatic against a simple uncluttered background of a wall or evergreen shrub; the flowers are ideal for cutting.

Agapanthus thrive in moist, well-drained, fertile soil with plenty of sun. They dislike winter wet, especially in low temperatures; deciduous species should be given a dry mulch of bark or bracken and evergreen forms should be grown in containers that can be moved to a frost-free position. Well-established, mature plants produce the most flowers; avoid dividing clumps too often.

Agapanthus africanus ♀ produces clumps of evergreen foliage and heads of deep blue, trumpet-shaped flowers on stems up to 90cm (3ft) in height; 'Albus' ♀ is pure white. *Agapanthus campanulatus* has deciduous foliage with pale to dark blue trumpet flowers on stems 80–120cm (32–48in) high; **var. *albidus*** is white.

SOME FINE AGAPANTHUS HYBRIDS

'Blue Giant' Impressive heads of ink-blue flowers with dark stripes, carried on 1m (40in) stems.

'Blue Triumphator' (right) A little shorter than 'Blue Giant' with mid-blue, slightly pendulous flowers.

'Bressingham White' Similar to 'Blue Triumphator' but white.

'Lilliput' Dark blue flowers on stems reaching no more than 40cm (16in) high. Other dwarf cultivars include **'Gayle's Lilac'**, **'Snowball'** and the sky-blue **'Streamline'**.

'Loch Hope' ♀ Large, bright blue flowerheads on slender stems up to 1.5m (5ft) in height.

'Tinkerbell' Unique, with its dwarf, variegated foliage of green and creamy white. Not the hardiest agapanthus; shy in producing its pale blue flowers. Height 30cm (12in).

The distinctive species *Agapanthus caulescens* ♀ forms a short, fleshy stem sheathed in broad, deciduous foliage. Its heads of bell-shaped flowers are violet-blue, borne on stems to 1m (40in) high.

Over the years many wonderful garden hybrids have been produced, and have recently become more widely available through micropropagation. The hardy *Agapanthus* **Headbourne hybrids** are perhaps most commonly grown (see page 64).

Agastaches are underestimated plants. Their spikes of tightly packed,

AGAPANTHUS IN POTS

Agapanthus flower more freely when their roots are restricted, so growing them in pots is ideal. In summer they can be placed in full sun and kept well watered. With the onset of colder weather, they can be moved to a sheltered position near the house, or overwintered in a greenhouse or a conservatory.

Agapanthus 'Blue Triumphator'

tubular flowers and bracts are extremely long-lasting and come in shades of white, orange, pink, blue and purple. The grey-green leaves are aromatic and vary from narrow to broad and nettle-like, carried on upright stems. There are species native to Asia and the USA; all are drought-tolerant plants, thriving in fertile, well-drained soil in full sun; many are winter tender.

Agastache urticifolia has upright, 60cm (24in) stems of nettle-like leaves, topped in summer with spikes of pink-blue flowers. 'Alba' is a white form. *Agastache rugosa* is similar in habit. 'Golden Jubilee' is a striking cultivar: an overwintered crown of crinkled green-purple foliage grows into an upright, bright golden yellow plant, a perfect setting for the lavender flowers (see page 92). A hybrid of *Agastache foeniculum* (see page 50), *Agastache* 'Blue Fortune' has exceptionally showy mauve-blue spikes on stems 75–90cm (30–36in) high. These are the hardiest forms, and those most often seen.

Of the more tender agastaches, the following are worth growing for their flowers borne from midsummer through to autumn. *Agastache aurantiaca* 'Apricot Sprite' has 40cm (16in) stems laden with pale orange flowers. *Agastache* 'Painted Lady' produces compact, grey-green foliage on 50cm (20in) stems topped with captivating

flowers of pink-orange. *Agastache* 'Tutti-frutti', 60cm (24in) high, is very aromatic with lipstick-pink flowers.

Astrantias are delightful plants, both subtle and elegant. From a clump of glossy, deeply divided, palmate leaves, lightly branched stems carry a number of unusual pincushion-like flowerheads, set against ruffs of sharply divided, coloured bracts. The flowers appear from midsummer onwards, and can be cut for drying.

(continued on page 155)

Agastache 'Blue Fortune'

Agastache 'Painted Lady'

153

Peruvian lilies (Alstroemeria)

Alstroemerias, the Peruvian lilies, provide luxuriant colour in the late summer border. Originating from South America, they have tuberous roots and form spreading clumps of erect, fleshy, grey-green stems with lance-shaped leaves. Loose clusters of intricately patterned, lily-like flowers appear at the tips of the stems for several weeks from midsummer onwards. They make excellent, long-lasting cut flowers.

Alstroemerias like full sun and are surprisingly hardy. When planted in free-draining soil they will survive temperatures as low as −10°C (14°F); extra protection can be given with a dry mulch of bark or bracken. After two to three years, an established clump will have developed tubers deep enough to avoid all but the most penetrating frost.

Bare-root tubers can be planted 20cm (8in) deep in autumn or early spring. Plant pot-grown stock in spring, protecting any emerging shoots from frost with horticultural fleece. The lush stems, up to 1m (40in) high, find their way through adjacent plants that lend support. If accommodating neighbours are absent, artificial support may be required.

Alstroemeria aurea, a favourite since the mid-1900s, has bright orange-yellow flowers streaked in red on the inner surface. **'Dover Orange'** has the same red markings on deep orange petals, while **'Lutea'** is canary yellow with brown-flecked inner petals.

Alstroemeria psittacina **'Royal Star'** is less hardy than other alstroemerias. It has lightly variegated, dark green foliage with white margins, and produces subtle but gorgeous green and dark red flowers.

Alstroemeria ligtu **hybrids** are seed-raised from hybrids between the species *Alstroemeria ligtu* and *Alstroemeria haemantha*. They are hardy and reliable. Flowers are usually in shades of pink, with inner petals flushed yellow and streaked white, red or purple.

Alstroemeria **hybrids** Demand for alstroemerias as cut flowers has inspired breeders to develop a wonderful range of hybrids that are produced in volume by micropropagation. The larger-flowered hybrids make superb garden plants, albeit more expensive than species and old garden varieties.

'Spitfire' Yellow-flushed pinky red flowers with brown flecks; gold-variegated foliage.

'Apollo' ♀ White flowers with yellow throats and inner petals marked chocolate brown.

OTHER ALSTROEMERIA HYBRIDS

'Evening Song' Pink-red flowers flushed yellow and flecked deep mauve.

'Glory of the Andes' Fragrant, golden flowers with red-brown markings; variegated foliage.

'Orange Glory' ♀ Flowers are orange-red flushed golden orange and flecked red-brown.

'Red Beauty' Glowing pinkish-red flowers flushed with yellow and flecked chocolate-red.

Astrantia major

Native to alpine woods and meadows of Asia and Europe, astrantias grow easily in most gardens, thriving in moist, rich soil in sun or partial shade. Most self-seed and some species have become naturalized in parts of England.

Astrantia major has flowers of greenish pink to purple-red surrounded by white to pinkish-white bracts traced with green veining. There are many named selections, all growing 30–90cm (12–36in) high; most bloom again in autumn. *Astrantia major alba* has white heads, often tipped green, and is attractive with ferns and *Euphorbia amygdaloides* subsp. *robbiae*♥ (see page 57). **'Claret'** is wine red, **'Ruby Wedding'** is a lighter shade of red, and **'Rubra'** dark wine red. *Astrantia major* subsp. *involucrata* produces greenish-white flowers and bracts. **'Shaggy'**♥ (previously known as 'Margery Fish') is a popular selection featuring very long, sharply cut bracts with green tips. *Astrantia major*

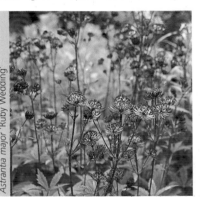

Astrantia major 'Ruby Wedding'

'Sunningdale Variegated'♥ has large, dark green leaves attractively marked with creamy white (see page 100).

The species *Astrantia maxima*♥ has less impressive foliage, but compensates for this with its 60cm (24in) stems of pale pink flowers and mid-pink bracts. *Astrantia* **'Hadspen Blood'**, a hybrid of *Astrantia major* and *Astrantia maxima* raised at Hadspen, Somerset, is a fine dark red cultivar of similar height, which blooms throughout the season.

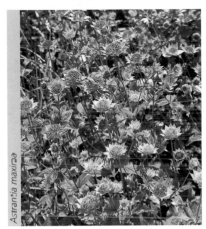

Astrantia maxima

Campanulas are a feature of gardens in early summer, and their display is continued by later-flowering varieties as the season progresses. They thrive in neutral to alkaline, well-drained soil in sun or part shade. (See also page 40.)

Campanula carpatica♥, often found in rock gardens, is a useful plant for the front of the border, the edge of a path or a container. It forms a neat mound, 30cm (12in) high, of bright,

CAMPANULAS FOR SHADE

Many campanulas are useful plants for partial shade, where they will grow and flower as well as they do in sun. Both *Campanula latiloba* and *Campanula latifolia* varieties are a good choice, as is the robust and floriferous *Campanula lactiflora* (see page 40), which will also colonize unkempt grassy areas.

Campanula 'Kent Belle'

crisp green foliage generously studded with buds and flowers. The upturned, bell-shaped, white to blue blooms appear unfeasibly large and, at times, almost completely obscure the plant. A number of forms have a more compact height of 15cm (6in), often with larger flowers in various shades of lavender to blue. The white *Campanula carpatica* f. *alba* **'Weisse Clips'** (WHITE CLIPS) and blue *Campanula carpatica* **'Blaue Clips'** (BLUE CLIPS) are readily available seed-raised selections.

Campanula **'Kent Belle'**♥ produces rosettes of toothed green leaves and 50cm (20in) stems carrying surprisingly large, shining purple-blue flowers. The colour is striking, the habit ungainly.

Campanula latifolia♥ is a tall, upright perennial over 1m (40in) high. The large tubular, bell-shaped flowers appear between the uppermost leaves. *Campanula latifolia* var. *alba* is white; **'Brantwood'** is deep purple-blue, and a more modest height at 75cm (30in).

Campanula latifolia var. *alba*

From a lush rosette of foliage, *Campanula latiloba* produces stout stems, 90cm (3ft) high, clothed in cupped, starry, rich lavender flowers. 'Highcliffe Variety'♀ is deep mauve-blue; 'Percy Piper'♀ is lavender-blue. (See also page 83.)

Campanula punctata forms a clump of 30cm (12in) stems bearing flowers of creamy white flushed pink, red spotted within. Individual blooms are pendent, bell-shaped and impressively large at 5cm (2in) long. *Campanula punctata* 'Hot Lips' is similar in colour and very free-flowering. 'Pantaloons' is unusual in that its petals are gently recurved to reveal a protruding inner layer. 'Wedding Bells' is similar but white. *Campanula punctata* f. *rubriflora* 'Cherry Bells' produces numerous rich pinkish-red bells on 50cm (20in) stems.

The vigorously spreading *Campanula takesimana* has glossy leaves and 50cm (20in) stems carrying pink-flushed white bells, speckled maroon inside.

Campanula trachelium, known as bats in the belfry, has nettle-like leaves and woody-based stems up to 80cm (32in) high. Outward-facing, tubular, bell-shaped, purple-blue flowers with lightly recurved petals grace the top of the stems. 'Bernice' has fully double, lilac-blue flowers; var. *alba*, the semi-double 'Alba Flore Pleno' and the fully double 'Snowball' are all white.

Catananche caerulea is a charming flower of Mediterranean meadows that will succeed in most gardens. Also

Catananche caerulea 'Major'

known as blue cupidane or Cupid's dart, it bears solitary dark-eyed, lilac-blue cornflower-like heads, 5cm (2in) across, on slender stems of over 50cm (20in), above a low-growing clump of narrow, grey-green leaves. The generally larger flowerheads of *Catananche caerulea* 'Major'♀ are of similar colouring on 45cm (18in) stems; 'Alba' is pure white; 'Bicolor' has a distinct flush of bright purple at the centre of each white flower. All will be in bloom from mid-summer onwards.

These are fully hardy, but short-lived perennials often treated as biennials; they produce flowers more prolifically in

their second year. Full sun and well-drained soil increase longevity.

By midsummer the cornflower blooms of *Centaurea montana* are nearly over, but exuberant *Centaurea hypoleuca* 'John Coutts' is still going strong (see page 133), and yet other centaureas are about to reach their peak. These late-blooming centaureas are easily accommodated perennials, requiring free-draining, moderately fertile soil in a sunny position.

Centaurea dealbata often needs support, with stems reaching 90cm (3ft). Each white-centred flowerhead is surrounded by a feathery ruff of bright pink. The divided foliage is light green. *Centaurea dealbata* 'Steenbergii' is rather more aggressive in habit, but its thuggish behaviour is forgiven on sight of the gorgeous deep pink flowers with pink-white centres, borne on 60cm (24in) stems. *Centaurea pulcherrima* has cream-centred pink blooms on stems 40cm (16in) high.

Preferring a moister soil, *Centaurea macrocephala* forms a robust clump of broad mid-green leaves, which diminish in size as they progress up the stout stems, to 1.5m (5ft) high. Quite unlike *(continued on page 158)*

(continued on page 158)

CATANANCHE IN GRASS

Catananche caerulea is suitable for naturalizing in grass, growing happily in areas managed as wildflower meadows (see page 54). Its charming blue flowers fulfil the role of cornflowers and are particularly pretty with the soft pink mallow, *Malva moschata*.

Centaurea macrocephala produces bold artichoke-like blooms, making a strong statement in the yellow border with the lighter foliage and flowers of achilleas.

Montbretias (Crocosmia)

Natives of South Africa, crocosmias (montbretia) have been in cultivation since the early 17th century. *Crocosmia × crocosmiiflora* thrives in the mild, damp climate of south-west England and, having escaped from gardens, has become widely naturalized there.

Crocosmias overwinter by means of underground corms that awake in late spring to produce pleated, sword-shaped leaves 50–100cm (20–40in) long. From midsummer onwards, slender, lightly branched, upright or arching stems bear a succession of funnel-shaped flowers up to 5cm (2in) long, in fiery shades of yellow, orange and red. The rounded, segmented seed capsules that follow are also attractive.

These handsome plants enjoy fertile soil, moist but free-draining. In areas of persistent frost the shelter of a sunny wall is appreciated. They will grow in partial shade but need full sun to flower well.

Crocosmias can be bought as dry corms, usually in early spring; these are planted 6–8cm (2½–3in) deep in clumps of 9–12. Pot-grown plants can be planted from late spring onwards; where conditions are less than ideal, these tend to be more successful. Lift and divide clumps in spring every few years to maintain vigour and flower quality.

Crocosmia 'Lucifer' ♀ is the most popular and widely planted of all crocosmias. It is extremely robust and reaches 1.2m (4ft) in height. It comes into flower early, bearing large, rich red blooms, and looks stunning with the blue-grey foliage of *Rosa glauca* ♀ and the terracotta and ochre flowers of achilleas.

Crocosmia × crocosmiiflora is the result of crossing the starry, mid-orange flowers of *Crocosmia aurea* with the more tubular, red *Crocosmia pottsii*. One of the hardiest, its vigorous, somewhat invasive growth produces stems of orange, occasionally yellow blooms. It has given rise to a rich array of cultivars, growing to around 60cm (24in).

'Carmin Brillant' ♀
Produces fiery red flowers.

'Emily McKenzie' Vigorous and free-flowering with long-lasting, open, dark orange flowers splashed with red.

GOOD CROCOSMIA X CROCOSMIIFLORA CULTIVARS

'Gerbe d'Or' Golden yellow buds open to bright canary-yellow blooms.

'Jackanapes' Unusual bicoloured flowers of orange-red and yellow.

'Lady Hamilton' Golden yellow flowers flushed with pale orange.

'Soltatare' ♀ Lovely bronzed foliage and pale orange-yellow flowers.

'Star of the East' ♀ Fully open, starry, bright orange flowers, paler towards the centres.

Crocosmia masoniorum ♀ is hardier than most, and taller at over 1m (40in), with striking orange-red blooms. These face upwards at the stem tips; with most other crocosmias, the flowers point forwards under the stems. 'Rowallane Yellow' ♀ (above) is rich golden yellow with orange overtones.

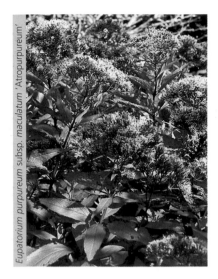

Eupatorium purpureum subsp. maculatum 'Atropurpureum'

Gaillardia pulchella

the other species, it forms large buds covered in brown, scale-like bracts, opening to a mass of fine golden yellow petals, similar in appearance to a thistle.

Coreopsis verticillata is a compact perennial, 30cm (12in) high, with wiry stems and fine narrow leaves. Small, starry yellow flowers are freely borne from midsummer (see page 27). 'Moonbeam' ♥ is pale yellow, an easier colour to mix with others.

Growing in moist to wet soil in sun or part shade, *Eupatorium purpureum* is a landmark of the late summer border. The stems, rising 2m (6ft) or so high, are furnished with tiers of coarse, pointed, mid-green leaves, making an effective backdrop to other plants. Domed heads of pink, pinkish-purple or white flowers are produced at the stem tips from mid-summer through to early autumn. The form *Eupatorium purpureum* subsp. *maculatum* 'Atropurpureum' ♥ is the most widely grown. The stems are reliably red, the colour often spreading to the foliage; the flowerheads are of a richer red.

Eupatorium rugosum is less often seen. Its nettle-like foliage reaches 1.5m (5ft) or more in height, and clusters of bright white flowers appear at the tips of the stems. *Eupatorium rugosum* 'Chocolate' ♥ is valuable for the rich

deep colouring of its foliage (see Good Companions, below, and see page 90).

Gaillardias (blanket flower) provide some of the brightest and most cheerful blooms in the border, the dual colouring of the daisy flowerheads shamelessly grabbing attention from midsummer into autumn. Two species, both American natives, are the parents of our garden hybrids. The perennial species *Gaillardia aristata* has flowerheads with sunny, mid-yellow, fringed ray-like petals surrounding blood-red, button-like centres, while the ray florets of the annual *Gaillardia pulchella* are

predominantly red with a variable rim of yellow. Both thrive in the full sun of grasslands and rocky slopes, the latter species in desert conditions, making them undemanding of the gardener even in the hottest of summers.

Gaillardia hybrids and cultivars are short-lived perennials, and are often treated as bedding plants. Give them a free-draining winter location sheltered from wet to increase their longevity. They are easily propagated from seed, most producing flowers within a year; alternatively try taking root cuttings in autumn and winter.

GOOD COMPANIONS

The pale yellow sunflower blooms of *Helianthus* 'Lemon Queen' ♥ (1) are carried on tall plants and look stunning set against the wine and flame autumn foliage of *Cotinus* 'Grace' (2).

The dark purple-brown foliage of *Eupatorium rugosum* 'Chocolate' ♥ (3) is sumptuous with the red, purple and pink foliage of *Berberis thunbergii* f. *atropurpurea* 'Rose Glow' ♥ (4).

Many selections are available; most are 60–75cm (24–30in) tall. *Gaillardia* 'Burgunder' is deep wine red, while 'Dazzler'♥ has orange-red ray florets tipped with yellow, around centres of deep red. 'Kobold', one of the most popular, is a compact, bushy plant only 30cm (12in) tall. It produces blood-red flowerheads tipped with mid-yellow for long periods of summer into autumn. 'Fanfare' is a more recent variety. Each flowerhead has a dark red centre surrounded by red tubular ray florets, tipped in bright yellow. It grows to 40cm (16in) and makes a wonderful cut flower.

Geraniums, prolific in spring and early summer, have yet more to offer in late summer. With neat or sprawling habits and leaves of varying size, shape and texture, the hardy geraniums are also blessed with variety of flower. (See also pages 48, 67 and 137.)

Geranium 'Ann Folkard'♥ flowers from midsummer into autumn, its striking magenta, black-eyed blooms seeming to float above the foliage. Scrambling stems bear attractive, maple-like leaves of bright yellow-green, maturing to mid-green. Growing 60cm (24in) tall, it makes excellent ground cover and will spread over a large area in sun or semi-shade. (See also page 93.)

Geranium × *oxonianum*, too, is in bloom from midsummer to autumn, bearing wave upon wave of mid-pink, starry flowers. Forming a vigorous clump of toothed, segmented foliage, 80cm (32in) high, it is an effective ground-cover plant. 'A.T. Johnson'♥ is a favourite cultivar, with a wealth of pale pink flowers. The larger, more widely spaced petals of 'Sherwood' are white flushed mid-pink at the tips, with deep pink veins. *Geranium* × *oxonianum* f. *thurstonianum* has narrow, deep pink petals, often notched at the tips, with white centres to the flowers. The double form 'Southcombe Double' has multi-layered mid-pink petals.

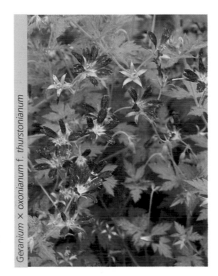

Geranium × *oxonianum* f. *thurstonianum*

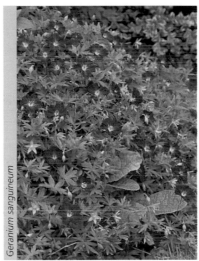

Geranium sanguineum

Geranium sanguineum forms a neat mat, 20cm (8in) high, of fine, soft green leaves, deeply cut into narrow fingers. Numerous upward-facing, cup-shaped flowers hug the foliage; they are deep pink in the species, white in the case of 'Album'♥, purple-pink for 'New Hampshire Purple', and deep pink-red on the extremely compact 'Shepherd's Warning'♥. The popular *Geranium sanguineum* var. *striatum*♥ grows to about 10cm (4in) high, and bears pale pink flowers with darker veining.

Geranium wallichianum 'Buxton's Variety'♥ is always sought after. It has superb saucer-shaped flowers, each with a large white centre, generously

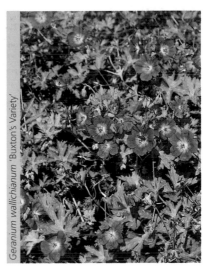

Geranium wallichianum 'Buxton's Variety'

margined sky blue and veined in bluish purple. Trailing, branched stems, 30cm (12in) high, carry the flowers from mid-summer to autumn, when they age to shades of pinkish blue and purple.

Few other perennials make such an impact in late summer plantings as the glorious **heleniums**. Clumps of sturdy stems clothed in lance-shaped mid-green leaves are topped with a wealth of daisy-like flowerheads in shades of yellow through orange-red, with bold yellow to golden brown centres. At up to 1.5m (5ft) tall, they have a dramatic effect mid-border.

In the wild they grow in the moist meadows and prairies of North and Central America. There are annual and biennial heleniums, but those that are commonly grown in gardens are the herbaceous perennial species and their hybrids. All reliably hardy, they are perfect for a sunny border, thriving in fertile, moist, well-drained soil. The shorter ones are self-supporting, but the taller varieties may need support. Most begin to flower in midsummer and go on right through autumn. *Helenium* 'Baudirektor Linne'♥ has satin red-brown petals with brown centres. 'Butterpat'♥ is bright yellow with golden yellow centres. 'Rubinzwerg'♥ has orange-red petals surrounding

159

Helenium 'Sahin's Early Flowerer'

Helianthus 'Loddon Gold'

golden brown centres. **'Sahin's Early Flowerer'**♀ has yellow flowers with orange streaks arriving in early to mid-summer on more compact plants, 70cm (30in) high. (See also pages 42 and 52.)

The perennial forms of *Helianthus* (sunflower) are not as well known as the annual varieties, but they are valuable for sunny colour in late summer; most reach the relatively modest height of 1.5m (5ft). They like neutral to alkaline soil with a fair amount of moisture in full sun. *Helianthus* **'Gullick's Variety'**♀ is extremely free-flowering, producing masses of yellow blooms with purple-brown centres. **'Loddon Gold'**♀ has numerous fully double golden blooms on very upright, stocky stems. **'Lemon Queen'**♀ produces vibrant, pale yellow flowerheads (see Good Companions, page 158).

Many **inulas** are monumental plants, familiar but often not readily identified by gardeners. Dormant in winter and spring, they grow steadily through the summer, forming a robust clump of coarse, dark green leaves up to 25cm (10in) long, with stems of bright daisy-like flowerheads in shades of yellow to orange, from midsummer into autumn. Thriving in rich, moist soil and full sun, inulas are good for the edge of a bog garden and for the exotic border.

Inula magnifica produces hairy stems, almost 2m (6ft) tall, streaked dark brown-purple. In late summer these carry a stunning show of bright, golden yellow flowerheads, each one up to 15cm (6in) across. *Inula helenium*, more commonly grown as elecampane, has smaller, bright yellow flowers, borne on 1–2m (3–6ft) stems in mid- to late summer; it is prized for the medicinal property of its roots.

At about 45cm (18in) high, *Inula ensifolia* is altogether smaller, perfect for a patio container or border's edge. In mid- to late summer, bushy growth of grey-green leaves is topped by plentiful heads of golden yellow flowers.

Inula hookeri has sunshine-yellow flowers with brownish-yellow centres, borne on 70cm (28in) stems from late summer into autumn. It prefers partial shade, where its spreading roots and upright stems will quickly colonize uncultivated areas.

ANNUAL SUNFLOWERS

The annual sunflowers need little introduction, familiar for their giant growth of up to 5m (15ft), with flowerheads as big as dinner plates. While *Helianthus annuus* itself is no more than a towering novelty, many of the new shorter varieties are useful late-flowering plants to fill gaps in the border. Easily raised from seed, they quickly reach heights of around 1.5m (5ft). They have larger flowers than the perennial sunflowers, in a richer colour range; their shades of yellow, russet, orange and brown associate particularly well with dahlias.

Inula hookeri

Kirengeshoma palmata

Monarda 'Croftway Pink'

Flowering in roughly the same period in similar conditions are the closely related *Telekia* and *Buphthalmum*. **Telekia speciosa** is another bold beauty growing almost 2m (6ft) tall, with large, broad, dark green leaves and branched stems carrying yellow, daisy-like flowerheads. Tolerating much drier conditions, **Buphthalmum salicifolium** is superb for a Mediterranean border; its 60cm (24in) stems of fine foliage bear a succession of bright yellow daisies.

Kirengeshoma palmata is a Japanese treasure forming a clump of dark red, slender, gently arching stems, 1m (40in) high, clothed in maple-like leaves. In late summer, each stem ends in a lightly branched arrangement of nodding, tubular, canary-yellow flowers with slightly recurved, waxy petals. This robust, hardy perennial is by nature a woodland plant, requiring lime-free, rich, moist soil in dappled shade. An annual mulch of leaf mould is beneficial.

Monardas (bee balm or bergamot) are wonderful garden plants from North America. They form dense clumps of upright stems clothed in aromatic, mint-like, mid- to dark green leaves, which are sometimes bronzed purple. The individual flowers are similar to those of sage and mint, but are much larger. At the top of stems 1m (40in) high, neat, leaf-like pink, purple or red-flushed bracts open to reveal stunning heads of tubular, two-lipped flowers, in white or shades of pink, red and violet. Often the stem extends beyond the first flowers to develop yet another tier. Typically the flowers are borne from midsummer into autumn. A situation in full sun or partial shade is required, in reasonably fertile, reliably moist soil.

Of the many monardas available, most are derived from *Monarda didyma*, a species with bright red or pink flowers above red-tinged bracts. **Monarda**

PREVENTING MILDEW ON MONARDAS

Although monardas are very garden-worthy plants, they are rather prone to powdery mildew. In late summer, it is common to see plants with entirely grey foliage as a result of infestation by the fungus. To try to prevent the problem, do not let the roots dry out from early summer on; plants under stress are far more susceptible. At first signs of attack spray with a fungicide and water plants thoroughly.

'Beauty of Cobham' has purple-bronzed foliage with pale lilac-pink flowers above pinkish-purple bracts. 'Croftway Pink' produces bold heads of mid-pink flowers. 'Mahogany' has rich red-brown bracts and flowers of bright pinkish red. 'Schneewittchen' (SNOW WHITE) is a pure white variety with green bracts. 'Violet Queen' is rich violet-purple, good with orange and red kniphofias.

Oenotheras (evening primrose) are well known for their fragrant flowers opening at dusk, although some species open at dawn. They are native mainly to the Americas, but some popularly planted biennial varieties have become naturalized in Europe, where they are a fairly common sight on roadside verges. They thrive in fertile, free-draining soil in full sun, but dislike wet conditions.

Oenothera fruticosa is a short-lived perennial responsible for many familiar garden hybrids. Upright, branched red stems, up to 80cm (32in) tall and with small dark leaves, bear clusters of deep yellow, funnel-shaped flowers, which

(continued on page 164)

Penstemons

There are over 250 species of penstemon, all natives of the Americas, and the innumerable hybrids derived from them are among our most popular herbaceous perennials. Selected for their bushy, upright habit and large, tubular or bell-shaped flowers, they bloom from midsummer into early winter in mild areas and mostly retain their foliage throughout the year. As a rule those with broader, larger leaves are less hardy than those with fine, narrow leaves.

When introduced in the late 1700s, penstemons were regarded as short-lived perennials. The plant hunter Reginald Farrer later described them as having 'a crowded hour of glory rather than a longer existence of mere usefulness'. Over the years we have learned more about how to grow them; as a result, and through hybridization and selection, penstemons today are hardier than many people realize.

Penstemons thrive in poor, free-draining, slightly alkaline soil, ideally in full sun. In wet conditions

Penstemon 'Raven' ♥ is an upright cultivar, reaching 90cm (3ft) in height. The leaves are broad and dark. The spikes of large tubular flowers are carried at the top of the stems from early summer through to late autumn. The darkest, rich purple, they are a perfect contrast to silver foliage plants.

some plants struggle to survive the winter. On heavy soils add grit when planting and spread gravel on the soil surface. Do not plant too deeply. Removing spent flower stems maintains vigour and encourages further flowering. Some species can be grown from seed and the garden cultivars propagated by cuttings.

Penstemon hybrids always produce healthy shoots at the base of the plant so it is tempting to cut stems back to ground level and allow the new shoots to take over. However, cutting back hard in spring results in plants that are late to come into flower. It is better just to tidy the plants, removing any remaining seedheads and any dead or damaged growth; the overwintered stems will then start to flower in early summer.

Penstemon heterophyllus is a low, spreading plant with lax stems, up to 30cm (12in) high, and narrow, shining green leaves. Small, pink-flushed blue flowers are produced early in the season, usually with intermittent blooms later. **'Catherine de la Mare'** ♥ (above) is excellent, with dark green foliage and brilliant blue flowers with lavender-blue markings.

OTHER GOOD PENSTEMON HYBRIDS

All grow 60–90cm (24–36in) high.

'Evelyn' ♥ Numerous small, bright pink flowers.

'George Home' ♥ Small wine-red flowers.

'Hidcote Pink' ♥ Pale pink flowers, delicately streaked crimson.

'Stapleford Gem' ♥ Distinctive lilac-blue flowers flushed pink-purple, with white throats striped purple.

'White Bedder' ♥ (also known as 'Snow Storm') Conical white flowers that age with just a hint of pink.

'Windsor Red' Narrow, white-throated, vibrant red flowers.

Penstemon pinifolius ♥, a spreading sub-shrub, is a favourite for scree. It has needle-like leaves on 40cm (16in) stems with bright red flowers. Cultivars include **'Wisley Flame'** ♥ with orange-red flowers, and **'Mersea Yellow'**.

Penstemon campanulatus Upright and semi-evergreen, with slender stems 30–70cm (12–28in) high. Flowers are small and numerous, in shades of pink to purple to violet. Early flowering.

Penstemon barbatus, a hardy species, reaching over 1m (40in) in height. With its blue-green foliage and rosy red flowers with bearded lips, it attracted much attention at the Royal Botanic Gardens, Kew, when it was introduced in 1793.

Penstemon digitalis 'Husker Red' Rosettes of dark green foliage, deep red when young, from which 60cm (24in) stems of small pinkish-white flowers emerge as summer progresses.

Penstemon hartwegii ♥ Stems up to 1m (40in) high carry a glorious show of nodding purple-red tubular bells with white throats.

Penstemon 'Andenken an Friedrich Hahn' ♥ (also known as *Penstemon* 'Garnet') is an old favourite, one of the hardiest of the penstemon hybrids, with fine foliage and large tubular, bell-shaped wine-red flowers. Its light habit and prolific flowers make it a perfect subject for the mixed border, where it will prolong the season of the early shrub roses. Height 75cm (30in).

Penstemon 'Alice Hindley' ♥ Large flowers of iridescent lilac-blue are carried on light spikes 90cm (3ft) high. It has a vigorous habit and good foliage. Grown as an alternative to the well-known but somewhat unreliable 'Sour Grapes' ♥.

Penstemon smallii Glossy, bronze-green basal leaves and numerous stems of bearded, lavender-purple flowers, white striped within. Prefers moister soil. Height 60cm (24in).

163

Autumn

As dewy mornings develop into mellow days and colder nights warn of impending frosts, the softer, warm-blooded blooms of summer make way for the brave and beautiful flowers of autumn. Delicate colours and graceful habits belie their hardiness, many continuing their display into early winter. Against the fiery tints of autumn foliage, the rich blues and purples of asters sing out all the louder. Evergreens provide a dark backdrop to the delicate pastel blooms of anemones.

The pale mauve-pink of *Anemone × hybrida* 'September Charm' is delightful in dappled shade in the soft light of autumn.

Anemones that flower in autumn are delightful perennials that have been grown in gardens for many generations, finding a welcome both in the cottage garden and in the grand herbaceous border. Popularly known as Japanese anemones, they have maple-like leaves and branched stems of up to 1m (40in) tall that, from late summer, produce airy clusters of silver buds and simple, saucer-shaped flowers with golden stamens. These anemones enjoy moist, fertile soil and are useful for their shade tolerance. Once established, they spread freely through the border, which may not suit carefully composed plantings.

Varieties belonging to *Anemone hupehensis* tend to flower from mid- to late summer, while those coming from *Anemone vitifolia* start to bloom later, continuing through autumn. *Anemone × hybrida* cultivars are the results of hybridizing the two species.

Anemone hupehensis bears either white or pink flowers on stems 80cm (32in) tall. **'Hadspen Abundance'** ♥ has pale and darker pink in the same flower, and blooms over a long period. *Anemone hupehensis* var. *japonica* has flowers with more numerous narrow

The single pink flowers of *Anemone hupehensis* 'Hadspen Abundance' clash happily with the vibrant autumn shades of heleniums.

petals, borne on stems often over 1m (40in). 'Pamina'♥ is a more compact alternative, at 50cm (20in), and its neatly double flowers are of a beautiful deep pink. 'Prinz Heinrich' (PRINCE HENRY)♥ produces a lovely show of semi-double, rose-pink blooms.

Anemone × hybrida 'Honorine Jobert'♥, with 1.2m (4ft) stems of large, single, pure white flowers, is the finest of the autumn anemones (see Good Companions, page 177). It looks stunning when planted against a dark evergreen hedge. 'Königin Charlotte' (QUEEN CHARLOTTE)♥ produces large semi-double, silky pink blooms on stems 1m (40in) tall. 'September Charm'♥

has an abundance of pale pink blooms. 'Whirlwind' is white and double, but lacks the sophistication of the single varieties. (See also page 46.)

Asters, which are best known for the Michaelmas daisies of the cottage garden, deliver an unrivalled show of colour late in the season. Their daisy flowers have a delightful simplicity and are good mixers both in the border and as cut flowers. Most of the popular hardy perennial species form clumps of upright stems clothed in lance-shaped mid-green leaves. Native to much of the northern hemisphere, most enjoy full sun or part shade in moderately fertile, moist but well-drained soil. Although some will tolerate dry conditions, any prolonged extremes of dry or wet will cause stress, increasing susceptibility to powdery mildew in some varieties.

Aster amellus provides a wonderful range of shades: flowerheads up to 5cm (2in) across are borne on stems of 30–60cm (12–24in). 'Brilliant' has bright pink blooms; 'Veilchenkönigin' (VIOLET QUEEN)♥ is rich violet; 'King George'♥ is lilac-blue. These asters flower for a long period and their mid-green foliage is far less prone to mildew.

Aster ericoides delivers a mass of much smaller white flowers, on stems 1m (40in) tall, throughout autumn. 'Brimstone'♥ has unusual creamy-white sprays; 'Blue Star'♥ is sky blue; and 'Golden Spray'♥ produces waves of golden-centred white flowers with just a hint of pink. 'Pink Cloud'♥ is a hazy pale pink and is seldom troubled by mildew. Other asters with small flowers in light sprays include *Aster lateriflorus* 'Prince', 60cm (24in) high, with starry white flowers with rosy-red centres and the added bonus of purple-red young growth ageing to dusky green. Every flower arranger will be familiar with the commercially grown *Aster pilosus* var. *pringlei* 'Monte Cassino'♥, with its graceful sprays of dainty white, yellow-centred daisies and dark green foliage; it grows 1m (40in) tall. (See also page 51.)

Aster × frikartii is a real autumn treasure, flowering for long periods. Considered by many to be the best, *Aster × frikartii* 'Mönch'♥ produces flowers of a wonderful lavender-blue with prominent yellow centres. Growing 60–90cm (24–36in) high, it is resistant to mildew so can be given a place at the front of the border, where its light form will not obscure other plants behind.

The Michaelmas daisy, *Aster novi-belgii*, is rather blighted by its readiness to succumb to mildew, but with due care can still play a valuable role among

(continued on page 174)

Aster × frikartii 'Mönch'

Anemone hupehensis var. *japonica* 'Prinz Heinrich' (PRINCE HENRY)

171

Dahlias

Dahlias have been a gardeners' passion for generations. Species from Central America and Mexico found their way into European gardens from the mid-17th century, and they soon became fashionable blooms of high society. Today their colourful flowers brighten so many gardens and are popular subjects for competition.

Dahlias excel for their variety of flower form, which ranges from small and daisy-like to large and spherical, and includes blooms resembling peonies, waterlilies and anemones. The colour range too is astonishing, from whites and creams to deep reds and purples, including a wide choice of pastel shades. Plants are bushy and grow from tuberous roots, producing stems bearing leaves with toothed, oval leaflets, which in some cases are beautifully bronzed or deep red.

The dahlias with smaller, relatively simple flowers are excellent garden plants: in bloom from midsummer through to autumn, their colours suit bold planting schemes, and their flower form looks at home in the traditional border. They are also excellent for cutting.

Dahlias are easy to grow, given fertile, free-draining soil and a sunny position. Dry tubers can be planted where they are to flower in mid-spring, or started into growth under glass in early spring. Pinch the tips of new growth to encourage stout stems. Protect from frost; dahlia shoots are tender and susceptible to cold.

In regions where winters are severe, tubers are best lifted when the foliage is knocked back by the first frost. Remove all soil and lay out the tubers to dry; then place in a dry medium such as sand and store in a frost-free, airy location. Check for fungal infections from time to time and treat as necessary with a fungicidal dust such as sulphur.

In a sheltered position on free-draining soil, many gardeners have success overwintering dahlias outside. Dry tubers are inexpensive and readily available, so failures are easily replaced. Pot-grown plants are sold in early summer and provide instant impact.

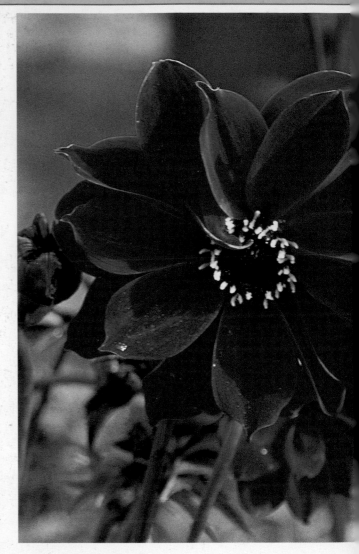

Dahlia 'Bishop of Llandaff' ♀ is the most popular dahlia for general planting. Dark chocolate foliage, reaching 90cm (3ft) or more high, throws tall stems of semi-double, dark-eyed, bright scarlet flowers. As the blooms mature, golden stamens ring the centres. This is a stunning plant, combining well with *Verbena bonariensis* ♀. *Dahlia* 'Tally Ho' ♀ offers a shorter version, at a height of 60cm (24in) or more.

For propagation, softwood cuttings can be taken when tubers start into growth in spring. The cuttings will produce fully developed plants in their first season and tubers by the following autumn. Tuber size varies according to variety, but it is improved by feeding with a high-phosphate fertilizer during the growing season.

Dahlia 'Moonfire' ♀, at 70cm (28in) high, is a favourite for patio containers. Its dark, red-brown foliage is the perfect setting for the numerous single golden-orange, red-centred flowers produced in long succession from midsummer through to late autumn.

Dahlia 'Roxy' Single, bright magenta flowers on dark, dusky red stems above chocolate foliage. Height 60cm (24in)

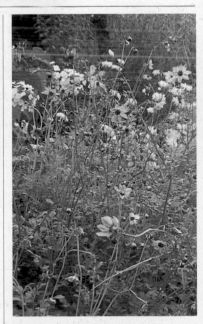

OTHER GOOD DAHLIAS FOR BORDERS

Dahlia 'Arabian Night' Small, double, upward-facing flowers of the darkest red. Height 1m (40in) or more. Good for cutting.

Dahlia 'Chimborazo' Dark red outer petals with an inner circle of shorter, yellow-tipped petals. Height 1.5m (5ft). Suits informal planting.

Dahlia 'Grenadier' Similar in colour to 'Bishop of Llandaff' and equally good. Double, deep scarlet flowers; excellent dark foliage. Height 90cm (3ft) or more.

Dahlia coccinea, one of the original species, has small, single, rich orange flowers and dusky green foliage. Height is 60cm (24in).

Dahlia 'David Howard' ♀ produces delightful small, double, apricot-orange blooms above dark bronzed foliage. Height 90cm (3ft). It was discovered as a seedling of 'Bishop of Llandaff' in the late 1950s and has been enjoyed ever since.

Dahlia merckii Numerous small, single flowers in shades of lavender-pink with yellow centres; has lush growth and a looser habit, 1.5m (5ft) high.

other late flowers (see page 40). The New England aster, *Aster novae-angliae*, a native of North America, seems resistant to mildew and its robust stems of bloom, in excess of 1m (40in), produce a reliable, loud display. 'Barr's Pink' has semi-double flowers of lipstick pink with gold centres; 'Mrs S.T. Wright' is lilac-pink; 'Rubinschatz' is pinkish red, and 'Violetta' violet-pink.

Chrysanthemums are usually thought of as beauties planted in neat rows at the back of the vegetable plot, carefully nurtured, supported and dis-budded in order to produce the finest of blooms. Some chrysanthemums are less demanding and grow happily among other perennials in the border, prolonging the flowering season with their mellow shades, including pink, red and purple, as well as yellow and white. The flowers are borne on woody-based, upright stems, clad with dark green, oval, deeply or shallowly cut leaves, which are distinctly aromatic. A sunny site in reasonably fertile, free-draining soil is required, enriched with plenty of well-rotted manure for best results.

The **Rubellum Group** consists of named selections or hybrids between *Chrysanthemum rubellum* (now *Chrysanthemum zawadskii*) and other notable species. These are hardy border perennials, also good for cutting. All

Chrysanthemum 'Clara Curtis'

Chrysanthemum Rubellum Group

have yellow-centred, daisy flowerheads on stems usually up to 75cm (30in) high, in late summer and early autumn.

Chrysanthemum 'Clara Curtis' is a favourite, with deeply divided foliage and stems carrying long-lasting sprays of single mid-pink flowerheads. 'Emperor of China' is taller, at over 1m (40in), and has double, pale pink-white flowers with red-bronzed foliage in late summer and autumn. 'Mrs Jessie Cooper' has larger, semi-double, vibrant red flowers, 10cm (4in) across. 'Nancy Perry' has deep pink, semi-double flowerheads.

Rubellum Group chrysanthemums are divided in autumn; healthy divisions can be replanted or potted in a frost-free situation to replace any winter losses. Members of this group tend to be less

susceptible to many of the pests and diseases that affect chrysanthemums; as part of the border, they should remain largely trouble-free.

The florists' spray chrysanthemums, developed mainly for cutting and for exhibition, are not such hardy creatures. They grow 80–140cm (32–56in) high and flower from late summer into autumn. There is a fine range of flower forms: alongside the singles, doubles and semi-doubles are the spherical or pompon heads made up of layer upon layer of ray-like petals; those resembling a large daisy with a broad central disc are referred to as 'anemone-centred'. The florists' chrysanthemums are usually propagated from basal cuttings, best taken in late spring.

CHRYSANTHEMUM LEAF MINER

This insect pest burrows through the leaf blade between the upper and lower surfaces, manifesting itself as a progressive filigree pattern of light green to buff appearing throughout the leaf. It obviously causes extensive damage to the foliage so early identification and eradication is desirable. Pick off and destroy affected leaves as they appear. Treat the plant with a systemic insecticide if the problem persists.

GOOD COMPANIONS

The yellow-centred lavender-blue flowerheads of *Aster* × *frikartii* 'Mönch' ✿ (1) sit well above the bright pink blooms of *Nerine bowdenii* ✿ (2).

As autumn progresses, the wispy leaves of *Carex buchananii* ✿ (3) reflect the warm tones of the fading blooms of *Sedum* 'Herbstfreude' (AUTUMN JOY) ✿ (4).

Chrysanthemum 'Buff Margaret' has fully double, rounded heads 9cm (3in) across in a creamy honey-orange. 'Enbee Wedding' ♀ has single pinkish-white flowers, effective against a dark shrub or hedge. 'Pennine Oriel' ♀ has large, anemone-centred flowers of buff-white with pale yellow centres.

Echinaceas (coneflower) produce their daisy-like flowerheads on upright, leafy stems from late summer into autumn. After the petals have fallen, the cone-like seedheads remain attractive into winter. Most varieties are derived from the rich reddish-purple *Echinacea purpurea*, some especially familiar through their use in prairie plantings (see page 51).

Other excellent varieties to grace the autumn garden include *Echinacea purpurea* 'Indiaca', which is similar to the species, but in some flowers there are more petals appearing from the top of the cone. This 'double-decker' effect is a random occurrence, not to be found on every bloom. *Echinacea purpurea* 'Razzmatazz' also resembles the species except that the central cone of each flowerhead is replaced with a mass of shorter, notched petals, not unlike a fully double dahlia. *Echinacea purpurea* 'Jade' has single flowers with white, green-tipped petals and dark green cones. All grow to 1m (40in) high.

Two other prairie echinaceas are somewhat lighter in habit, and their flowers consist of much narrower ray-like petals around the central cone. *Echinacea angustifolia* is dainty and pale pink, and a favourite of butterflies. *Echinacea paradoxa* is similar but mid-yellow. A new hybrid, *Echinacea* 'Art's Pride', shares this flower form, with narrow petals of rich mid-orange around each cone; it makes a delightful garden plant and a lovely cut flower.

Like many prairie plants, echinaceas like full sun and rich, well-drained soil with an adequate supply of moisture.

Echinacea 'Art's Pride'

Where conditions are too dry, plants are slow to become established.

Kniphofias (red hot poker or torch lily) have been popular garden plants since Victorian times. Some start to flower from early summer, others peak in late autumn. Their bright, torch-like flowers suit hot colour schemes and excel with the warm shades of autumn. (See also pages 42 and 68.)

Kniphofia caulescens ♀, also called the Lesotho red hot poker, grows to 1.2m (4ft) high and provides glorious heads of pinkish-orange flowers, which mature to lime yellow as they open from bottom to top. The glaucous, evergreen foliage is attractive in itself. The flowers of the slightly shorter *Kniphofia* 'Percy's Pride' start off lime yellow, but turn to creamy yellow as they mature. *Kniphofia* 'Erecta', 90cm (3ft) tall, carries its flowers upside down when in tight bud but, on opening, each tubular flower points skywards in a show of fiery orange-red.

Physalis alkekengi ♀ (Chinese lantern) reaches its full glory in early autumn, when its large, deep orange, papery lanterns glow against a mass of yellowing foliage. During early summer its spreading stems of diamond-shaped leaves and small, starry cream flowers command little attention. By late season plants carry a succession of blooms alongside developing green lanterns and those already turning orange.

Close inspection of the lanterns reveals a shiny orange berry at the centre of each. The berries become more visible as winter progresses and the lanterns lose their colour, exposing their intricate skeletal frames.

Physalis likes well-drained soil in sun or partial shade, and is best in a location where its vigorous habit will cause least mischief. Growing up to 75cm (30in) tall, the stems become rather lax and undisciplined and may need support. There are dwarf selections growing to 50cm (20in) that are more controllable.

Physalis alkekengi

DRYING CHINESE LANTERNS

Chinese lanterns (*Physalis alkekengi*) are wonderful for winter decoration in the home. Cut the lanterns as they mature, remove any remaining yellow leaves and support the stems in a tall vase without water until dry. Wooden skewers or thin canes may be needed to keep the stems straight. Just three stems in a slender ceramic vase make a superb contemporary arrangement.

Sedums

Sedums are well known for attracting butterflies and bees, which search for nectar in the tiny, star-shaped flowers that crowd the flat flowerheads. Many are grown in planters and rock gardens, their diminutive foliage borne on trailing stems forming dense mounds or mats, but they also have a role to play elsewhere in the garden. *Sedum kamtschaticum*♡, for example, is excellent in scree or at the front of the border. Its dark, spoon-shaped leaves and clustered yellow flowers are also useful to fill gaps between bearded iris rhizomes.

The taller herbaceous species form clumps of upright, unbranched stems bearing oval to rounded-oblong, grey-green to blue-green, succulent leaves. They die down in winter, leaving behind a cluster of blue-green succulent buds. The flowers peak in late summer and autumn: flat heads of white or pink. When faded, the browned stems and mahogany heads can be left until spring to provide winter interest.

Sedums typically thrive in free-draining, shallow soils, preferring chalk. Mature clumps tend to collapse

Sedum 'Herbstfreude' (AUTUMN JOY)♡ has large, flat heads of rich pink flowers on 60cm (24in) stems. The blooms turn coppery pink then mahogany and last well into early winter.

in autumn if grown in moist, fertile sites, so grow-through supports may be necessary; annual division and replanting will also help to avoid the problem. Sedums are easy to propagate by stem cuttings, taken at any time in the growing season.

Sedum telephium, 60cm (24in) high, has heads of purple-pink flowers above pale grey-green foliage. The cultivar **'Matrona'** has larger, rounded leaves; **'Munstead Red'**, a Gertrude Jekyll plant, has darker foliage with a distinct purple flush and pleasant, rich brown-red flowers. *Sedum telephium* subsp. *maximum* **'Atropurpureum'**♡ has striking purple foliage (see pages 73 and 91).

Sedum erythrostictum is little more than 30cm (12in) high, with heads of greenish-white flowers. These are particularly attractive in the variegated cultivar **'Frosty Morn'** (above), which has clear white leaf markings. (See also page 97.)

Sedum spectabile♡ (ice plant) has light blue-green foliage and stems 45cm (18in) high bearing pink flowers. **'Iceberg'** (above) has pure white flowers above pale foliage. **'Brilliant'**♡ has bright pink blooms; **'Septemberglut'** (SEPTEMBER GLOW) is darker. **'Indian Chief'** has rich pink flowers and grey-green leaves with boldly serrated edges, supposedly resembling the feathers of a headdress.

OTHER GOOD SEDUMS

Sedum **'Ruby Glow'**♡ Forms a sprawling clump to 25cm (10in) high. Leaves are grey and flowers deep wine red.

Sedum aizoon **'Euphorbioides'** Forms a spreading clump of 35cm (14in) stems, with green succulent leaves and yellow flowerheads.

Rudbeckias are North American beauties found growing in moist, often heavy soils of plains and foothills, where they thrive in full sun or partial shade. The hardy herbaceous perennial species *Rudbeckia fulgida* (commonly known as black-eyed Susan) and *Rudbeckia laciniata* are excellent garden plants, easy to grow and reliable, provided they have an adequate supply of moisture as the flowers develop.

Rudbeckia fulgida var. *sullivantii* 'Goldsturm' ♀ is a striking plant that produces a mass of golden, black-eyed daisy flowerheads from late summer well into autumn on stems up to 90cm (3ft) high. It is superb planted with grasses or against the dark backdrop of purple foliage. (See page 53.)

Rudbeckia laciniata has rather stringy, tall stems up to 4m (13ft) in height, with pale, deeply cut leaves. The flowers consist of pale green-yellow cones dressed in recurved, narrow petals of bright yellow. The fuller, more prolific flowers of 'Herbstsonne' ♀ make a dramatic impression at the back of the border. 'Goldquelle' ♀ is more modest in height, with sumptuous double, bright yellow flowers which, when fully open, reveal shorter, green-yellow petals obscuring the central cone.

Rudbeckia occidentalis, 90cm (3ft) tall, is a favourite of garden designers. A collar of sharply pointed green bracts cradles a dark, almost black, egg-shaped cone with a narrow band of bright yellow pinhead anthers. The cultivar 'Green Wizard' has striking flowers with more conspicuous green bracts.

Schizostylis coccinea is a South African native with showy scarlet blooms. It forms a clump of semi-evergreen, narrow, sword-like mid-green foliage, from which 60cm (24in) flower spikes emerge in late autumn, each carrying up to eight open, starry blooms in shades of pink, red or white. There are a number of named forms and

Rudbeckia occidentalis 'Green Wizard'

Schizostylis coccinea

cultivars: **f.** *alba* is white; 'Viscountess Byng' is dainty pale pink; 'Jennifer' ♀ produces large flowers of mid-pink; 'Sunrise' ♀ is a rich shade of salmon pink and 'Major' ♀ a lovely satin red. All look good with silver foliage plants.

Schizostylis are often still in bloom at Christmas, and they make excellent cut flowers. They thrive in a position in full sun with moist, but free-draining soil. In cooler areas, they must have a sheltered situation, protected from cold, drying winds, with the benefit of a dry mulch in winter. Even so, the flower spikes may be damaged by frost.

Solidagos (golden rod) have long been a strong feature of the autumn garden. Excellent plants to encourage wildlife, they are much loved by late pollinating insects. Their green-gold flowers are good mixers in the border and they supply light relief from some of the bolder blooms. (See page 53.)

Tricyrtis, the toad lilies, may not be the showiest of autumn flowers, but their muted colours and exquisite beauty suit the season well. Useful plants in shady situations, they bring contrasting form and detail to plantings of ferns and hostas. (See page 59.)

GOOD COMPANIONS

The pure white petals and golden stamens of *Anemone* × *hybrida* 'Honorine Jobert' ♀ (1) stand out beautifully against the rich burgundy leaves of *Cotinus coggygria* 'Royal Purple' ♀ (2).

With its delicately patterned flowers, *Tricyrtis formosana* ♀ (3) makes a delightful companion for *Heuchera micrantha* var. *diversifolia* 'Palace Purple' (4) in moist soil in semi-shade.

177

Winter

Most herbaceous perennials retreat safely underground in winter, hiding beneath the surface until the warmer days of spring. Yet evergreen perennials still provide foliage interest – heucheras, ajugas, ophiopogons, epimediums and bergenias are among those that defy the cold – and a few brave souls join the winter-flowering shrubs and produce delicate but hardy blossoms. These are all the more welcome as reminders of the pleasures to come, and all the more wonderful in the way that, paying no heed to the elements, they challenge the frost and snow.

When considering winter flowers *Helleborus niger*♀, commonly called the Christmas rose, is the first that comes to mind. A pure white beauty, it will defy the winter gloom, although often waiting until late in the season to produce its finest flowers. From a clump of dark, semi-evergreen, leathery leaves emerge numerous short, reddish-brown flower stems, about 30cm (12in) high, each carrying up to three nodding buds of folded white petals. These open to outward-facing, saucer-shaped white flowers, sometimes with a hint of pink, but always ageing to a lovely shade of creamy pink before setting seed.

Native to regions of Germany, Austria, Switzerland, Italy and Slovenia, *Helleborus niger* is a truly hardy perennial. Cultivation in the garden is not always easy; often the plant is given too much shade and moisture, which results in spotting of the leaves and badly marked flowers. In the wild this hellebore is found growing on limestone in fairly dry coniferous woods or in open meadows. In the garden an open, well-drained position suits it best, on fertile, neutral to alkaline soil. Some protection from slugs and snails is desirable; a grit mulch over the soil surface is ideal.

A number of named selections are available, often with subtle variations to the excellent flowers of the species. *Helleborus niger* subsp. *macranthus*

The brave winter flowers of soft purplish-pink *Cyclamen coum* and purest white *Galanthus nivalis* appear among the inky foliage of *Ophiopogon planiscapus* 'Nigrescens'.

Helleborus niger

Iris unguicularis

has more glaucous foliage, with larger white flowers. **Helleborus niger 'Potter's Wheel'**, when true to name, has more bowl-shaped flowers, which are white with pale green centres. **Helleborus niger Harvington hybrids** are reliable, free-flowering plants with pure white blooms. There are also forms of *Helleborus niger* with marbled or silver leaves. (For other hellebores, see pages 180–81.)

GROWING CHRISTMAS ROSES IN POTS

Helleborus niger can be grown in a pot of loam-based compost. Stand the pot in a sunny spot in the garden for the summer and keep it well watered. In winter, when flower buds appear, move it close to the house. The blooms can be enjoyed without venturing too far into the garden and the plant will gain some protection from winter wet.

Iris unguicularis ♀ (formerly known as *Iris stylosa*) produces beautiful fragile blossoms from a dense clump of narrow, evergreen, grass-like foliage 30cm (12in) tall. The deliciously scented flowers are a vibrant blue-mauve, with the lower petals (falls) displaying an elaborate flash of yellow, framed in white stripes.

This is a native of countries such as Greece and Turkey; in the garden, the ideal situation for it is the dry soil at the base of a sunny wall. Left undisturbed, a mature plant will produce a succession of blooms, starting in early winter and continuing into spring. The flowers sit low down in the foliage, so removing damaged or brown leaves will help to reveal the full beauty of the blooms.

Iris foetidissima ♀ excels in winter, not with showy flowers but with brightly coloured seedheads. The plant forms a clump of sword-shaped, dark, evergreen foliage. a useful spiky form against neighbouring flowers and foliage throughout the seasons. The rather dull purple flowers, on 40–80cm (16–32in) stems, go almost unnoticed in early summer, but without them the winter treat of scarlet berries nestled in large splitting capsules could never be enjoyed. Stems bearing the distinctive seedheads can be cut for indoor display.

Found naturally in much of Europe, *Iris foetidissima* was often prescribed by medieval herbalists as a purgative. The plant has a pungent smell, like that of raw beef, when the foliage is crushed or damaged, hence its common names stinking iris and stinking gladwyn; but such an unfortunate odour is quickly forgiven when considering its garden merits. This is a versatile plant, happily performing in almost any free-draining soil and tolerating full sun, but thriving in full to partial shade and alkaline soil.

Iris foetidissima

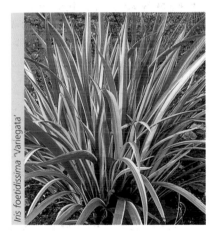

Iris foetidissima 'Variegata'

A small number of varieties to the species are available: **Iris foetidissima var. citrina** produces yellow flowers, while **Iris foetidissima 'Fructu Albo'** has unusual white winter berries. **Iris foetidissima 'Variegata'** ♀ has deep green foliage striped creamy white. An excellent hardy foliage plant, it tolerates hostile conditions and looks good all (continued on page 182)

Lenten roses (Helleborus × hybridus)

No garden should be without the classic beauty of the Lenten rose. Its colourful yet subtle shades brighten the darkest days of winter, giving a glimpse of eagerly awaited spring. *Helleborus × hybridus* is in fact a large group of garden hybrids, the offspring of *Helleborus orientalis* and other hellebore species. Many of the parent species are native to regions of Greece, Turkey and the Caucasus and have featured in gardens for the past two centuries. *Helleborus × hybridus* began to reach gardeners in the mid-1900s, assisted by many keen enthusiasts and nurserymen.

These hellebores form a clump of semi-evergreen, leathery, mid- to dark green leaves from the base of which appear thick stems, up to 45cm (18in) high, each carrying up to four pendent buds, sheathed in soft new leaves. The buds open to outward-facing, saucer-shaped flowers. The promiscuous nature of the plant has led to great variety in flower colour: shades of green, white, cream, yellow, pink, red and burgundy, through to slate grey. Pink to dark red speckles are a common feature, as if paint has been flicked from a brush and landed on the flowers in distinct spots or a fusion of tiny flecks.

Some forms of pink through to burgundy have darker veining on the petals. A rare delight are those with semi- to fully double flowers; scarcer still are anemone-flowered forms, with short ruffled petals packed into the centre of the more typical outer ones.

Micropropagation of these hellebores has given poor results, so the numbers of named clones are small, and they command high prices. There are some seedling strains, such as the Ashwood Garden hybrids, Ballard's Group, Blackthorn Group and the Hillier hybrids. These offer selections of some or all of the flower forms and colours described above, but because they are seedlings they do show variation.

Helleborus × hybridus has beautiful flowers, enchanting both in the garden and for indoor decoration. Unfortunately they wilt and die if stems are cut and put in water. Instead just the flowers should be picked, and floated on a bowl of water. They look wonderful used in this way and the exquisite detail of each bloom can clearly be seen.

Helleborus × hybridus planted among hemerocallis (daylilies), which will provide both colour and shade in summer as next year's hellebore flowers develop.

CULTIVATING LENTEN ROSES

The many forms of *Helleborus* × *hybridus* are undemanding plants, thriving in most moist, well drained sites, but preferring neutral to alkaline soil. Vigour is seriously inhibited in very wet or dry conditions. They enjoy the dappled shade of trees or shrubs, and look delightful planted with evergreen ferns or spring bulbs, such as snowdrops (*Galanthus nivalis* ♀) or *Cyclamen coum* ♀. Purchase pot-grown plants of flowering size; these can be planted at any time. Buying plants in flower is ideal since the exact colour can be seen.

In autumn or early winter, before the flowers appear, remove any brown or damaged foliage. Some gardeners prefer to remove all mature foliage, in order to enjoy the emerging flower stems; new leaves will soon be produced once the flowers are over.

As the flowers fade, remove any weeds around the plants and carefully loosen the soil surface. Hellebores seed themselves readily and seedlings will appear later in the year all around the mother plants. These should be left where they are until the following spring, then transplanted to make room for the next crop. The seedlings will vary in flower colour – and hopefully result in some pleasant surprises. Alternatively, the seed can be collected when ripe and sown immediately in a coldframe, protected from birds and mice.

Established plants can be divided, but this may seriously affect the health and vigour of both the mother plant and its offshoots. The best time for dividing or moving plants is late summer or early autumn, just as cooler conditions encourage a flush of new root growth.

Ophiopogon jaburan 'Vittatus'

plants come even close to matching its glossy, almost black, broad, grass-like leaves, which grow in tight evergreen tufts (see Good Companions, below). Ophiopogons are members of the lily family, and have charming bell-shaped, purple-white flowers during summer, followed by shiny black berries.

Native to China and Japan, they grow on fertile, moist but well-drained soil in dappled woodland shade. In the garden, a site in full sun is preferable because it intensifies the blackness of the leaf. The slowly spreading foliage reaches 30cm (12in) in height and forms a thick, weed-suppressing carpet, the darkness of which looks sensational underneath golden-leaved evergreen shrubs such as *Euonymus japonicus* 'Chollipo' ♀ and *Choisya ternata* SUNDANCE ('Lich') ♀.

The foliage of *Ophiopogon jaburan* **'Vittatus'** is less dramatic but perfectly lovely, reaching 60cm (24in) high. Each pale green leaf is striped creamy white, and the small white summer flowers are followed by violet-blue berries. Not as hardy as *Ophiopogon planiscapus*, it needs a very well-drained site in winter, in the shelter of a sunny wall. Cover with fleece if temperatures persistently fall below –3°C (27°F).

year (see Good Companions, below). Dark purple, semi-evergreen heucheras are glorious against its strong, creamy-white variegation. Though prone to rust, its foliage is less susceptible than that of the green form.

Evergreen foliage comes to the fore in the winter garden. With competition from deciduous plants much reduced, those that retain their leaves now take centre stage, particularly if the shape or colour of the foliage is either unusual or dramatic. *Ophiopogon planiscapus* **'Nigrescens'** ♀ is a natural choice. Few

Primula **Cowichan** series are rather a surprise in the winter garden. They are members of the Polyanthus Group of primulas and share many of their relatives' attributes, but they should definitely be considered as more than winter bedding plants.

Cowichan primulas produce robust, winter-hardy rosettes of rounded-oblong, bronzed, dark green leaves. From late winter to early spring, they bear elegant, reddened stems, showing off clusters of simple, saucer-shaped, velvet flowers in shades of cream, yellow and apricot as well as white, blue,

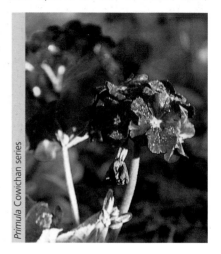

Primula Cowichan series

purple and deep satin red; each has just a hint of yellow in the centre. Compared to many of the more brazen forms in the Polyanthus Group, Cowichan primulas bring a more subtle, sophisticated touch to the garden.

Plants may start to bloom in early winter and continue through spring. Although a severe frost may spoil the early flowers, a succession of blooms will always follow. Grow them in any reasonably fertile, humus-rich, moist but well-drained soil, in full sun or partial shade. They are perfect for containers or for planting beneath the bare winter stems of shrubs such as the red-barked dogwood, *Cornus alba*. After flowering, the foliage rosettes will thicken, forming useful, weed-suppressing ground cover.

GOOD COMPANIONS

The shiny purple-black foliage of *Ophiopogon planiscapus* 'Nigrescens' ♀ (1) is stunning when planted beneath the bare, powdery white stems of *Rubus cockburnianus* (2).

The flame-coloured wands of *Cornus sanguinea* 'Winter Beauty' (3) contrast with the creamy-white striped foliage of *Iris foetidissima* 'Variegata' ♀ (4).

Left undisturbed, the mahogany flowerheads of sedum stand throughout winter.

BEAUTIFUL REMAINS

As the last summer and autumn flowers fade many gardeners rush to strip away the remnants of flowers and foliage. But, left alone, many border plants will keep their structure, their drying stems a reflection of former glory, yet still captivating in their own right.

Some essential maintenance must be done at this time of year: for example, mulching dormant perennials vulnerable to frost and collecting seed, whether for use next season or simply to avoid self-sown seedlings. But the big clean up is best left until early spring: the dead growth helps to insulate against hard frosts as well as providing winter interest and often seeds for birds and animals.

Towards the back of the border the light filigree form of *Foeniculum* (fennel) contrasts with the heavier upright rods of faded **verbascums**. **Echinops** often hold their rounded thistle heads, and the flat heads of *Achillea filipendulina* **'Gold Plate'** ♀ become a lovely golden brown. The cones of **echinaceas** and **rudbeckias** remain deep black-brown, persisting in the border long after the colourful petals have fallen.

Above the tight grey-green rosettes of its dormant winter shoots, *Sedum spectabile* ♀ still holds stout stems of large, flat chestnut heads, the remnants of its ruby autumn brilliance.

The reddened stems and rounded heads of *Angelica gigas*, blackened by frost, persist alongside the oblong cones of the teasel, *Dipsacus fullonum*, and surrounded by the once rampant growth of **gypsophila**. Eryngiums such as *Eryngium × oliverianum* ♀ retain brown, rounded cones, still encircled by dramatic spiny bracts. Among the most intriguing winter remains are those of the plant commonly called Chinese lantern, *Physalis alkekengi* ♀. The papery lanterns lose their rich orange colour, leaving intricate skeletal frames, each one imprisoning a single shrivelled fruit waiting to release its seeds.

Ornamental grasses excel at this time. Plumes of **cortaderias** (pampas grass) above evergreen, arching foliage, feathery spikes of silvery **miscanthus**, swirling mists of **stipas** and fluffy tails of **pennisetums** all contribute to the winter scene.

Frost etches the silhouettes of winter, snowfall emphasizes shapes and hides imperfections. Low sun changes colour and outline. The winter garden is a magical place above and below ground. While we enjoy the delights of the more minimal landscape, those deciduous herbaceous perennials are waiting expectantly for warmer days to come.

Faded remains of summer glory are transformed by hoar-frost in midwinter.

183

Authors' choice:
favourite perennial planting groups

There are vast numbers of herbaceous perennials in cultivation, and this book contains a selection of those that we consider to be the best. From these we have chosen some proven favourites that are easy to grow and rewarding. We have put them together into suggested planting groups that will give a long season of interest as well as providing variety in form or texture. Among these planting combinations you should find one to suit just about any situation in your garden.

1. DARK FOLIAGE AND HOT COLOURS FOR FULL SUN
Maximum height 2m (6ft)

 Crocosmia 'Lucifer' ♟ (page 157) Sword-shaped leaves and rich red flowers from midsummer.

 Foeniculum vulgare 'Purpureum' (page 90) Fine, feathery foliage of soft bronze; yellow flowers.

 Dahlia 'Moonfire' ♟ (page 173) Dark chocolate foliage and golden orange flowers in summer.

 Lysimachia ciliata 'Firecracker' ♟ (page 91) Dark foliage on upright stems; starry yellow flowers.

 Shrub planting partner: *Physocarpus opulifolius* 'Diabolo' ♟ (to 3m/10ft) Upright habit and deep burgundy foliage; a perfect background shrub.

2. LIME AND YELLOW FOR A SUNNY SITUATION
Maximum height 1.2m (4ft)

 Alchemilla mollis ♟ (page 46) Soft green leaves and frothy lime flowers in summer.

 Hemerocallis 'Hyperion' (page 138) Narrow, grass-like foliage; large, pale yellow flowers in summer.

 Euphorbia characias (page 113) Evergreen, grey-green foliage; bold, yellow-green flowers in early spring.

 Leucanthemum × *superbum* 'Aglaia' ♟ (page 142) Yellow-eyed white summer flowers; dark leaves.

 Shrub planting partner: *Philadelphus coronarius* 'Aureus' ♟ (to 2m/6ft) Spring foliage lime-yellow, strong yellow in summer. Fragrant white flowers.

3. BLUE, PURPLE AND MAGENTA FOR A SUNNY SITUATION
Maximum height 1m (40in)

 Geranium psilostemon ♟ (page 48) Tall habit; vivid magenta-pink, black-centred flowers in summer.

 Penstemon 'Raven' ♟ (page 162) Deep purple flowers summer and autumn. Upright, evergreen.

 Salvia × *sylvestris* MAY NIGHT ♟ (page 43) Violet-blue flowers in late summer. Compact, upright.

 Heuchera 'Amethyst Myst' (page 89) Dark purple, glossy, waved leaves. Evergreen.

 Shrub planting partner: *Buddleja* 'Lochinch' ♟ (to 2m/6ft) Silver-grey leaves and large sprays of scented, lilac-blue flowers in late summer.

4. SILVER AND WHITE FOR A DRY, SUNNY SITUATION
Maximum height 1m (40in)

 Eryngium bourgatii 'Oxford Blue' ♟ (page 67) Silver-grey foliage; silver-blue flowers in summer.

 Artemisia 'Powis Castle' ♟ (page 103) Finely cut silver foliage on sprawling, shrubby stems.

 Centranthus ruber 'Albus' (page 65) Fresh green leaves and frothy white flowerheads in summer.

 Stachys byzantina 'Silver Carpet' (page 103) Soft, felted silver-grey leaves in a low mat.

 Shrub planting partner: *Cistus* × *obtusifolius* 'Thrive' (90cm/3ft) Small, dark, evergreen leaves. White, yellow-eyed flowers in early summer.

5. GREEN AND WHITE GROUND COVER IN SHADE
Maximum height 80cm (32in)

 Euphorbia amygdaloides var. *robbiae* ♀ (page 57) Dark green leaves in whorls on short, upright stems. Lime-green flowers in spring.

 Helleborus foetidus ♀ (page 114) Dark green leaves divided into narrow leaflets. Pale green flowers in early spring. Evergreen.

 Brunnera macrophylla 'Jack Frost' (page 106) Attractive silver-green foliage and bright blue forget-me-not flowers in early spring.

 Lamium maculatum 'Beacon Silver' (page 62) A mat of pale green-silver leaves, narrowly edged dark green. Pink-purple flowers in summer.

 Hosta 'Patriot' (page 98) Bold, deep green, heart-shaped leaves broadly edged with white. Lilac flowers in midsummer.

 Shrub planting partner: *Skimmia* × *confusa* 'Kew Green' ♀ (to 1m/40in) Evergreen, glossy leaves; cream-green scented flowers in early spring.

6. EASY-TO-GROW MIX FOR SUN OR SEMI-SHADE
Maximum height 1m (40in)

 Astrantia major (page 155) Starry, greenish-pink flowers on straight stems above a mound of foliage through summer and into autumn.

 Geranium 'Johnson's Blue' ♀ (page 48) Dark-veined, lavender-blue flowers in early to midsummer, often again in autumn. Attractive cut foliage.

 Penstemon 'Andenken an Friedrich Hahn' ♀ (page 163) Rounded bush of evergreen foliage. Wine-red flowers through summer and autumn.

 Paeonia officinalis 'Rubra Plena' ♀ (page 146) Attractive mid-green foliage and large, very double, ruby-red flowers in early summer.

 Nepeta 'Six Hills Giant' (page 42) Grey-green, aromatic foliage and fine spikes of lavender-blue flowers throughout summer.

 Shrub planting partner: *Sambucus nigra* 'Black Lace' (to 2m/6ft) Vigorous stems with finely cut, purple-black leaves. Pinkish flowers in early summer.

7. BOLD FOLIAGE FOR SEMI-SHADE AND MOIST SOIL
Maximum height 2m (6ft)

 Euphorbia griffithii 'Fireglow' (page 122) Upright stems crowned with vivid orange-red flowers in late spring. Good autumn foliage colour.

 Hosta sieboldiana var. *elegans* ♀ (page 107) Large, bold, silver-blue architectural leaves. Spikes of pale lilac flowers in midsummer.

 Lobelia 'Queen Victoria' ♀ (page 76) Shining, rich red-purple foliage. Spikes of vivid scarlet flowers on dark stems in late summer.

 Ligularia 'The Rocket' ♀ (page 76) Green, toothed leaves on black stems. Spikes of tiny, deep yellow flowers in midsummer.

 Bergenia purpurascens ♀ (page 111) Bold, leathery foliage that turns deep mahogany-red in autumn. Purple-red flowers in spring.

 Shrub planting partner: *Cornus alba* 'Gouchaultii' (to 2m/6ft). Soft green, yellow-variegated leaves flushed pinkish red. Red stems in winter.

8. BLUE AND WHITE FOR SEMI-SHADE
Maximum height 1m (40in)

 Hosta 'Halcyon' ♀ (page 107) Wonderful, elegant blue-green leaves. Spikes of greyish-lavender flowers in midsummer.

 Aquilegia alpina (page 120) Pretty divided, fern-like leaves of bluish green. Slender stems of inky-blue flowers in late spring. Self-seeds freely.

 Dicentra 'Langtrees' ♀ (page 106) Fern-like foliage of silver-grey. Delicate stems of pinkish-white flowers in spring.

 Pulmonaria 'Roy Davidson' (page 115) Pale ice-blue flowers above strongly spotted foliage that remains in good condition throughout the season.

 Iris sibirica 'Flight of Butterflies' (page 75) Narrow, upright, sword-like leaves and dainty sapphire-blue flowers in early summer.

 Shrub planting partner: *Cornus alba* 'Sibirica Variegata' (to 1.5m/5ft) Foliage dark green and creamy white, often flushed pink. Red winter stems.

Index

Suffix *i* refers to illustrations. Page numbers in bold type indicate major references; numbers in italics indicate illustrations and captions only.

A

Aaron's rod see *Verbascum thapsus*
Acaena microphylla 28*i*
  A.m. 'Kupferteppich' (COPPER CARPET) 103*i*
Acanthus 20, 80, **130–1**
  A. dioscoridis 131
  A. hungaricus 131
  A. mollis 130
  A. spinosus 31*i*, 66, *123i*, **130**, *131i*
  A. 'Summer Beauty' 130–1
Acer palmatum
  A.p. 'Bloodgood' 45, 106
  A.p. 'Fireglow' 87*i*
Achillea 27, *73i*, 80, **131**, *156i*, *157i*
  A. clypeolata 104, 131
  A. 'Coronation Gold' 131
  A. 'Fanal' 131
  A. filipendulina 131; *A.f.* 'Cloth of Gold' 131; *A.f.* 'Gold Plate' *31i*, 32, 35, 131*i*, *166i*, 183
  A. 'Lachsschönheit' (SALMON BEAUTY) 131
  A. millefolium 131; *A.m.* 'Cerise Queen' 131; *A.m.* 'Lilac Beauty' 131; *A.m.* 'Paprika' 131
  A. 'Moonshine' 43, 131
  A. ptarmica 131–2; *A.p.* 'Boule de Neige' 132
  A. sibirica var. *camschatica* 'Love Parade' 131
  A. 'Summerwine' 131*i*
  A. 'Terracotta' 131
  A. 'Walther Funcke' 131
acidity/alkalinity 19
Aconitum 24, 31, **46**, **132**
  A. carmichaelii var. *trupellianum* 'Kelmscott' 46
  A. 'Spark's Variety' 40, 46*i*
  A. 'Stainless Steel' 46
Actaea
  A. cimicifuga 17, 86
  A. racemosa 58
  A. simplex 62; *A.s.* Atropurpurea Group 86; *A.s.A.G.* 'Brunette' 86, *87i*
Aegopodium podagraria 'Variegatum' 21*i*, *97i*–100
aeoniums 38
African blue lily see *Agapanthus*
Agapanthus 9, 29, **64–5**, **152–3**
  A. africanus 152*i*; *A.a.* 'Albus' 152*i*
  A. 'Blue Giant' 153
  A. 'Blue Triumphator' 153*i*
  A. 'Bressingham White' 153
  A. campanulatus 142, 152; *A.c.* var. *albidus* 152
  A. caulescens 153
  A. 'Gayle's Lilac' 153
  A. Headbourne hybrids 64*i*–65, 153
  A. 'Lilliput' 153
  A. 'Loch Hope' 153
  A. 'Snowball' 153
  A. 'Streamline' 153
  A. 'Tinkerbell' 153

growing in pots 153
Agastache 42, 153
  A. aurantiaca 'Apricot Sprite' 153
  A. 'Blue Fortune' 153*i*
  A. foeniculum 50–1, 153; *A.f.* 'Alabaster' 50*i*–51
  A. 'Painted Lady' 153*i*
  A. rugosa 153; *A.r.* 'Golden Jubilee' 92*i*, 153
  A. 'Tutti-frutti' 153
  A. urticifolia 153; *A.u.* 'Alba' 153
Ajuga 86, **118–19**
  A. genevensis 118
  A. 'Little Court Pink' 119
  A. pyramidalis 118
  A. reptans 60, 118; *A.r.* 'Atropurpurea' 27, *57i*, *63i*, **86**, 118*i*; *A.r.* 'Burgundy Glow' 86; *A.r.* 'Catlin's Giant' 27, 86, 119*i*; *A.r.* 'John Pierpoint' 119; *A.r.* 'Multicolor' 119; *A.r.* 'Variegata' 118
Alcea 31, *130i*, **132**
  A. 'Chater's Double' 132
  A. rosea 132; *A.r.* 'Majorette' 132; *A.r.* 'Nigra' 132*i*
  A. rugosa 132*i*
  rust on 132
Alchemilla mollis 27, *46i*, *184i*
  companions for 30*i*, 40, 45, *47i*, 67, 82, 88, *184i*
  cultivation of 17, 22*i*, 23, 27, 29*i*, 60
Allium cristophii 30*i*, *67i*
Alstroemeria 154
  A. 'Apollo' 154*i*
  A. aurea 154; *A.a.* 'Dover Orange' 154; *A.a.* 'Lutea' 154
  A. 'Evening Song' 154
  A. 'Glory of the Andes' 154
  A. haemantha 154
  A. ligtu 154; *A.l.* hybrids 154
  A. 'Orange Glory' 154
  A. psittacina 'Royal Star' 154
  A. 'Red Beauty' 154
  A. 'Spitfire' 154
Althaea 132
  A. armeniaca 132
  A. cannabina 132
Amaryllis belladonna 124
Anaphalis triplinervis 65, 102*i*
Anchusa 119
  A. azurea 119; *A.a.* 'Loddon Royalist' 119*i*; *A.a.* 'Opal' 119
Anemone
  A. blanda 58, *59i*, *112i*, 115
  A. hupehensis 170–1; *A.h.* 'Hadspen Abundance' 170–1*i*; *A.h.* var. *japonica* 170–1; *A.h.v.j.* 'Pamina' 171; *A.h.v.j.* 'Prinz Heinrich' (PRINCE HENRY) 171*i*
  A. × *hybrida* 32, 40, 46, 170–1; *A.* × *h.* 'Honorine Jobert' 46*i*, 171, *177i*; *A.* × *h.* 'Königin Charlotte' (QUEEN CHARLOTTE) 46, 171; *A.* × *h.* 'September Charm' *170i*, 171; *A.* × *h.* 'Whirlwind' 171
  A. vitifolia 170
Angelica gigas 13, 183
angel's fishing rods see *Dierama pulcherrimum*
Anne's Grove Gardens, Ireland *143i*
Anthemis **119–21**
  A. 'Beauty of Grallagh' 119
  A. 'Grallagh Gold' 119
  A. punctata subsp. *cupaniana* 119–21, *126i*
  A. sancti-johannis 119

A. tinctoria 29, 66, **119**; *A.t.* 'E.C.Buxton' 119*i*; *A.t.* 'Sauce Hollandaise' 39, 119*i*
Anthriscus sylvestris 90
  A.s. 'Ravenswing' *86i*, 90*i*
Antirrhinum majus 34
Aquilegia 120
  A. alpina 120*i*, *185i*
  A. canadensis 120
  A. coerulea 120
  A. flabellata 120
  A. longissima 120
  A. McKana Group 15, 120*i*
  A. vulgaris 120*i*; *A.v.* 'Nivea' 120*i*
Arabis alpina subsp. *caucasica* 'Variegata' 96
Armoracia rusticana 'Variegata' 100*i*
Artemisia 14, 29, **51**, **65**, **104–5**
  A. absinthium 'Lambrook Silver' 104
  A. alba 'Canescens' 65, 105
  A. ludoviciana 51, 105; *A.l.* 'Silver Queen' 51, 105*i*; *A.l.* 'Valerie Finnis' 47, 51*i*, 105, 119
  A. pontica 65, 67*i*, 105
  A. 'Powis Castle' 65, 89, 102–3*i*, *184i*
  A. schmidtiana 30*i*, 65, 105; *A.s.* 'Nana' 105, 125
  A. stelleriana 65; *A.s.* 'Boughton Silver' *91i*, 105*i*
Arum italicum
  A.i. 'Pictum' 60
  A.i. subsp *italicum* 'Marmoratum' 60*i*
arum lily see *Zantedeschia aethiopica*
Aruncus dioicus 74*i*, 79*i*
Asarum 61
  A. caudatum 61
  A. europaeum 58, 61*i*
Asclepias tuberosa 52
Asphodeline lutea **70**, 80, 104
Aspidistra elatior 'Milky Way' 62
Aster 29, *39i*, **40**, *40i*, **51**, 83, **171**, **174**
  A. amellus 171; *A.a.* 'Brilliant' 171; *A.a.* 'King George' 171; *A.a.* 'Veilchenkönigin' (VIOLET QUEEN) 171
  A. ericoides 171; *A.e.* 'Blue Star' 171; *A.e.* 'Brimstone' 171; *A.e.* 'Golden Spray' 171; *A.e.* 'Pink Cloud' 51, 171
  A. × *frikartii* 171; *A.* × *f.* 'Mönch' 51, 171*i*, *174i*
  A. lateriflorus 51; *A.l.* 'Horizontalis' 51; *A.l.* 'Prince' 90, 171
  A. novae-angliae 40, 174; *A.n.* 'Barr's Pink' 174; *A.n.* 'Mrs S.T. Wright' 174; *A.n.* 'Pink Victor' 40*i*; *A.n.* 'Rubinschatz' 174; *A.n.* 'Septemberrubin' (SEPTEMBER RUBY) 40; *A.n.* 'Violetta' 174
  A. novi-belgii 40, 171; *A.n.* 'Eventide' 40; *A.n.* 'Marie Ballard' 40; *A.n.* 'Patricia Ballard' 40
  A. pilosus var. *pringlei* 'Monte Cassino' 171
Astilbe **74–5**
  A. 'Bressingham Beauty' 75
  A. 'Cattleya' 75
  A. chinensis var. *pumila* 75
  A. 'Deutschland' 75
  A. 'Fanal' 75
  A. 'Jo Ophurst' 75
  A. 'Weisse Gloria' 75
Astrantia 42, **153–5**
  A. 'Hadspen Blood' 155
  A. major 82, 155*i*, *185i*; *A.m.* alba

155; *A.m.* 'Claret' 155; *A.m.* subsp. *involucrata* 155; *A.m.i.* 'Margery Fish' 155; *A.m.i.* 'Shaggy' 155; *A.m.* 'Rubra' 155; *A.m.* 'Ruby Wedding' 155*i*; *A.m.* 'Sunningdale Variegated' 100*i*
  A. maxima 155*i*
Aubretia 'Argenteovariegata' 97
autumn planting 19, 20
Award of Garden Merit (AGM) ✿ 5

B

baby's breath see *Gypsophila paniculata*
bachelor's buttons see *Ranunculus aconitifolius*
balloon flower see *Platycodon grandiflorus*
banana 8
Banks, Joseph 11
Baptisia **132–3**
  B. alba 132–3; *B.a.* var. *macrophylla* 133
  B. australis 40, 66, **132***i*, *133i*
  B. 'Purple Smoke' 133
bare-root plants 16
barrenwort see *Epimedium*
bats in the belfry see *Campanula trachelium*
bearded irises 20, 124–125
bear's breeches see *Acanthus*
bee balm see *Monarda*
bellflowers see *Campanula*
Berberis thunbergii f. *atropurpurea* 'Rose Glow' 45, *158i*
bergamot see *Monarda*
Bergenia 61, **110–11**
  B. 'Abendglocken' (EVENING BELLS) 111
  B. 'Abendglut' (EVENING GLOW) 111
  B. 'Bressingham Ruby' 111
  B. 'Bressingham White' 111
  B. ciliata 110
  B. cordifolia 61; *B.c.* 'Purpurea' 110–11
  B. 'Morgenröte' (MORNING RED) 111
  B. purpurascens 111*i*, *117i*, *185i*
  B. 'Silberlicht' (SILVERLIGHT) 111*i*
  B. 'Wintermärchen' (WINTER FAIRY TALES) 111
Betula 96
  B. nigra 112*i*
bindweed 39
birthroot see *Trillium erectum*
bishop's mitre see *Epimedium*
blanket flower see *Gaillardia*
bleeding heart see *Dicentra spectabilis*
bloody dock see *Rumex sanguineus*
Bloom, Alan 12, 39, 73
blue cupidane see *Catananche caerulea*
blue-eyed grass see *Sisyrinchium angustifolium*
blue fescue see *Festuca glauca*
borders
  colour in 34–5, 184–5
  herbaceous 38–43
  mixed 44–9
  plant shapes in 28–33
  preparation 18–19
  see also colour schemes; foliage; maintenance; soil
botanical latin 14–15
botrytis 146
Bowles, E.A. 12

PICTURE CREDITS

The publishers would like to acknowledge with thanks all those whose gardens are pictured in this book.

All photographs were taken by Andrew McIndoe or Kevin Hobbs with the exception of:

Blackmore & Langdon: 135a
Crûg Farm Plants: 127c
Patricia Elkington: 28c, 123a, 126 Good Companions (3) , 174b
John Hillier: 112 Good Companions (3)
Kelways: 125b, 125d, 146
Notcutts Nurseries Ltd: 87a
Jane Sterndale-Bennett: 89b, 94b, 99a, 120b, 128a, 129a, 177 Good Companions (4)
Terry Underhill: 40b, 61b, 71a, 87c, 95b, 112a, 123b, 124, 126a, 126b, Good Companions 129 (3), 148c, 174a
Whetman Pinks Ltd: 81b, 136a, 136b

INDEX